SUDARSHAN CHAKRA STRATEGIC STUDIES SERIES

MIND WARS

The New Battlefield of Information Warfare

SUDARSHAN CHAKRA STRATEGIC STUDIES SERIES

MIND WARS

The New Battlefield of Information Warfare

Maj Gen PK Mallick, VSM (Retd)

Foreword by

Lt Gen NS Raja Subramani, PVSM, AVSM, SM, VSM

Vice Chief of The Army Staff

Colonel of Garhwal Rifles & Garhwal Scouts

PENTAGON PRESS LLP

First published in 2025 by
PENTAGON PRESS LLP
206, Peacock Lane, Shahpur Jat
New Delhi-110049, India
Contact: 011-26490600

Typeset in AGaramond, 11.5 Point
Printed at Aegean Offset Printers, Greater Noida

ISBN 978-81-993527-0-4

Disclaimer: The views and opinions expressed in the book is the individual assertion of the Author. The Publisher does not take any responsibility for the same in any manner whatsoever. The same shall solely be the responsibility of the Author.

www.pentagonpress.in

This book is dedicated to

Lt Gen Gautam Banerjee, PVSM, AVSM, YSM (Retd)

For constantly encouraging me to write the book.

Contents

Lt Gen NS Raja Subramani, PVSM, AVSM, SM, VSM
Vice Chief of The Army Staff
Colonel of Garhwal Rifles & Garhwal Scouts

Integrated Headquarters of
Ministry of Defence (Army)
New Delhi - 110011

Foreword

In an era when the speed of ideas often outpaces the speed of bullets, Information Warfare has moved from the margins of military thought into the centre of strategic planning. This book, *Mind Wars: The New Battlefield of Information Warfare* by Maj Gen PK Mallick is therefore both timely and indispensable. It maps the contours of a battlefield that is simultaneously ancient—rooted in the age-old contest for hearts and minds—and radically modern, shaped by algorithms, artificial intelligence and an ever-more-pervasive digital ecology.

Maj Gen Mallick offers readers a rare combination: encyclopaedic breadth and operational clarity. Across its extensively referenced chapters, the work surveys conceptual foundations, doctrinal debates and the technical tools that enable contemporary influence campaigns. It explains foundational ideas—from the three-dimensional model of the information environment to the compression of strategic, operational and tactical levels under digital conditions—and then shows how those ideas translate into concrete practice: cyber-enabled information operations, psychological operations, narrative and cognitive warfare and the weaponisation of social media. The book also performs the vital service of situating these phenomena in geopolitical context, offering case studies on State and non-State actors whose campaigns and countermeasures define our present security environment.

What sets Maj Gen Mallick's book apart is its insistence on the human dimension. Technology widens the aperture through which information flows, but it is people—messengers, audiences, analysts and decision makers—who remain the decisive variable. Maj Gen Mallick repeatedly underscores that credibility, cultural empathy and narrative craft are not soft adjuncts to technical prowess; they are essential capabilities. Likewise, the chapters on cognitive warfare and AI-driven radicalisation highlight an uncomfortable truth: the most advanced tools can amplify human vulnerabilities as much as they can augment human strengths. The policy prescriptions and institutional recommendations offered here are practical and prudent: building cross-agency coordination, investing in media literacy and cognitive resilience and establishing clear legal and ethical guardrails.

Readers will also find value in the comparative treatment of major actors. The analyses of China's algorithmic approaches, Russia's reflexive control and Pakistan's institutionalised IW mechanisms help illuminate how different political systems exploit and regulate the information domain in divergent ways. The hypothetical operational planning chapters chart the operational logic of influence campaigns while repeatedly reminding us of the ethical and strategic pitfalls inherent in such work.

For practitioners, scholars and informed citizens alike, this book provides both a primer and a reference. It is a call to seriousness for policymakers, militaries and civil society: defending open, democratic societies in the information age requires not only technical investment but also institutional imagination, cross-disciplinary expertise and ethical restraint.

I recommend this book to anyone seeking to understand how the contests of the twenty-first century are waged—and how they might be restrained, regulated and where necessary, defended against. The battlefield of the mind is not an abstract theatre; it is where nations' futures are decided. This study helps sharpen our vision for that contest and points towards the durable institutions and civic competencies we will need if truth, trust and democratic governance are to endure.

Lt Gen NS Raja Subramani, PVSM, AVSM, SM, VSM
Vice Chief of The Army Staff
Colonel of Garhwal Rifles & Garhwal Scouts

Acknowledgements

After my staff tenure at Divisional Headquarters, Baramulla, I was posted to Military College of Telecommunication Engineering (MCTE), Mhow, in the mid-1990s. Immediately after the First Gulf War, the term "Information Warfare" gained significant traction. The first assignment I got at MCTE was to be a member of a Study Group on Information Warfare.

In those days, the Internet was emerging and not much information was available. We conducted extensive visualisation, analysis, kite flying, debates and studying over numerous hours to produce the final study report.

Since then, I have become increasingly interested in the subject and over the past 25 years, I have written numerous peer-reviewed papers, contributed chapters to books and delivered talks at various venues.

As technology improved in leaps and bounds, the character of warfare kept changing; vast amounts of information were available at the click of a button, including social media and LLMs. I find that many discussions on Information Warfare are taking place. I felt there is a lack of clarity on the understanding of the concept of Information Warfare.

I decided to take a fresh look after more than a quarter of a century since the term 'Information Warfare' was introduced and attempt to clarify many of the emerging issues.

The journey of conceptualising, researching, writing and refining this book has been as intellectually demanding as it has been rewarding. I am grateful to the analysts and practitioners who generously shared their experiences and perspectives, whether in government agencies, think tanks or the technology sector, while respecting the necessary boundaries of classified information. While I cannot name them individually, the contributors who shared their experiences under the condition of anonymity, your courage in speaking out about the real-world impacts of Information Warfare is deeply appreciated.

I extend my sincere thanks to the Librarian and staff of the Manohar Parrikar Institute for Defence Studies and Analyses (MP-IDSA), especially Shri Mukesh Kumar Jha and Ms. Hitakshi, as well as the National Defence College, New Delhi Library and its staff, Shri J.K. Yadav and Shri G.C.K. Rai. The way they went the extra mile to provide me with all the necessary inputs is indeed commendable.

The team at Pentagon Press took on this project with enthusiasm and professionalism, recognising the urgency of addressing Information Warfare in our current political and technological climate. The editorial direction, copyediting and design work were all carried out with patience and precision. I would like to extend my sincere appreciation to the editorial and production team at Pentagon Press LLP. My sincere thanks to Shri Rajan Arya, the proprietor of Pentagon Press LLP, for giving me the freedom to express myself yet gently guiding me to make the text more readable.

My profound appreciation goes to my family—my bedrock and my constant source of inspiration. To my beloved partner, Ratna, your boundless patience, understanding and emotional fortitude throughout the demanding process of researching and writing this book has been nothing short of heroic. I thank you, from the bottom of my heart.

To my daughters, Piyali and Pritha, your ability to listen, offer perspective and remind me of the bigger picture has kept me grounded. Your curiosity and enthusiasm for learning inspired me to make this work accessible and meaningful to anyone interested in the subject.

This book would not have been possible without the intellectual generosity of two of my mentors: Lt Gen Gautam Banerjee, PVSM, AVSM, YSM (Retd) and Maj Gen Raj Mehta, AVSM, VSM (Retd). They have consistently encouraged me throughout the writing of the book at every step—my deepest regards to both of them.

I am grateful to Lt Gen Kanwar Vinod Kumar, AVSM, the Signal Officer-in-Chief and Maj Gen T.M.P. Kumar of Directoratre General Signals, for making the logistics available to me to write this book.

I will be failing in my duty if I do not acknowledge the role of my research assistant, my Man Friday, Hav Sunder Singh, for his painstaking typing, organising the book, providing practical suggestions and generally keeping my morale up. No amount of praise is enough for him.

I hope this book contributes to a better understanding of Information Warfare and helps equip readers with the knowledge needed to navigate an increasingly complex information landscape.

The views expressed here are my own and do not necessarily reflect the positions of any institution or organisation with which I am affiliated.

The responsibility for all errors or omissions in this work are mine.

New Delhi
31 July 2025

Maj Gen PK Mallick, VSM (Retd)

List of Abbreviations

5G	Fifth-Generation
AI	Artificial Intelligence
APTs	Advanced Persistent Threats
AQI	Al Qaeda in Iraq
AR	Augmented Reality
ARSTRUC	Army Force Structure Transformation
BBG	Broadcasting Board of Governors
BCIs	Brain-Computer Interfaces
C2W	Command and Control Warfare
C5ISRT	Command, Control, Computing, Communications, Cyber, Intelligence, Surveillance, Reconnaissance and Targeting
CA	Civil Affairs
CCP	Chinese Communist Party
CCTV	Central Television
CERT	The National Computer Emergency Response Team
CGTN	China Global Television Network
CIA	Central Intelligence Agency
CII	Critical Information Infrastructure
CiMiC	Civil-Military Cooperation
CIO	Information Operations
CNA	Computer Network Attack
CND	Computer Network Defence
CNE	Computer Network Exploitation
CNO	Computer Network Operations
COCOMs	Combatant Commands

CSD	Countering State-sponsored Disinformation
CW	Cyber Warfare
CYL	Chinese Communist Youth League
DDoS	Distributed Denial-of-Service
DIA	Defense Intelligence Agency
DIME	Diplomatic, Informational, Military and Economic
DOD	Department of Defense
DSPD	Defense Support to Public Diplomacy
EW	Electronic Warfare
FSB	The Federal Security Service of the Russian Federation
GEC	Global Engagement Center
HUMINT	Human Intelligence
ICCR	Indian Council for Cultural Relations
ICCs	International Communication Centres
ICD	Information Confrontation Doctrine
IDF	Israel Defense Forces
IE	Information Environment
IIO	Inform and Influence Operations
IIWAM	Influence/Information Warfare and Manipulation
ILD	International Liaison Department
IO	Information Operation
IRA	Internet Research Agency
IS	Islamic State
ISF	Information Support Force
ISI	Inter-Services Intelligence
ISIS	Islamic State of Iraq and Syria
ISKP	Islamic State Khorasan Province
ISPR	Inter-Services Public Relations
ITO	Information Technical Operations
IW	Information Warfare
JeM	Jaish-e-Mohammad
LeT	Lashkar-e-Taiba

LLM	Large Language Models
MBN	Middle East Broadcasting Networks
MCIA	Marine Corps Intelligence Activity
MDO	Multi Domain Operations
MILDEC	Military Deception
MISO	Military Information Support Operations
MR	Mixed Reality
MSS	Ministry of State Security
NCCIA	National Cyber Crimes Investigation Agency
ODNI	Director for National Intelligence
OIE	Operations in the Information Environment
OPSEC	Operations Security
OSINT	Open-Source Intelligence
PA	Public Affairs
PD	Public Diplomacy
PLA	People's Liberation Army
PSYOPS	Psychological Operations
PSYWAR	Psychological Warfare
PTI	Pakistan Tehreek-e-Insaf
RFA	Radio Free Asia
RFE/RL	Radio Free Europe/Radio Liberty
SC	Strategic Communication
SIGINT	Signal Intelligence
SMART	Specific, Measurable, Achievable, Relevant and Time-Bound
SMP	Social Media Platforms
SSD	Strategic Studies Detachment
SSF	Strategic Support Force
SVMs	Support Vector Machines
TAO	Taiwan Affairs Office
TIADs	Theatre Information Advantage Detachments
TTP	Tactics, Techniques, Procedures
TVE	Terrorist and Violent Extremist Actors

UFWD	United Front Work Department
USAID	The United States Agency for International Development
USASOC	US Army Special Operations Command
VNSA	Terrorists and Violent Non-State Actors
VOA	Voice of America
VR	Virtual Reality
XR	Extended Reality

Chapter I

Introduction

The third wave brings with it a new form of conflict—information war—in which the key strategic asset is knowledge, not brute force and the battlefield extends to media, cyberspace and public perception."

—Alvin and Heidi Toffler in *War and Anti-War: Survival at the Dawn of the 21st Century*

Information Warfare (IW) is not a new concept. The roots of Information Warfare can be traced to the fundamental role that information has always played in a conflict. From ancient times, the ability to gather intelligence, deceive adversaries and influence public opinion has determined the outcomes of wars and revolutions. Its scope and impact have expanded exponentially with the arrival of the digital age.

Information Warfare now encompasses cyber operations, psychological manipulation, disinformation campaigns and the strategic use of data to influence, disrupt or dominate adversaries. It is a multi-dimensional battlefield where State and non-State actors, from superpowers to rogue hackers, vie for control over the flow of information and the perceptions it shapes.

Information Warfare is about power—the power to shape narratives, influence decisions and control outcomes without necessarily resorting to kinetic force. Today, information is not merely a tool of war; it is the battlespace itself. The objective is clear: to shape the decisions, actions and beliefs of adversaries, often without firing a single shot.

The consequences of Information Warfare extend far beyond the military sphere. Attacks on information systems can disrupt economies, undermine democratic processes and erode social cohesion. The manipulation of narratives and social media campaigns can sway elections, incite unrest or erode trust in institutions. The spread of disinformation can polarise societies, delegitimise authorities and incite violence.

Cyber operations can cripple critical infrastructure or steal sensitive data with a few keystrokes. State and non-State actors alike exploit vulnerabilities in information systems, seeking to gain an advantage under the garb of ambiguity and deniability. The lines between peace and war, civilian and combatant, truth and falsehood have become increasingly blurred.

Democratic nations themselves employ sophisticated Information Operations, both defensively and offensively. Information Warfare is not the domain solely of States and armies. Corporations wage information campaigns to protect their reputations and market positions. Non-State actors, from terrorist organisations to activist groups, leverage Information Warfare tactics to advance their causes. Even individuals, armed with nothing more than a smartphone and a social media account, can engage in Information Warfare by spreading disinformation, launching harassment campaigns or engaging in coordinated inauthentic behaviour. The democratisation of technology has lowered the barriers to entry, making Information Warfare a truly global and pervasive phenomenon.

To understand Information Warfare, it is essential to appreciate the interplay of technology, strategy and human psychology. The information sciences—spanning philosophy, logic, information theory, decision theory and semiotics—provide the conceptual foundation for analysing how information is created, processed and used in conflict. Technologies such as, sensors, networks, Artificial Intelligence and data analytics enable the rapid collection, fusion and dissemination of knowledge, transforming the tempo and scale of operations.

As we confront the challenges of Information Warfare, several key questions arise. How can societies defend themselves against the invisible and deceptive threats of Information Warfare? What ethical and legal frameworks should govern the use of information as a weapon? How can truth and trust be preserved in an age of manipulation and deception? And what role should individuals, organisations and governments play in shaping the future of the information domain?

When anyone can publish content that appears authoritative, when Artificial Intelligence can generate convincing but false information at scale and when traditional gatekeepers of information have lost much of their influence, how do societies establish and maintain shared standards of evidence and reasoning? The epistemological challenges posed by Information Warfare extend far beyond politics and national security, touching every aspect of human knowledge and belief.

Policy makers and military leaders have understood the strategic significance of Information Warfare. In recent decades, governments have developed doctrines, policies and capabilities to both defend against Information Warfare threats and exploit opportunities for offensive action.

The modern battlefield is no longer limited to land, sea and air; it has expanded to include space. It includes cyberspace, information and psychological domains. As adversaries adapt to the changing character of war, nations must develop effective Information Warfare strategies. In the context of South Asia, the enduring rivalry between India and Pakistan—fuelled by historical animosity, territorial disputes and terrorism—necessitates a sophisticated and calibrated Information Warfare campaign.

India, with its growing technological capabilities and democratic information ecosystem, is well-positioned to leverage Information Warfare as a strategic tool. The Indian Information Warfare campaign should aim not only to deter aggression and discredit adversarial narratives but also to blend psychological insight, technological prowess and Strategic Communication to influence perceptions, reduce the adversary's internal cohesion and bolster India's image as a responsible regional power, thereby projecting India's values.

Managing public expectations is an even bigger challenge in the face of stunningly successful military operations. In the case of Operation SINDOOR, even some respectable persons decried the ceasefire. The government is aware of the exact situation on the ground, the enemy's reaction, international opinion and diplomatic status. The government does not rely solely on media reports. Unless these public passions are managed, they will rebound on the government with unrealistic expectations during the next crisis.

The war for information is not around the corner—it is already here. The only question is whether we will be prepared to fight it.

This book aims to provide a comprehensive examination of Information Warfare, encompassing its principles, practices, technologies and implications. Drawing on insights from history, theory and real-world operations, it offers a systems-level understanding of how information has become both the prize and the weapon in contemporary conflict. The chapters ahead will examine:

- Foundations of Information Warfare
- Components of Information Operations (IO)
- Psychological Warfare
- Artificial Intelligence as a Tool for Online Radicalisation
- Social Media
- Psychological Warfare and Various Terms
- Narrative and Cognitive Warfare
- China and Cognitive Warfare
- Perception Management
- Sentiment Analysis
- Surprise, Deception and Psychological Warfare
- Country Studies—Pakistan, China and Russia
- Cautionary Thoughts
- Hypothetical Information Warfare Plan against Greenland by India
- Recommendations
- Conclusion

The battle for hearts and minds has always been central to human conflict, but never before has it been waged with such technological sophistication, global reach and potential for societal disruption. The invisible battlefield of Information Warfare may determine the fate of democratic institutions, international stability and social cohesion in ways that conventional military conflicts cannot. This book is an attempt to map that battlefield, understand its dynamics and chart a course towards a more resilient and truth-oriented Information Environment.

In this book, the human dimension of Information Warfare is addressed. The book grapples with the defensive challenges posed by Information Warfare. How can democratic societies protect themselves against information attacks without sacrificing the fundamental freedoms of speech and expression that define them? What role should technology companies play in moderating content and combating disinformation? How can educational institutions prepare citizens to navigate an increasingly polluted Information Environment, one that is often manipulated and deceptive? These questions have no easy answers, but they demand serious consideration from policy makers, technologists, educators and citizens alike.

Chapter II

Foundations of Information Warfare

> *I began to understand that I was caught up in two wars: one fought on the ground with tanks and artillery and an information war fought largely, though not exclusively, through social media. And, perhaps counter-intuitively, it mattered who won the war of words and narratives (rather) than who had the most potent weaponry.*
>
> —**David Patrikarakos**, *War in 140 Characters*, 2017.

Information Warfare involves the use and management of information to gain a competitive advantage over an opponent. The scope of Information Warfare encompasses a range of activities designed to influence, disrupt, corrupt or usurp the decision-making process of adversaries while protecting one's own information systems and processes.

Information Warfare is a critical component of modern military strategy, designed to influence the cognitive dimensions of adversaries, allies and civilian populations. It extends beyond the traditional battlefield, leveraging information to achieve strategic objectives by controlling narratives and shaping perceptions. The ability to influence the thoughts, emotions and behaviours of target audiences can determine the outcome of both conventional and unconventional conflicts.

Unlike conventional warfare, Information Warfare transcends the battlefield, affecting the hearts and minds of civilian populations and military leaders alike. The impact of these operations often becomes apparent only months or years after their execution. Yet, their success can decisively alter the course of history, while their failures, though subtle, can have devastating consequences.

In the era of information saturation, where news cycles are rapid and social media platforms facilitate the instant spread of information, controlling the narrative has become a pivotal aspect of modern military strategy.

Information Warfare integrates Cyber Operations, Electronic Warfare, Psychological Operations, Military Deception and Operational Security to dominate the information space.

In recent decades, the rise of digital technology and social media has transformed the landscape of Information Operations. The ability to disseminate information rapidly and widely has amplified the impact of psychological campaigns. Adversaries can now reach global audiences with tailored messages, exploiting the fragmented nature of modern information consumption. This evolution necessitates a more sophisticated and integrated approach to Information Warfare, incorporating cyber operations, data analytics and Artificial Intelligence to influence perceptions and shape narratives in real-time. Information Warfare operates on the principle that information itself is a critical asset and controlling the flow and integrity of information is essential for achieving strategic and tactical objectives.

The evolution of Information Warfare is closely tied to advancements in digital and cyber technologies. Historically, Information Warfare has been a component of military strategy, with ancient civilisations employing various forms of propaganda and deception to influence adversaries. However, the digital revolution has transformed the landscape of Information Warfare, introducing new capabilities and challenges.

Governments and military organisations recognise the potential of digital platforms to influence public opinion, conduct espionage and disrupt adversary operations. The ability to reach global audiences instantaneously and anonymously became a powerful tool in the arsenal of information warriors.

Information Warfare strategies have been employed in various contemporary conflicts. During the Arab Spring, social media played a crucial role in mobilising protestors and disseminating information, both supporting and undermining different regimes. In the conflict between Russia and Ukraine, cyber attacks and Information Operations have been used extensively to influence perceptions and disrupt military operations. These examples illustrate the critical role of Information Warfare in modern conflict and the necessity for military professionals to understand and counter these tactics.

Protecting one's information systems and processes is equally important in Information Warfare. Ensuring the security and integrity of communication networks, data repositories and critical infrastructure is essential for maintaining operational effectiveness. This involves implementing robust cybersecurity measures, conducting continuous monitoring and threat assessments and developing resilient information systems capable of withstanding adversary attacks.

The ethical and legal considerations of Information Warfare also warrant attention. The use of disinformation and manipulation in Influence Operations raises questions about the ethical implications of these tactics. While achieving strategic objectives is paramount, maintaining adherence to international laws and norms is crucial for preserving legitimacy and avoiding unintended consequences. Balancing operational effectiveness with ethical constraints is a complex challenge that military professionals must navigate.

As Information Warfare continues to evolve, the future will likely see further integration of advanced technologies, such as, Artificial Intelligence, Machine Learning and Quantum Computing. These technologies offer new opportunities for enhancing the effectiveness of Information Operations and protecting against adversary threats. However, they also introduce new risks and challenges that require continuous adaptation and innovation.

Information Warfare is a vital component of today's warfare, encompassing a wide range of activities aimed at influencing perceptions and controlling information. The evolution of digital and cyber technologies has transformed the landscape of Information Warfare, creating new opportunities and challenges. Understanding the relationship between Information Warfare and Cyber Warfare and integrating these capabilities into strategic planning is essential for achieving and maintaining a competitive advantage in the information domain.

HISTORICAL EVOLUTION OF INFORMATION WARFARE

From the beginning, the battle over information has been a part of warfare. In the Mahabharata, during the great battle of Kurukshetra, information was used to kill Guru Dronacharya and King Shalya as the Charioteer of Karna used psychological means to affect the mind of the great warrior Karna. The use of information as a tool in warfare and its emphasis on accurate intelligence for decision superiority over a mightier foe have been enunciated in Chinese military strategist Sun Tzu's book, *The Art of War*, which dates back to the fifth century BC. In 480 BC, during the Battle of Thermopylae, Persian ruler Xerxes employed intimidation tactics to weaken the resolve of the Greek City-States.

When the Mongols, under the leadership of Genghis Khan, were sweeping across Eurasia in the thirteenth century, they employed spies to deliberately spread news of the atrocities they had committed against cities that did not surrender, instilling fear and confusion among their enemies. Mongols would also drag branches behind their horses to raise dust clouds, an early and effective form of deception and disinformation, which suggested their armies were far larger than they actually were. The clear goal was to defeat the enemy before firing a single shot. This tactic was so effective that it often led to the surrender of cities without a fight.

Alexander the Great 336 to 323 BCE used cultural assimilation to subdue dissent and maintain conquered lands.

In 1870, Otto von Bismarck incited the French into a very unfavourable declaration of war against Prussia by manipulating the reported text of one telegram. These earliest strategists laid the foundation for the Information Warfare strategy in modern times.

During World War I and World War II, both the Allied and Axis powers developed extensive propaganda apparatuses, utilising print media, radio broadcasts and films to influence public opinion and demoralise enemy forces. These efforts laid the groundwork for modern Psychological Operations, demonstrating the effectiveness of coordinated and strategic information campaigns.

The Cold War marked a significant period of innovation and expansion in Information Warfare. The ideological battle between the United States and the Soviet Union spurred the development of comprehensive influence strategies, including covert operations, psychological campaigns and information dissemination. This era saw the establishment of specialised institutions and the integration of Psychological Operations into broader military and intelligence frameworks.

Nearer home, during the 1971 Bangladesh Liberation War, the Chief of the Indian Army appealed to Pakistani soldiers to surrender through a radio broadcast. The leaflets were dropped over the location of Pakistani troops as a part of Psychological Warfare.

In a Foreword to the RAND Corporation's Report on the Changing Role of Information in Warfare, Andrew W. Marshall stated prophetically in 1998:

- Information advances will affect more than just how we fight wars. The nature and purpose of war itself may change. The manner in which wars start, how they end, their duration and the nature of the participants may change as shifts in the relative power of States and non-State entities occur.
- New technologies have both positive and negative effects on national security. Together, advances create new vulnerabilities; new threats create new opportunities. We should resist the temptation to view the changes documented here as either wholly bad or wholly good. Instead, we need to understand that profound technological changes are inevitably two-sided.
- The US Department of Defense (DOD) has little control over the pace and direction of the information revolution. Although the DOD played a significant role in developing, refining and implementing new information technologies in the past, today the technological envelope is being pushed primarily by the commercial sector. DOD needs to manage a difficult transition from being a pioneer to being a leading user. This transition will require not only keeping abreast of new technological developments but also accepting that technology will no longer be developed exactly to military specifications.
- The increasing capacity to produce, communicate and use information will have a significant impact on every area of national security. Information is everywhere. As a result, we will not be able to understand how these new technologies will change our own jobs unless we understand how they will change the jobs of others. The advent of the information age will require, as never before, that we

take a broader perspective and avoid stovepipes that close our eyes to changes taking place outside our own spheres of direct responsibility.

DEFINING INFORMATION WARFARE

While there is currently no official United States government definition of Information Warfare, some US DOD doctrines define Information Warfare not as a strategy but as a subset of Operations in the Information Environment (OIE) conducted during both sub-conventional warfare and during warfighting to dominate the Information Environment (IE) at a specific place and time.[1]

The US Secretary of Defense later characterised Information Operations (IO) in JP 3-13 as "the integrated employment, during military operations, of information-related capabilities in concert with other lines of operation to influence, disrupt, corrupt or usurp the decision making of adversaries and potential adversaries while protecting our own."

The RAND Corporation defined Information Warfare as: "Information Warfare is a conflict or struggle between two or more groups in the Information Environment".

Dan Kuehl of the National Defense University defines Information Warfare as "military offensive and defensive actions to control/exploit the environment."

The UK has defined Information Operations as: A staff function to analyse, plan, assess and integrate information activities to create desired effects on the will, understanding and capability of adversaries, potential adversaries and audiences in support of mission objectives.[2]

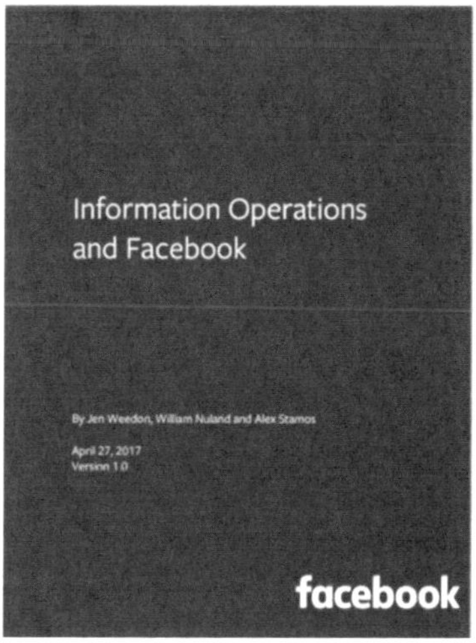

Facebook has published an interesting White Paper on Information Operations. It defines Information Operations as:

Actions taken by organised actors (governments or non-State actors) to distort domestic or foreign political sentiment, most

frequently to achieve a strategic and/or geopolitical outcome. These operations can employ a combination of methods, such as, false news, disinformation, or networks of fake accounts, aimed at manipulating public opinion.

According to the IBM Centre for the Business of Government, Information Operations are deliberate campaigns to influence others' wills, in which the mechanism of influence is not the use or threat of violence, but rather non-violent, non-kinetic methods aimed at shaping others' perceptions, motivations and convictions. In the information domain, human cognition is key terrain. The weapons used on that terrain include violence, viral memes, speeches and any other methods by which human cognition may be influenced.

Information Warfare versus Information Operations

Information Warfare occurs at the strategic level, while Information Operations involve using various information-related capabilities to implement the strategy. The operational level is when campaigns and major operations are planned, conducted and sustained to achieve strategic objectives within theatres or other operational areas. Operations link these strategic objectives with particular tactics, techniques and procedures to achieve them.

Information Warfare may be a preamble to an armed conflict. Information Operations set the conditions to gain the support of locals, "winning the hearts and minds." Alternatively, Information Warfare may be an end in itself, achieving the goal without the use of force. Information Operations take place at the operational level, linking information-related capabilities and tactics to a broader strategy. They are essential during all phases of a military operation.

However, in this book, Information Warfare and Information Operations have been used interchangeably, meaning the same.

There is a difference between Cyber Warfare and Information Warfare. Both deal with information. Cyber Warfare does it exclusively in its digitised and operationalised form. Information Warfare does so in a much broader sense. With Information Warfare, information itself is the weapon.

Information Operation Domain

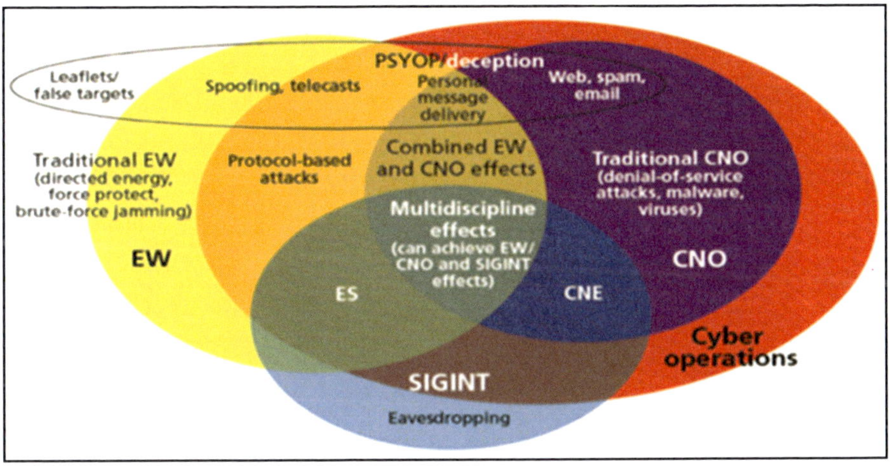

Source: CERDEC I2WD. RAND, MG1113-5.2

INFORMATION ENVIRONMENT

The Information Environment (IE) has emerged as a critical domain in modern conflict where data is created, disseminated and consumed. It encompasses traditional media, social platforms, algorithms and Artificial Intelligence, all of which shape how information is accessed and interpreted. It shapes perceptions, influences decisions and can decisively affect outcomes across political, military, economic and social spheres. The Information Environment is increasingly contested, with both State and non-State actors leveraging information as a tool and weapon.

The Information Environment is part of the operational environment. Any activity that occurs in the Information Environment domain, simultaneously takes place in and affects, one or more of the operational environment domains.

The Information Environment is becoming increasingly complex. It has a crucial importance in military planning and operations. Activities occurring in and through the Information Environment have a substantial impact on military operations and outcomes. Commanders and staff at all levels must be aware of the Information Environment in all its complexity and the likely impacts it will have on current and planned military operations.

In 2017, the US DOD updated its Doctrine for the Armed Forces and categorised information as the seventh joint function of the military, alongside the joint functions of command and control, intelligence, fires, movement and manoeuvre, protection and sustainment.

The aggregate of social, cultural, linguistic, psychological, technical and physical factors that affect how humans and automated systems derive meaning from, act upon and are impacted by information, including the individuals organisations and systems that collect, process, disseminate or use information.

—Joint Publication 3-04, *Information in Joint Operations,* September 2022

The UK has defined Information Environment as: An environment comprised of the information itself, the individuals organisations and systems that receive, process and convey the information and the cognitive, virtual and physical space in which this occurs.[3]

Informational Power

The ability to use information to support the achievement of objectives and gain an information advantage. The essence of informational power is the ability to exert one's will through the projection, exploitation, denial and preservation of information in pursuit of objectives.

—Joint Publication 3-04, *Information in Joint Operations,* September 2022

Operations in the Information Environment (OIE)

Military actions involving the integrated employment of multiple information forces to affect drivers of behaviour by informing audiences, influencing foreign relevant actors, attacking and exploiting relevant actor information, information networks and information systems and protecting friendly information, information networks and information systems.

— Joint Publication 3-04, *Information in Joint Operations,* September 2022

Strategic Communication, Public Diplomacy, Public and Civil Affairs and Cyberspace Operations may be integrated and employed by information forces. These efforts may take place in and throughout each of the global domains, including air, land, sea, space and cyberspace, as well as in various forms unrelated to cyberspace, such as, distributing pamphlets, engaging in cultural exchanges, jamming or broadcasting targeted communications and implementing foreign aid programmes.

Cyberspace is a global domain within the Internet comprising the interdependent network of information technology infrastructures and resident data, including telecommunications networks, the Internet, computer systems and embedded processors and controllers.

Context for Operations in the Information Environment

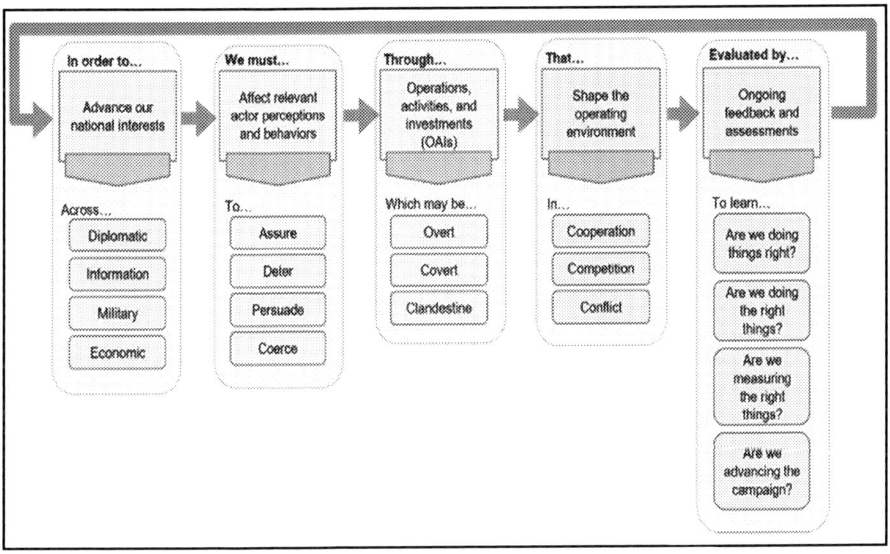

Source: Air Force Doctrine Publication 3-13, Information in Air Force Operations, 1 February 2023, https://www.doctrine.af.mil/Portals/61/documents/AFDP_3-13/3-13-AFDP-INFO-OPS.pdf

Recent developments in the entertainment industry and social media have brought about significant changes in the Information Environment. Entertainers, advertisers, politicians and others have always tried to build audiences with attention-grabbing techniques. The attention economy, which translates online views of content into money, has made it almost impossible for humans to turn away. The same methods can expose individuals to information that is specifically designed to reinforce their biases and prevent them from engaging in objective analysis of facts.

An example of cyber-based exploitation is YouTube. Algorithms produce videos for viewers based on their previously viewed content. This is more concerning when combined with big data. The manipulation and targeted use of information are creating threats to democracy that are as real as military threats.

Information-capable adversaries can promote narratives that exploit social divisions, strategically target information and selectively manipulate the truth. Cyber-enabled Information Operations are a threat to democracies. Democratic nations will have to come to grips with the modern Information Environment.[4]

All instruments of national power, including Diplomatic, Informational, Military and Economic (DIME), can be projected and employed in the Information Environment.

Strategy, Information and Power are intimately linked

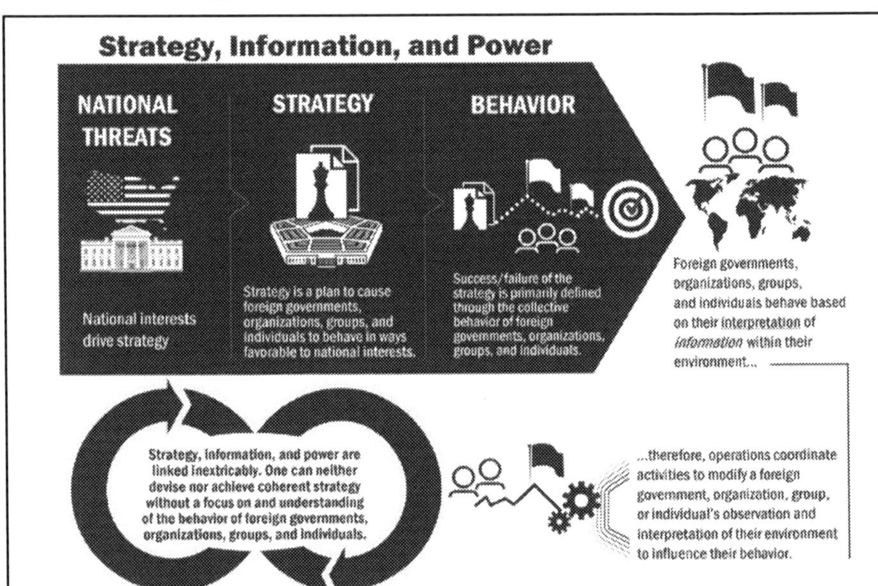

Source: US Government Accountability Office, Information Environment: Opportunities and Threats to DOD's National Security Mission, Washington DC: GAO, 21 September 2022, https://www.gao.gov/products/gao-22-104714

INFORMATION ENVIRONMENT DIMENSIONS

The recent model of the Information Environment focuses on the transmission, processing and storage of information within three interrelated but distinct dimensions: physical, informational and cognitive domains. Information Warfare is conducted in three dimensions:[5]

- **The physical layer**. Command and control systems and associated infrastructure.
- **The informational layer.** Networks and systems where information is stored.
- **The cognitive layer.** The minds of people who transmit and respond to information.

Three Dimensions of the Information Environment

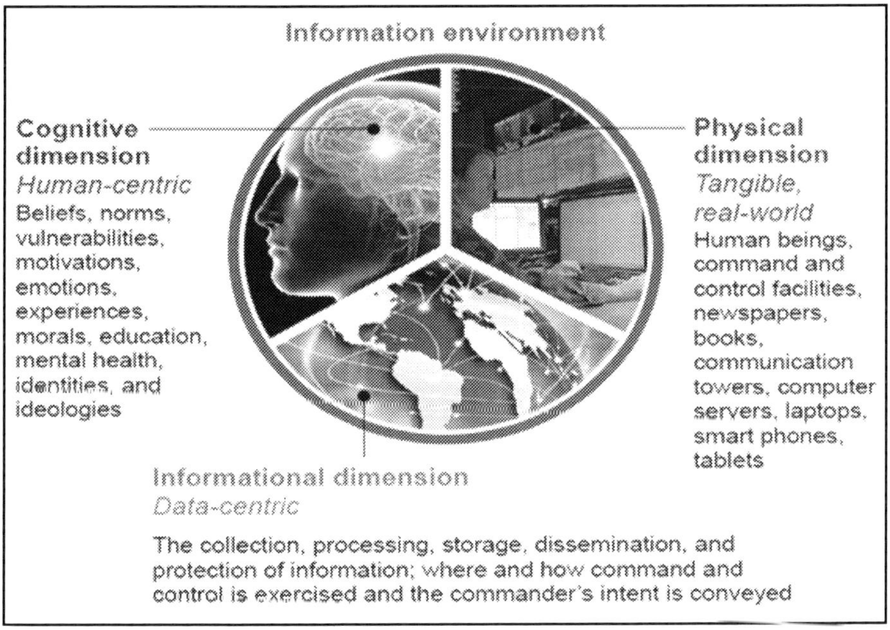

Source: GAO analysis of Department of Defense information: U.S. Air Force/Capt. Justin Brokhoff, GAO-22-1047

Types	*Affects*	*Examples*
Physical	Content	• The physical world and its content, particularly that which enables and supports exchanging ideas, information and messages. • Information systems and physical networks. • Communications systems and networks. • People and human networks. • Personal devices, handheld devices and social media graphical user interface. • Mobile phones and personal digital assistants.
Informational	Code	• Collected, coded, processed, stored, disseminated, displayed and protected information. • Information metadata, flow and quality. • Social media application software, information exchange and search engine optimisation. • The code itself. • Any automated decision-making.
Cognitive	Context	• The impact of information on the human will. • The contextualised information and human decision making. • Intangibles, such as, morale, values, worldviews, situational awareness, perceptions and public opinions. • Mental calculations in response to stimuli, such as, liking something on a social media application.

Source: The Conduct of Information Operations, ATP 3-13.1, October 2018, https://irp.fas.org/DODdir/army/atp3-13-1.pdf

Human Dimensions	*Information Dimensions*	*Physical Dimensions*
• **Relevant Actors** – Military Leaders – Civilian Leaders – Key influencers – Groups – Organisations – Populations • **Drive of behaviour** – Attitude – Cognition – Culture – Desire – Emotion – Instinct – Laungage – Memory – Perception	• **Ideas** – Narratives – Messages – Themes • **Data** • **Software** • **Information** – Friendly – Neutral – Threat	• **Inherent informational aspects of operations Terrain** • **Weather** • **Electromagnetic radiation** • **Communications** – Computer networks Internet – Cellular networks – Print – Television – Radio – Satellite Constellations • **Bandwidth** • **Storage**

The Information Environment is increasingly Digital and Wireless

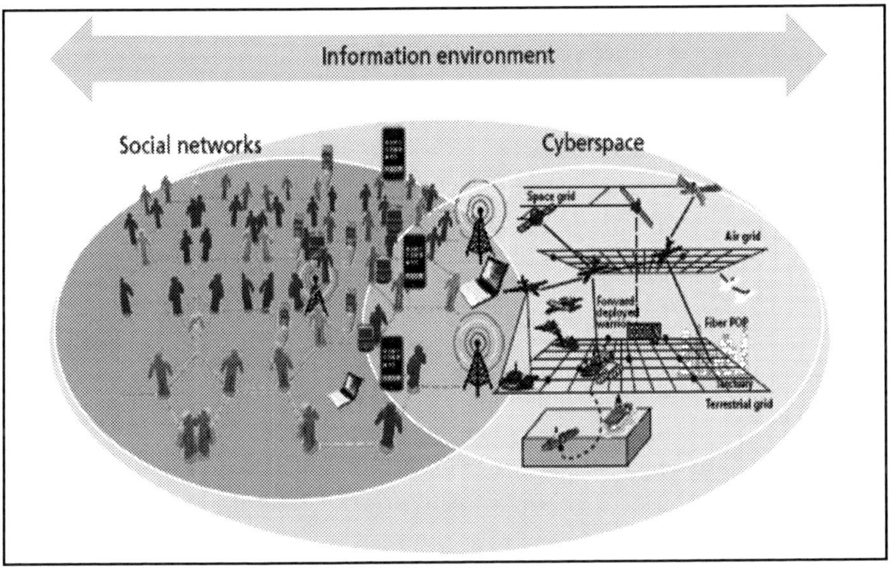

Source: RAND Corporation MG 1113-2.1

IBM defines the information space as:

- The information space is a chaotic system, as slight variations in conditions can have a dramatic impact on how information traverses space and time. Information Operations can be compared to weather forecasting and fluid dynamics. While an actor may set out with a clean narrative, that narrative will likely be disrupted by changing contexts, unanticipated perspectives and complex interactions with other narratives.
- Any visualisation of this mélange of data points must be useful to decision makers at multiple echelons. Such a visualisation requires a dataset that encompasses data from the entire information space, not just social media and that can be overlaid onto visualisations of the land, air, sea and cyber domains.
- Although the information domain is large, it must remain bounded. With decades of practice, US adversaries have developed rigorous Information Warfare doctrines. Delineating activities that do and do not fall within the bounds of Information Operations allow for a more useful understanding and visualisation of these activities.

The information domain can be viewed as the sum of the wills, decision-making capabilities and resulting choices to act of each actor, where the will is the composite of convictions, perceptions and influences that drive action.

This definition distinguishes the information space from cyberspace, which encompasses the electromagnetic spectrum and the physical infrastructure that harnesses those wavelengths. Cyberspace contains data that affects the information domain; cyberspace is not the totality of the information domain. Analogue containers of information outside cyberspace—such as, gestures, conversations, symbols and press reports—are just as relevant to the information domain as these same data contained within cyberspace.

Targeting

Targeting is the process of selecting and prioritising targets and matching the appropriate response to them, considering operational requirements and capabilities. A target may be an area, complex, installation, force, equipment, capability, function, individual, group, system, entity or behaviour identified for possible action to support the Commander's intent, objectives and guidance. Targets relate to objectives at all levels—strategic, operational and tactical. The nature of the target or threat, the conditions of the mission variables (mission, enemy, terrain, weather, troops and support available, time available and civil considerations) and the desired outcomes determine whether actions need to be lethal or non-lethal.

Various targeting processes that contribute to decision-making and mission accomplishment

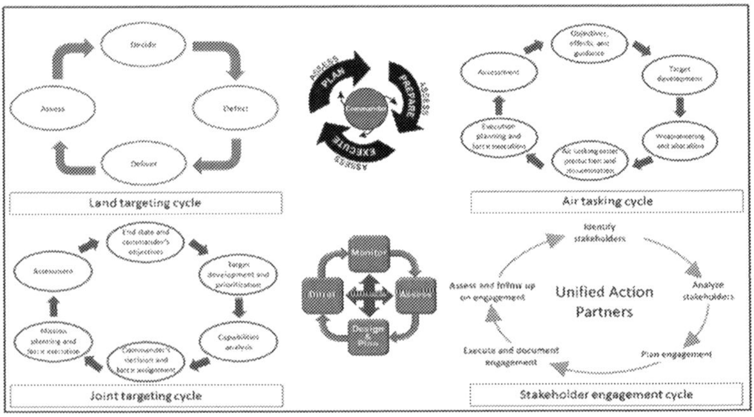

Source: GAO Report on Contested Information Environment, January 2023, https://www.gao.gov/assets/gao-23-105608.pdf

Different categories of information that may be used in OIE include the following:

Propaganda. The propagation of an idea or narrative that is intended to influence, similar to psychological or Influence Operations. It can be misleading but true and may include stolen information. A government communicating its intent, policies and values through speeches, press releases and other Public Affairs can be considered propaganda.

Misinformation. The spreading of unintentionally false information. Examples include internet trolls who spread unfounded conspiracy theories or web hoaxes through social media, believing them to be true.

Disinformation. Unlike misinformation, disinformation is intentionally false. Examples include planting false news stories in the media and tampering with private and/or classified communications before their widespread release.

OODA Loop in Theory and Practice

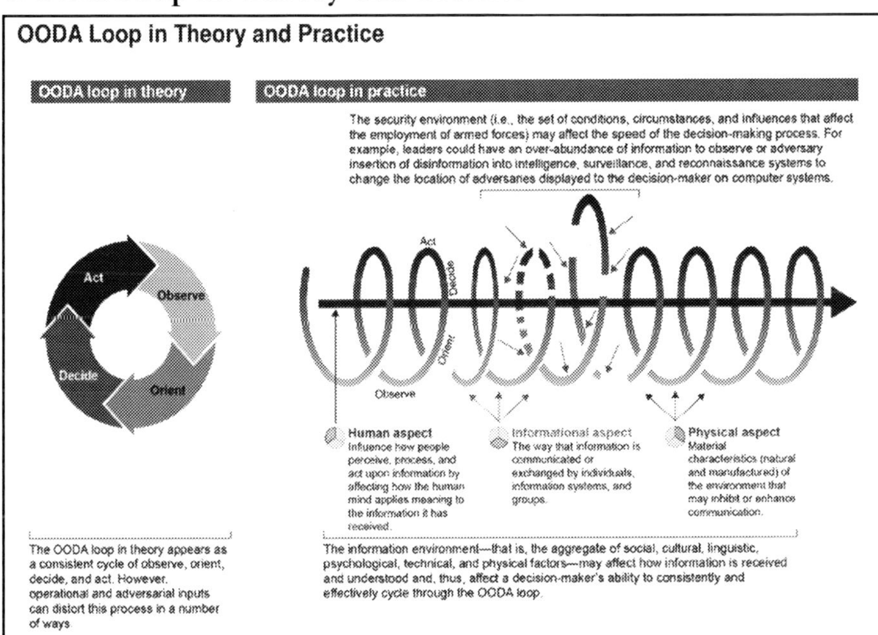

Source: GAO Report on Contested Information Environment, January 2023, https://www.gao.gov/assets/gao-23-105608.pdf

Examples of Adversary Actions That Can Affect Military Leader Decision-Making in a Contested Information Environment

Adversaries can disrupt military decision-making through cyberattacks (disabling communications), deepfake propaganda (spreading false information), Electronic Warfare (jamming sensors), social media manipulation (sowing confusion) and AI-driven disinformation (distorting reality). These actions degrade situational awareness, delay responses and erode trust in command structures in a contested Information Environment.

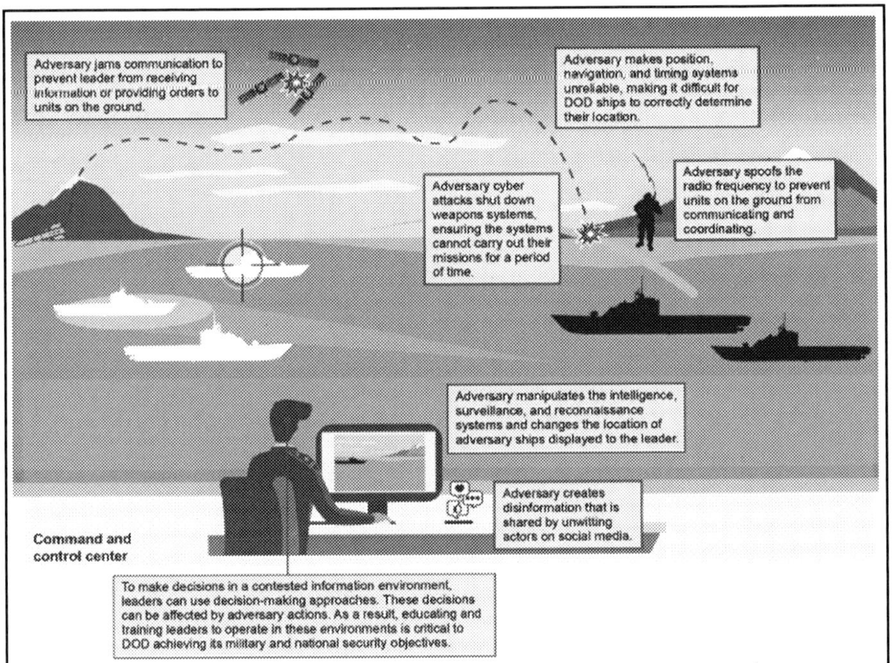

Source: GAO Report on Contested Information Environment, January 2023, https://www.gao.gov/assets/gao-23-105608.pdf

Institutional Challenges for Armed Forces Related to the Information Environment

The Armed Forces face difficulties in adapting to modern Information Warfare. These include integrating advanced cyber, AI and data analytics into traditional structures, overcoming bureaucratic resistance to change and ensuring secure, real-time information sharing across domains. Armed forces must counter disinformation, protect critical networks and train personnel in digital warfare while maintaining ethical and legal standards. The rapid evolution of technology demands agile policies, joint interoperability and new doctrines, posing significant institutional hurdles for militaries accustomed to conventional warfare paradigms. This requires institutional reforms to operate effectively on the information-driven battlefield.

Institutional Challenges

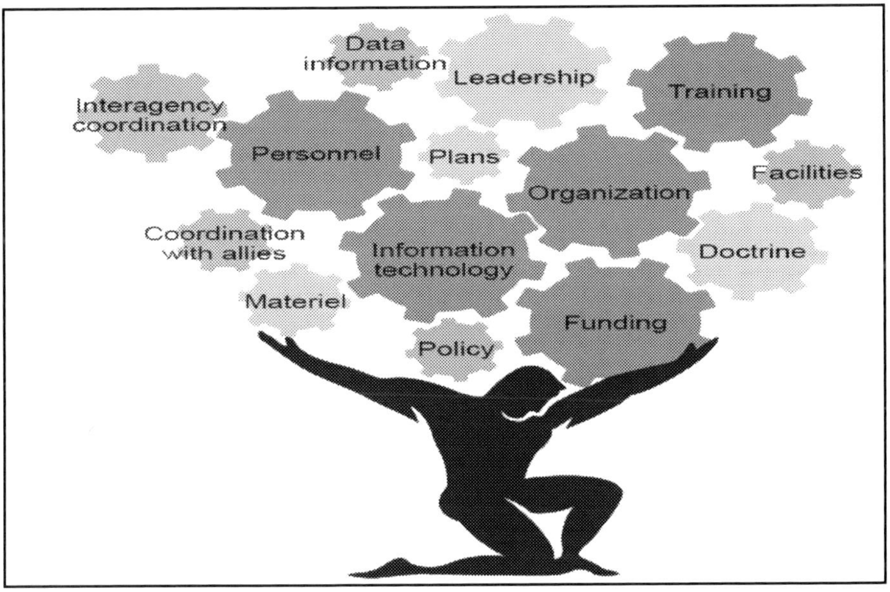

Source: GAO Report on Information Environment, September 2022, https://www.gao.gov/assets/gao-22-104714.pdf

INFORMATION COMPRESSES THE LEVELS OF WARFARE

Information Technology, particularly in cyber and information domains, blurs the traditional distinctions between strategic, operational and tactical levels of warfare. In modern conflicts, information flows rapidly across all levels, enabling real-time decision-making and coordination. Cyber operations, social media and data analytics enable tactical actions, such as, a drone strike, to have strategic impacts instantly, while strategic decisions can directly influence battlefield outcomes.

Information acts as a force multiplier, accelerating decision-making and integrating actions across all levels, making warfare more interconnected and dynamic. This compression transforms how military operations are planned, coordinated and executed across the entire spectrum of conflict.

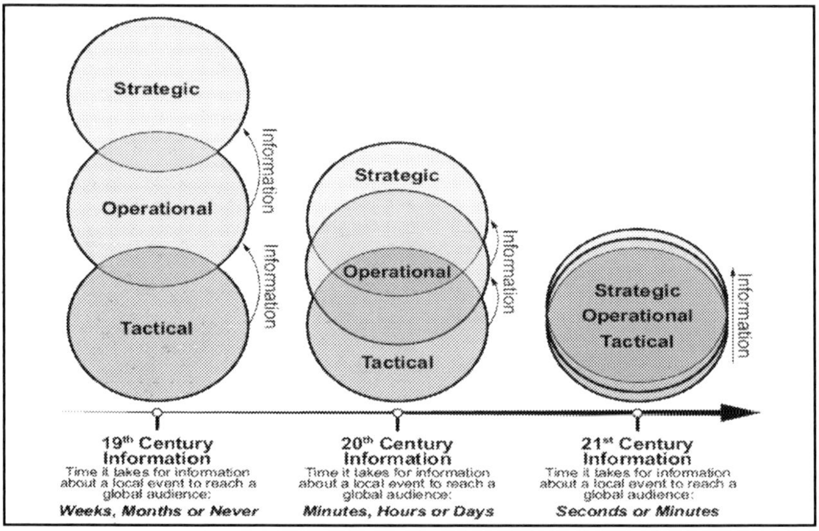

Several guiding questions need to be addressed:[6]

- What is the best unit of analysis for understanding Information Operations?
- What would constitute centres of gravity in Information Operations and/or inflexion points?
- How do we identify, assess and visualise them?
- Are mass and momentum applicable in the information domain?

Specific questions which need deliberation are:

- In the current era, how do Information Operations impact governments and stakeholders?
- How can emerging technologies facilitate the faster and more reliable development of a common operating picture and understanding, enabling effective decision-making?
- What challenges and opportunities do Information Operations provide to swift and effective decision-making? What communications do they have with other domains?
- How should governments and stakeholders combat misinformation as a tool of modern conflict?
- How can Information Operations be best visualised alongside other domains?

Emerging Technologies Associated with the Information Environment

As Information Warfare continues to evolve, the future will likely see the further integration of advanced technologies, including Artificial Intelligence, machine learning and quantum computing. These technologies offer new opportunities for enhancing the effectiveness of Information Operations and protecting against threats from adversaries. However, they also introduce new risks and challenges that require continuous adaptation and innovation.

Several emerging technologies have the potential to accelerate change and introduce both opportunities for and threats to the Information Environment. A variety of technologies, including Artificial Intelligence (AI) and Machine Learning, Quantum Computing, Social Media Platforms, Deepfakes and Bots, could have either a positive or negative effect on the Information Environment.

Artificial Intelligence

Artificial Intelligence (AI) is being leveraged in warfighting operations for intelligence analysis, battlefield data fusion, autonomous vehicles and lethal autonomous weapon systems. Non-warfighting applications include financial transaction resolution, predictive maintenance, security clearance vetting and health screening analysis. However, AI introduces significant cybersecurity risks. AI-powered malware can mutate rapidly, exploit vulnerabilities and conduct precise, large-scale cyber attacks, accelerating and automating Cyber Warfare while enabling stealthier, more persistent threats.

Big data enables the unprecedented speed at which information is collected by connected devices, accumulating massive amounts of data that can be used for actionable insights, improved decision-making and a competitive advantage. Information gathered through shopping loyalty programmes, credit cards, online shopping and social networking has increased available data exponentially. Analysis of this big data can predict political attitudes, affiliations, household income and many other personal details. This type of analysis can be used to narrow down the information to receptive audiences.

AI systems are themselves vulnerable to manipulation and deception, particularly as critical decision-making and authentication processes are increasingly automated. As reliance on AI grows, so does the potential impact of cyber incidents.

To counter these challenges, the government must strengthen its cybersecurity initiatives, address weaknesses in information security programmes and enhance its responses to cyber incidents, ensuring robust protection, as AI deployment expands.

Quantum Technologies

Quantum Technologies harness the smallest particles of energy and matter to collect, generate and process information in ways far beyond current capabilities. Quantum sensors promise more precise measurements for science, industry and navigation, offering critical benefits, such as maintaining timing and position accuracy even when GPS is unavailable.

Quantum communications could enable highly secure, unhackable data transmission for businesses and governments, making eavesdropping extremely difficult.

Quantum computers may revolutionise fields like machine learning and cryptography, but they also pose significant security risks. A full-scale quantum computer could potentially break standard encryption, posing a significant threat to the current cybersecurity infrastructure. This would require the government to adapt its security measures to counter these new vulnerabilities.

Conversely, adversaries could utilise quantum communications to establish secure channels that are virtually impossible to intercept or decrypt. Thus, while quantum technologies offer transformative benefits, they also introduce serious national security challenges.

Social Media Platforms

Social media platforms enable users to create profiles, form networks, share content and interact with others. But its algorithms and user-driven networks can spread misinformation. Algorithms prioritise engaging content, often amplifying the distribution of certain content, which can include misinformation. Algorithms designed to boost engagement often prioritise and amplify certain posts, which can consist of false or misleading information. These platform characteristics present both threats and opportunities within the Information Environment, impacting how information is shared and perceived.

Deepfakes

Deepfakes is an AI-enabled technology that can be used to replace faces, manipulate facial expressions, synthesise faces and synthesise speech in video, photo or audio recordings. It is a powerful tool that can be used for exploitation and disinformation. Deepfakes could be used to influence elections or incite civil unrest or as a weapon of Psychological Warfare. Deepfakes could also lead audiences to disregard legitimate evidence of wrongdoing and undermine public trust in audiovisual content.

Bots

Bots are lines of computer instructions that work to execute tasks autonomously and repetitively. They can simulate the behaviour of human beings in a social network, interact with other users and share messages and information. Based on how the bots are developed, they can learn from response patterns or input values to respond to specific situations. Using these capabilities, the bots simulate users' behaviour, which could include the propagation of misinformation and disinformation.

Fifth-Generation Wireless Communications

Fifth-generation (5G) wireless networks are designed to deliver significantly faster speeds, support a greater number of devices and offer enhanced flexibility, reliability and security compared to current cellular networks. However, several challenges may limit the effectiveness and adoption of 5G. These include ongoing spectrum shortages, heightened privacy risks, persistent supply chain vulnerabilities in network equipment and the potential for new cybersecurity threats that could broaden the attack surface.

Extended Reality Technologies

Extended Reality (XR) encompasses technologies that blend the digital and real worlds, including Augmented Reality (AR), Mixed Reality (MR) and Virtual Reality (VR). AR overlays digital content onto real environments using devices like smartphones or AR glasses. MR utilises headsets to facilitate interaction between digital and real elements, whereas VR fully immerses users in digital spaces using head-mounted displays. XR technologies offer benefits, such as enhanced data sharing, collaborative digital workspaces, new methods for knowledge generation and decision-making and safer, more cost-effective training for complex or hazardous tasks like military operations.

Internet of Things

The Internet of Things (IoT) is a set of internet-capable devices, such as wearable fitness devices and smartphones, that interact with the physical environment and typically contain elements for sensing, communicating, processing and actuating. However, the National Security Agency of the US commented that IoT technologies, particularly smart medical devices, are an operational security concern. The US DOD identified numerous security risks with IoT devices that can generally be divided into risks with the devices themselves and risks with the devices' operational implications.

Two main categories of IoT security risks are inherent device vulnerabilities and broader operational consequences stemming from their use.[7]

THE INDIVIDUALISATION OF WAR

When people work on the internet for searching, reading, watching, shopping, dating and other miscellaneous activities, they leave a huge amount of data that the sensors collect. AI-enabled systems can analyse these vast amounts of harvested data to micro-target individuals. This micro-targeting could entail targeting key individuals with kinetic attacks. The effects can be delivered on the battlefield, close to it or away from it. Individualisation's greatest threat is to peacetime and crisis decision-making, but it may also contribute to disrupting large-scale combat operations.

This individualisation of war will change the psychology of war. The reach of new technology-enabled systems means that individual combatants, leaders and even their family members are more easily targetable. When this takes place, anyone considered a target by the adversary will not be safe.

We have seen this micro-targeting by Ukraine and Russia in the ongoing Ukraine War. Initially, Russians sent emails or social media messages to individual soldiers and their families about the futility of fighting the much stronger Russian forces. The Ukrainians have effectively and repeatedly tracked and targeted Russian military leaders. The effects can be delivered on the battlefield, close to it or away from it. Individualisation's greatest threat is to peacetime and crisis decision-making, but it may also contribute to disrupting large-scale combat operations. Israelis are now using the same technique to target Iran's military and political leaders.

Individuals and small units have at their disposal more sophisticated technologies to deliver tactical to strategic effects. By expanding the power of individuals, technology will increase uncertainty, about which actions are taken by a State, by those acting on behalf of a State or by those acting independently.

Chapter III

Components of Information Operations

INFORMATION OPERATIONS

The US government has theorised Information Operations (IO) as a purely military activity involving a set of tactics or capabilities. In the US DOD's 2003 version of the Joint Publication 3-13 and the Information Operations Roadmap, IO consists of five pillars:

- Computer Network Operations (CNO), which include Computer Network Attack (CNA), Computer Network Defense (CND) and Computer Network Exploitation (CNE).
- Psychological Operations (PSYOPS).
- Electronic Warfare (EW).
- Operations Security (OPSEC).
- Military Deception (MILDEC).

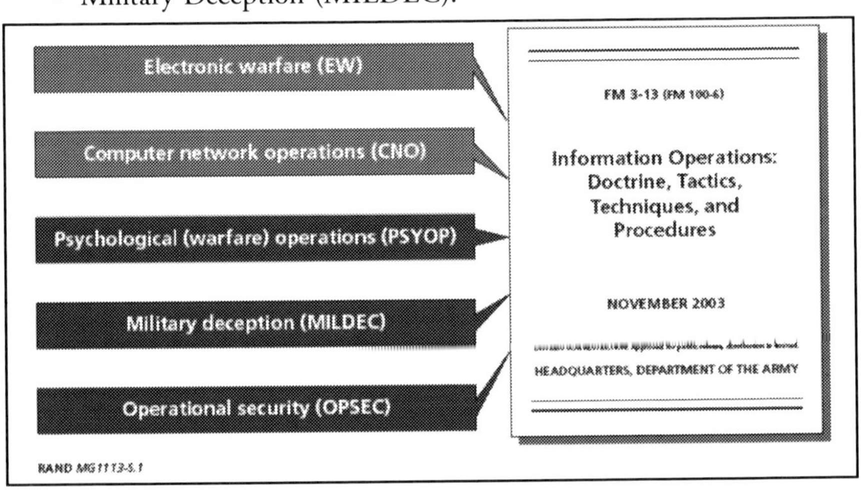

COMPUTER NETWORK OPERATIONS

With the advent of the US Cyber Command, the Computer Network Operations (CNO) became responsible for cyberspace operations, encompassing both their offensive and defensive aspects, with its own doctrine outlined in JP 3-12. In 2010, PSYOPS were reorganised as the Military Information Support Operations (MISO), to reflect a broader range of activities and the existing Military Information Support Teams, which consist of PSYOPS personnel deployed at US embassies overseas. JP 3-13.2 Military Information Support Operations replaced the term PSYOPS with MISO to "more accurately reflect and convey the nature of planned peacetime or combat operations activities." The name changes caused administrative confusion and some services reverted to the PSYOPS label.

PSYCHOLOGICAL OPERATIONS

Psychological Operations (PSYOPS) involve the prepared use of information (propaganda) to influence emotions, objective reasoning, motives and ultimately, the behaviour of foreign governments, organisations, groups and individuals. At the strategic level, PSYOPS involve the dissemination of information to influence foreign target audiences in support of a nation's goals and objectives. PSYOPS at the operational level are conducted to support the combatant commander's mission accomplishment, either independently or as an integral part of other operations.

ELECTRONIC WARFARE

Electronic Warfare is defined as military action involving electromagnetic and directed energy to control the electromagnetic spectrum or attack the enemy. Examples include jamming command and control systems, as well as satellites used for global positioning systems and radio communications.

OPERATIONS SECURITY

Operations Security is the system of identifying critical information and analysing friendly actions attendant to military operations and other activities.

MILITARY DECEPTION

Military Deception (MILDEC) is the act of knowingly misleading an adversary's military, paramilitary or violent extremist organisation decision-makers, thereby causing the adversary to undertake specific actions or inactions that contribute to accomplishing the friendly mission. A pillar closely related to PSYOPS, MILDEC focuses on the dissemination of false information or disinformation.

Strategic Communication, Public Diplomacy, Public and Civil Affairs and Cyberspace Operations may be considered as supporting capabilities. They may occur outside of cyberspace and may include tasks such as, distributing pamphlets, engaging in cultural exchanges and implementing Civil Affairs and foreign aid programmes to gain favour with a target population.

INFORMATION OPERATIONS IN CYBERSPACE

In JP 3-12, cyberspace is defined as "the global domain within the Information Environment consisting of the interdependent network of information technology infrastructures and resident data, including the Internet, telecommunications networks, computer systems and embedded processors and controllers." Some have criticised this as lacking the cognitive, human element that the Internet represents, which could adversely affect how the military organises, trains and equips for IO.[8]

Cyberspace serves as a force multiplier for Information Warfare activities. Social media and botnets can amplify a message or narrative, utilising all three information elements to create discord and confusion within a target audience. Cyberspace operations can be utilised to achieve strategic Information Warfare objectives. For example, an offensive cyber attack may be used to create psychological effects in a target population.

IO may be covert or overt. In covert operations, government sponsorship is denied if disclosed. The anonymity afforded by cyberspace can create an ideal battle space for conducting clandestine Information Operations. IO may also take place outside of cyberspace.

Intelligence Agencies

Earlier, intelligence agencies like the Central Intelligence Agency (CIA) were responsible for Information Warfare or Psychological Operations.

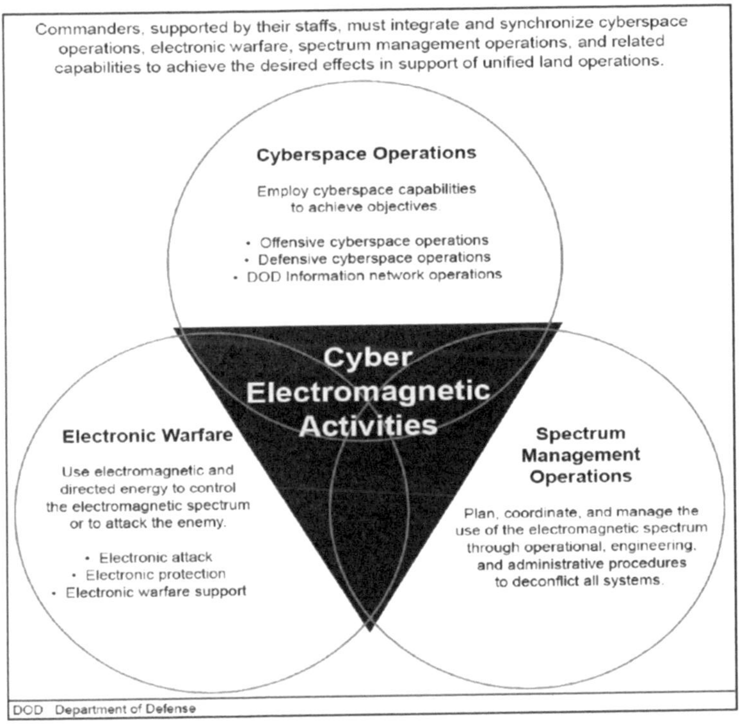

Source: FM 3-38 Cyber Electromagnetic Activities, February 2014, https://irp.fas.org/doddir/army/fm3-38.pdf

The Nation States and Terrorist Organisations

Both nation-states and terrorist organisations conduct Information Warfare to achieve strategic objectives. The US National Defense Strategy refers specifically to Information Warfare as a means through which "competitors and adversaries seek to optimise their targeting of our battle networks and operational concepts, while also using other areas of competition short of open warfare to achieve their ends."[9]

Information content is the key to the psychological operations. The means to deliver content or prevent delivery is critical for the technical function. Ultimately, most of what falls into the psychological realm can be redefined as Inform and Influence Operations (IIO). Most of what falls into the technical domain is considered Information Technical Operations (ITO). The dividing line between technical operations and Inform and Influence Operations is illustrated in the following diagram.

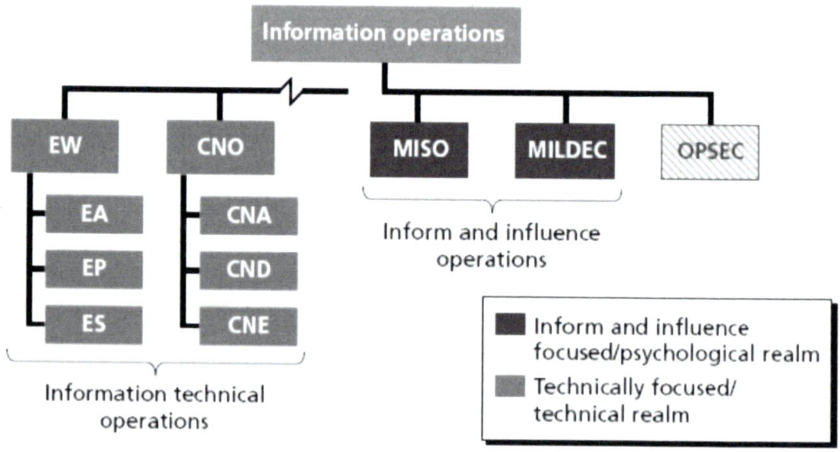

NOTE: CND = computer network defense.

Source: RAND MG1113-5.2

CYBER-ENABLED INFORMATION OPERATIONS

Cyber-Enabled Information Operations (CIO) are defined as the conduct of Information Warfare that utilises modern information technologies, such as social media, search engines, Artificial Intelligence and the Internet, as well as traditional communication media technologies.

The Information Environment broadly includes military information support operations, military deception, cyber operations, electromagnetic warfare, operations security and Information Operations.

Figure: Information Operations and Selected Information-Related Capabilities

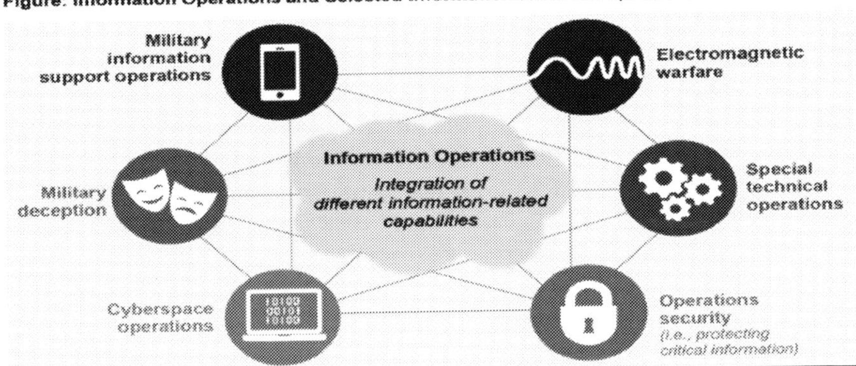

Source: GAO analysis of Department of Defence (DOD) information I GAO 21-525T

EXAMPLE OF DOD INFORMATION-RELATED CAPABILITIES

Military information support operation	**Military deception**	**Cyberspace operation**	**Electromagnetic warfare**	**Operations security**	**Special technical operation**
Planned operations to convey selected information and indicators to foreign audience them and ultimately the behavior of foreign governments, organisation, groups and individuals in a manner favorable to the originator's objectives.	Actions to deliberately mislead adversary military, paramilitary or violent extremist organisation decision makers, causing the adversary to take specific actions (or inactions) that will continue to the accomplished of the friendly mission.	The employment of cyberspace capabilities where the primary purpose is to achieve objectives in or through cyberspace.	Military action involving the use of electromagnetic and directed energy to control the electromagnetic spectrum or to attack the enemy.	A capability that identifies and controls critical information, indicators of friendly force actions attendant to military operations and incorporates countermeasures to reduce the risk of an adversary exploiting Vulnerabilities.	A process to plan and use specific systems and capabilities protected by special access programs.

Source: GAO analysis of Department of Defense (DOD) information | GAO 21-525T

Information Operation-Related Terms Defined by DOD and Others

DOD-Defined Terms	
Information Environment	The aggregate of individual organisation and systems that collect process, disseminate or act on information. This environment consists of three interrelated dimensions, which continuously interact with individuals organisations and systems. These dimensions are known as the physical, information and cognitive (or human) dimensions.
Information Operations	The integrated employment during military operations of information-related capabilities in concert with other lines of operations to influence, disrupt, corrupt or usurp the decision making of adversaries and potential adversaries while protecting our own.
Information-related capability	A tool, technique or activity employed within a dimension of the Information Environment that can be used to achieve a specific end. The DOD does not have a definitive list of information-related capabilities because any capability could be used in a way that meets the definition, according to DOD officials. A DOD official recently stated that the term 'information-related capability' will be retired from the common vocabulary; however, for this testimony, the term will continue to be used.
Non-DOD-Defined Terms	
Influence activities/ operations	The DOD's current dictionary does not refer to the terms "influence activities" or "Influence Operations." However, the DOD's 10 policy document refers to "influence activities" as an information-related capability, although the policy document does not define or describe these activities." In 2009, RAND issued a study on behalf of the US Army. In that study, RAND defines Influence Operations as "the coordinated, integrated and synchronised application of national diplomatic, informational, military, economic and other capabilities in peacetime, crisis, conflict and post conflict to foster attitudes, behaviours or decisions by foreign target audiences that further US interests and objectives." A key difference between this definition of Influence Operations and the DOD's definition of "Information Operations" is that RAND's definition includes all instruments of national power (i.e., diplomacy, information, military and economics). In contrast, the DOD's joint doctrine focuses on activities and operations conducted by the military.

Information Warfare	Neither the US government (as a whole) nor the DOD (as a department) have a definition for "Information Warfare." However, the Congressional Research Service notes that Information Warfare is a form of political warfare that targets a nation-state's government, military, private sector and general population, occurring at a level below that of armed conflict. Information Warfare is the range of military and government operations to protect and exploit the Information Environment. It consists of both offensive and defensive operations: the protection and assurance of one's own information (information security) and Information Operations to advance interests. As noted in the 2019 Report about the DOD's Information Operations, while the DOD does not have a clear definition for Information Warfare, we found that several of the Services were using the term. For example, it defines Information Warfare as the integrated application of capabilities to degrade, deny, deceive, or destroy an enemy's Information Environment or to enhance the effectiveness of friendly operations. Our Report also noted that the US Army has begun to use the term' Information Warfare' as well, but this change has not been reflected in doctrine or guidance.

Source: GAO analysis of Congressional Research Service, Department of Defense (DOD) and RAND information | GAO-21-525T

Protecting one's information systems and processes is equally important in Information Warfare. Ensuring the security and integrity of communication networks, data repositories and critical infrastructure is essential for maintaining operational effectiveness. This involves implementing robust cybersecurity measures, conducting continuous monitoring and threat assessments and developing resilient information systems that can withstand attacks by adversaries.

In the digital age, Information Warfare is generally viewed in terms of the attack surface of network-enabled information and communications systems. Whether the target for decision-makers is political or military, they mostly rely on internet-enabled infrastructure—from data stored in computers and code that enables it to work to sensors employed on the battlefield.

Cyber-enabled Information Operations are a threat to the well-being of democratic States, for democracies to come to grips with the modern Information Environment. Today, cyberspace appears to be an ideal platform for conducting Influence Operations. As Tim Stevens puts it, "Cyber Warfare of the future may be less about hacking electrical power grids and more about hacking minds by shaping the environment in which political debate takes place."[10]

Cyber-enabled disinformation, which undermines democracy and erodes governmental institutions, poses a significant threat to public safety and national security. It presents unique challenges to the armed forces. Those challenges are likely to worsen, with the ongoing advancement of technology and the increasing willingness of our adversaries to utilise the tool of disinformation to further their interests. Responding to these challenges will not be easy. It will require taking complex and controversial decisions about the responsibility of the private sector and foreign social media companies for our national well-being, as well as about restrictions on speech.

The information function helps commanders and staff understand and leverage the pervasive nature of information, its military uses and its application during all military operations. This function enables commanders to integrate the generation and preservation of friendly information, leveraging the inherent informational aspects of all military activities to achieve the commander's objectives and attain the desired end state.

Information Operations

The realm of Information Warfare extends beyond the psychological and perceptual using cyber means to encompass the use of digital and cyber capabilities to influence, disrupt or corrupt the information systems of adversaries. In today's digitised world, where information can traverse the globe in seconds, the ability to control or manipulate this flow is a powerful strategic asset. Understanding the relationship between Information Warfare and Cyber Warfare and integrating these capabilities into strategic planning is essential for achieving and maintaining a competitive advantage in the information domain.

The primary restriction on conducting any offensive psychological operation is to be truthful and not misleading. This was valid during the Cold War era. The introduction of the Internet, social media, search engines and other information technologies have changed the Information Environment by many orders of magnitude. The successes of Information

Warfare carried out by autocratic countries against democracies in recent times have exhibited that truth does not always prevail, in part because lies spread faster than truth. Authoritarian governments exercise maximum control and influence over the information that flows through their borders or into their spheres of influence. Conducting Information Operations against adversaries such as these countries or non-State actors, requires careful examination.

In September 2019, NPR reported on some Cyber Command activities aimed at causing psychological effects on adversaries. Specifically, Operation Glowing Symphony was planned to degrade and disrupt online efforts by the Islamic State for propaganda, communications, fundraising and recruitment. Most of this effort concentrated on creating an endless series of technology annoyances and time-wasting interruptions that significantly degraded and disrupted the workflow of the Islamic State's network operators.

Glowing Symphony activities conveyed selected information to the Islamic State network and cyber operatives, influencing their emotions, motives and objective reasoning and ultimately, the behaviour of the Islamic State in a manner favourable to the anti-Islamic State objectives of the United States. There is no clarity about the nature of integrating military forces specialising in Psychological Operations into cyber operations. Usually, this type of joint activity between cyber and psychological operations demands expects which is rare.

Cyber operations are essential instruments through which psychological effects can be generated. The expertise of the US Army Cyber Command lies in the information delivery aspect of Psychological Operations. The US Special Operations Command has developed extensive psychological and cultural knowledge on the information content side of Psychological Operations due to its long experience in executing Influence Operations. Bringing together the respective expertise of each Command should enhance the synergies possible between cyber-enabled Psychological Operations and offensive cyber operations. The competence required to conduct Psychological Operations goes beyond the skill set of cyber operators. The Cyber Commands are not particularly interested in acquiring such expertise.

The technical dimensions of combating adversarial Influence Operations are important. The expertise of cyber forces generally focuses on the information delivery side of cyber-enabled Psychological Operations. Contesting Information Warfare requires content. The issue of content, themes, etc., is the most critical part. The government must adopt a whole-of-government approach to bring together all relevant expertise from across government and the nation to address the problem.

Significant efforts are underway to enhance global cybersecurity. These activities and the funds that support them are centred around technical expertise in computer science, communications, mathematics and other related fields. Much less activity and funds are dedicated to understanding the science and practice of Psychological Operations. Practitioners of Psychological Operations must be familiar with social cognition and behavioural economics, as these are the fundamental psychological sciences underlying Influence Operations.

For defence against adversary Psychological Operations, the practitioners need critical thinking skills to resist propaganda. They need to learn techniques for inoculating against misinformation. For offensive operations against the Islamic State, persuasion techniques are required. Experts in marketing and advertising are crucial for executing these operations.

Use of Kinetic Power against Information Warfare

It was reported that two Israeli airstrikes against targets in Gaza were intended to hit Hamas cyber operation centres. A strike on 14 May 2019, is stated to have hit what Israeli Air Force sources called "a cyber-equipment storage site in the northern Gaza Strip belonging to Hamas military intelligence." The site was also serving as a data centre. The building also housed civilian media offices of NPR, the Associated Press and Al-Jazeera.

In a second airstrike on 19 May, the Israeli military said it hit a "hideout apartment that was used by the terror operatives for offensive cyber activity against Israeli targets." Security experts described this as the first kinetic response to a cyber attack.

STRATEGIC GOALS AND TACTICS OF CIO

A CIO campaign aims not to degrade a computer system's functional integrity, but to utilise those computer systems against the target to benefit the attacker's objectives. Many such activities are intended to shape a society's perceptions, choices and behaviours, and in some cases, render the target dysfunctional as a society. This is not merely propaganda, fake news or manipulation of perception. It is a battle over what people believe is reality and the decisions each individual makes based on those beliefs. The winners in this battle are the attackers who have convinced a large number of victims to make decisions that directly help the attackers.

China, Iran, Syria and the Islamic State have all carried out political warfare regularly via digital platforms and often augmented by cyber means against Western polities with increasing intensity and sophistication during the past few years.[11]

In the twenty-first century, digital platforms have become the primary sources of information that shape perceptions. Anyone can publish any kind of information, true or false. Digital platforms provide numerous advantages for current Information Operations, including the following:[12]

- **Low-cost publishing.** Only minimal resources are needed. The equipment used to capture and manipulate photos and videos is as ubiquitous as smartphones.
- **Elimination of "gatekeepers".** Information is published with no editorial oversight. Anyone can be a source of information.
- **Anonymity.** Information of any nature can be published and disseminated without having to reveal its true identity.
- **Precision targeting.** It is easier to tailor the narrative to what the audience has already agreed upon.
- **Automated amplification.** Automated accounts enable a comparatively small number of individuals to disseminate numerous narratives across a wide range of social media platforms and target diverse audiences.

Examples of objectives pursued by CIO[13]

Jarol Manheim, in his book Strategy in Information and Influence Campaigns, suggests a range of objectives pursued through CIO:[14]

- Reinforcing an existing perception, preference or attitude.
- Planting a new perception where none existed previously.
- Attaching a new preference to a current perception or linking a current perception to an existing belief system.
- Introducing a belief system to integrate existing perceptions or an attitude cluster to integrate existing lower-order attitudes.
- Inspiring action is based on a prevailing perception that is not linked to a sensible preference.
- Stirring action that occurs without reference to perceptions, preferences or attitudes.
- Inspiring action based on an existing attitude or preference or an existing attitude cluster or belief system.
- Changing a current, lightly held perception, preference or attitude or one that remains isolated or only loosely integrated into a belief system or attitude cluster.

How do we plan to achieve these objectives?

Once the objectives are selected to achieve through CIO, a strategic plan is formulated that answers a broad range of important questions like:[15]

- What types of information do you want to communicate and how will this help in achieving the goals you have aimed for?
- What categories of target audiences will it help you the most to influence in your intended ways?
- What do you know about the target audiences? What do those audiences want, value, need, fear and so on?
- What are the favourite means of information sharing and communication among the target audiences?
- How do the target audiences perceive the influencer now? What are those views based on?
- While pursuing your influence campaign objectives, what peer competition, potential allies and enemies should you keep in mind?
- How will you know which types of information resonate among the target audience and how will you adjust your efforts according to that analysis?

- Will you need to disguise the origins of the influence campaign using deception, proxies and digital influence mercenaries?
- How will you recognise that you have achieved your influence goals? What data will you analyse and when will you assess this?

Tactics

A large number of tactics have been identified to accomplish these goals. Some of them are:[16]

- Astroturfing (fake grassroots support), False amplification of critiques of opponents, marginal voices and false amplification of news.
- Impersonation of public figures and political allies.
- Defamation, Doxxing, Hacking and leaking documents.
- Interference with political processes, Intimidation and harassment.
- Dark advertising, Exploitation of content moderation systems, Shocking or graphic content, Scare stories.
- Playing both sides, Communications disruption, Hashtag poisoning, Spam, Algorithm exploitation and manipulation, Deepfakes.
- Dissemination of false, misleading or misattributed content, Impersonation of websites, restriction of availability of information to the public, dissemination of conspiracy theories.

A typical offensive strategy against a target population may consist of numerous steps:[17]

- Break down the population into communities based on various criteria, such as, hobbies, politics, interests, concerns and needs.
- Find the social dynamics of communication and the flow of ideas within each community.
- Locate who in each community is most susceptible to given types of messages.
- Find out what narratives of different types lead the discussion in each community.
- Using all of the above designs, push a narrative that is likely to succeed in displacing an unfavourable narrative with one that is more favourable.

- Utilise continuous monitoring and interaction to assess the success of your effort and make adjustments in real time.

Today, technologies exist that can perform each of these steps continuously and at a large scale. However, while current technologies support the manual application of psychological research results, they do not fully automate it. This would be the next stage in the development of technology.

Defensive Measures

The same technologies can be used for defensive purposes. For example, one can use these techniques to break down communities and detect efforts by opponents to push a narrative, as well as examine the content of that narrative. The technology can help researchers concentrate while searching massive amounts of social media data.[18]

Understanding what adversaries plan to do in the short term (one year) and medium term (three years) is crucial for building domestic defences. The following questions should serve as a starting point for developing own defensive measures:

- What are the strategic goals of an adversary's use of IO campaigns?
- Who are the targets of IO campaigns and why were they chosen?
- What are the objectives of IO campaigns against us and are there any specific timelines?
- Who is responsible for crafting each adversary's Information Operations (IO) strategy?
- What fiscal allocation is provided to those programmes?
- What government and non-government ministries, offices or groups are responsible for conducting IO? How and why are they selected?
- How are IO validated, measured and evaluated?
- What training is provided to tactical- and operational-level IO staff?
- What tactics are used in IO campaigns? How are they selected?[19]

Conflict occurs in cyberspace's Information Environment and involves the cognitive and emotional parts of the brain. Victory in Influence Operations occurs when the adversary willingly accepts and adopts the victor's political goals, not because the adversary lacks the means to resist but because the adversary no longer views the victor as an enemy. Knowledge, truth and confidence are all compromised due to the adversary's decision-making process being infected with fear, anger and uncertainty. There are no non-combatants in Influence Operations. Everyone, including governments, universities and news media, is a potential target. Influence Operations utilise the features of information technology, whereas cyber war leverages the benefits of information technology.

It is not easy to use Influence Operations against authoritarian regimes. Such regimes usually have strict information control systems that limit the types of communication citizens can access.

There has been a general decline of faith in government, mainstream media and other traditional institutions. People are assisted by algorithms that push information that data indicates will be of interest to them. This fragmented Information Environment makes it challenging to establish a shared national narrative that protects society against hostile influences.

Cyber-enabled disinformation, which undermines democracy and erodes governmental institutions, poses a significant threat to public safety and national security. It presents unique challenges to the armed forces. Those challenges are likely to worsen with the ongoing advancement of technology and the increasing willingness of our adversaries to utilise the tool of disinformation to further their interests. Responding to these challenges will not be easy. It will require making difficult and controversial decisions about the responsibility of the private sector and foreign social media companies for our national well-being, as well as about restrictions on speech.

The information function encompasses the management and application of information, as well as its deliberate integration with other joint functions, to influence the perceptions, behaviour, actions, or inactions of relevant actors and human and automated decision-making. The information function helps commanders and staff understand and leverage the pervasive nature of information, its military uses and its application during all military operations. This function enables commanders to integrate the generation and preservation of friendly information, leveraging the inherent informational aspects of all military activities to achieve the Commander's objectives and attain the desired end state.

Cyber Warfare and Information Warfare

The integration of cyber capabilities and Information Warfare was a critical turning point. Cyber Warfare involves the use of digital attacks to compromise, disrupt or destroy information systems and networks. These attacks can target critical infrastructure, communication networks, financial systems and military assets. The convergence of cyber operations with traditional Information Warfare tactics has created a more dynamic and complex operational environment. Understanding the relationship between Information Warfare and Cyber Warfare and integrating these capabilities into strategic planning, is essential for achieving and maintaining a competitive advantage in the information domain.

The relationship between Information Warfare and Cyber Warfare is symbiotic. Cyber operations enable the execution of Information Warfare strategies on a global scale. By exploiting vulnerabilities in digital systems, Cyber Warfare can amplify the effects of Psychological Operations, Perception Management and military deception. For example, cyber attacks can be used to disrupt communication channels, spread disinformation and manipulate data to create confusion. Information Warfare is a vital component of modern military strategy, encompassing a wide range of activities aimed at influencing perceptions and controlling information. The evolution of digital and cyber technologies has transformed the landscape of Information Warfare, creating new opportunities and challenges. Understanding the relationship between Information Warfare and Cyber Warfare and integrating these capabilities into strategic planning is essential for achieving and maintaining a competitive advantage in the information domain.

To exploit the impact of media and communication tools, sophisticated psychological techniques are often integrated into Influence Operations. These include:

Narrative Construction. Crafting compelling narratives that resonate with target audiences is fundamental. Narratives provide a framework that people use to make sense of information and a well-constructed narrative can be incredibly persuasive.

Emotional Appeals. Messages designed to evoke strong emotions can be highly effective in influencing behaviour. Fear, pride, anger and hope are common emotions that campaigns might target to achieve specific reactions.

Authority Appeals. Using authoritative sources or respected figures to convey messages can enhance the credibility of the information and increase audience acceptance.

Reciprocity and Conformity. These principles from social psychology are often leveraged to encourage target behaviour. For example, showing that many others have adopted a position can drive individuals towards conformity.

The cyber dimension of Influence Operations involves a range of tools designed to manipulate online Information Environments. These include:

Botnets. Automated programmes that can create or amplify content on social media, generating artificial trends or drowning out opposing viewpoints.

Hacking and Data Leaks. Gaining unauthorised access to private communications or databases can allow operators to release sensitive information strategically to influence public opinion or embarrass adversaries.

Fake News and Websites. Creating and disseminating false information through seemingly legitimate websites or news.

ANALYTICAL TOOLS

Data analytics play a crucial role in today's Influence Operations. Tools that evaluate big data can help operatives understand audience behaviours and preferences, allowing for the optimisation of message delivery based on real-time feedback. Analytics can track the reach and impact of campaigns, providing insights that guide strategic adjustments.

Sentiment Analysis

This involves analysing reactions and opinions from social media to gauge the emotional response to different messages and adapt strategies accordingly.

Audience Segmentation

Identifying specific groups within a larger population based on demographics, interests or behaviour allows for more targeted and effective messaging.

There is a difference between cyber-enabled Psychological Operations and offensive cyber operations. The competence required to conduct Psychological Operations goes beyond the skill set of cyber operators. The expertise of cyber forces generally focuses on the information delivery side of cyber-enabled Psychological Operations. Contesting Information Warfare requires content. The issue of content, themes, etc., is the most critical part. The government must adopt a whole-of-government approach to harness all relevant expertise from across the government and the nation to address the problem.

Considerable resources are invested in cybersecurity globally. These activities and the funds that support them are centred around technical expertise in computer science, communications, mathematics and other related fields. Much less activity and funds are dedicated to understanding the science and practice of Psychological Operations.

For defence against adversarial Psychological Operations, the practitioners need critical thinking skills to resist propaganda. They need to learn techniques for inoculating against misinformation. Experts in marketing and advertising are crucial for executing these operations.

INFORMATION OPERATIONS DURING MILITARY OPERATIONS

A wide variety of unit functions and activities can be adapted for the purposes of conducting Information Operations or serve as enablers to its planning, execution and assessment. Some of these include, but are not limited to:

- Commander's communications strategy.
- Presence, profile and posture.
- Physical security.
- Foreign disclosure.
- Physical manoeuvre.
- Civil-military operations.
- Special access programmes.
- Intelligence.
- Destruction and lethal actions.

INFORMATION OPERATIONS AND DECISIVE ACTION

Defend. In defensive IO, it seeks to create effects in the Information Environment that accomplish any one or a combination of the following (not all-inclusive):

The Commander. Commanders, at all levels, are responsible for understanding the threats their units face and knowing how to counter or defeat them. To affect the Information Environment to their advantage, Commanders should be aware of the following:[20]

- Every operation, to some extent, affects the Information Environment.
- IO planning is integral to operations from the start.
- Effects in and through the Information Environment, if essential to success, are part of the Commander's intent.
- Combat power cannot be optimised without IO.
- The war-fighting functions (particularly movement, manoeuvre and fires) produce effects in the Information Environment, whether intentional or not.
- IO is essential to operational success at all levels.
- All communication can quickly become global and have strategic consequences.
- IRCs can have long lead times to coordinate and employ and lengthy lag times before their effects are realised.
- The alignment of words, deeds and images is essential to building trust and confidence with relevant audiences in operations.
- IO requires prioritised intelligence support.
- Effects in the Information Environment are not always as expected; assessment is challenging and benefits from commanders' interest, prioritisation and support.
- IO can be constrained by policy and law, while the threat is often unconstrained in its use of information.

Three obstacles prevent the achievement of the desired IW state:

- A communication gap exists between Information Warfare subject matter experts and the formation commanders.
- Information Warfare capabilities are mostly highly classified. This makes planning difficult, as decision-makers across the various domains involved in the planning process may not be aware of a particular programme or capacity.
- More needs to be done to enable lower-level decision-makers to take the initiative.

INTELLIGENCE

Defence intelligence organisations provide detailed enemy orders of battle and other related and valuable products. Information Warfare professionals also gather such intelligence, which sometimes overlaps. There is a general lack of coordination and understanding between the Information Operations (IO) and intelligence communities, which adversely affects operational planning.

From the very beginning, intelligence organisations have been present at every level of the armed forces. Over such long periods, they have fine-tuned their organisation, doctrine, leadership, methods of gathering intelligence and analysis capabilities, as well as human resource policies. What distinguishes them from practitioners of Information Warfare is how each community compiles, sorts, analyses and uses information. A clear understanding of the Information Environment is the responsibility of intelligence practitioners. The ability to conduct operations in and through the Information Environment is the responsibility of IO practitioners.

There is friction between the intelligence and IO communities regarding the collection of information and the conduct of analyses necessary to support Operations in the Information Environment (OIE). Generally, there is a lack of understanding, shared processes and a shared lexicon about what the other community does. Gaps in knowledge hinder close coordination between the two communities, leading to reduced operational effectiveness.

Both intelligence and IO professionals need training to support and conduct OIE effectively. Training and education must grow as needs change.[21]

COMMAND AND CONTROL

Information Warfare has two aspects: the psychological and the technical. The information content is vital for the psychological part. The means to deliver content or counter its delivery are crucial to the technical function. There is logic behind most of what falls into the psychological realm being redefined as IO. Most of what falls into the technical realm should be considered cyber-electronic. The exception must be for operating and maintaining the networks, which itself is a vital and mammoth task.

Virtually all core, supporting and related capabilities of IO tend to operate within their own stovepipes. On the technical side, cyber operations, Electronic Warfare (EW), EMSO and so on, are all separate organisations. Correspondingly, PA and MISO have many overlapping objectives, capabilities and processes on the content side, but are separate and sometimes competing organisations. Suppose the vision of IO includes specific capabilities working together in seamless harmony. In that case, those capabilities need to be combined or placed under the tight control of a single integrating authority.

Currently, the authorities for Cyber and Electronic Warfare are not the same. The use of EW capabilities at all echelons has well-established tactics and procedures. Many policy changes are needed for cyber to enjoy the same level of permission, understanding and use. Training will have to be commensurate.

Ethical and Legal Considerations

The ethical and legal considerations of Information Warfare also warrant attention. The use of disinformation and manipulation in Influence Operations raises questions about the ethical implications of these tactics. While achieving strategic objectives is paramount, Adherence to international laws and norms is crucial for preserving legitimacy and avoiding unintended consequences. Balancing operational effectiveness with ethical constraints is a complex challenge that military professionals must navigate. It is imperative to develop and implement strategies that are both effective and ethically sound.

Typical Questionnaires for Conducting Information Warfare

In a series of Roundtable Discussions in Washington, D.C., Brussels and Honolulu, global leaders from the military, government, academia, and technology sectors converged to discuss three core challenges of visualising and countering information warfare: identifying reliable metrics for assessing the impact of psychological operations, developing adaptive frameworks for real-time response to disinformation campaign and integrating interdisciplinary expertise to anticipate emerging threats. These discussions emphasised the need for standardised questionnaires to systematically gather data on adversarial tactics, audience vulnerabilities and the efficacy of counter-narratives.

DOCTRINE OF THE INDIAN ARMY

The Indian Army's Doctrine, published in October 2004, gave out different forms of Information Warfare on page 20:

- Command and Control Warfare (C2W)
- Intelligence-Based Warfare
- Electronic Warfare
- Psychological Warfare
- Cyber Warfare
- Economic Information Warfare
- Network Centric Warfare

The Indian Army's doctrine was revised and published in November 2010. On page 53, the doctrine states, "IW battlespace deals with physical, information infrastructure and perceptual realms. From IA's perspective, IW will comprise Cyber Warfare, Psychological Warfare and Electronic Warfare."

The Indian Army's Land Warfare Doctrine, published in 2018, states that the Indian Army will develop capabilities to prosecute Information Warfare Operations over the entire spectrum of conflict, as well as in 'No War No Peace' scenarios, to achieve full-spectrum information dominance over the adversary. It will have the following components: Cyber Warfare (CW), Electronic Warfare (EW) and Psychological Warfare (PsyW).

Generally, people tend to use the term 'Information Warfare' to mean Psychological Warfare. Psychological Warfare is covered in detail in the next chapter.

Cyber Warfare in itself is a vast subject. Only cyber-related issues of Psychological Operations will be discussed.

Electronic Warfare is generally fought in a tactical battle area. Most of the information is classified. Electronic Warfare is not being covered in this book.

TYPICAL QUESTIONNAIRES FOR CONDUCTING INFORMATION WARFARE

Narrative construction can be one of the most challenging forms of Information Operations to implement, track or measure, but it can also be one of the most powerful. Successful narrative construction forms a political theory around tangible aspects of the cultural landscape and presents self-evident facts about the reality within which the narrative will be propagated. Such campaigns incorporate passive and active operations to shape discourse within and between societies. The success of this kind of societal effort is not entirely verifiable, as competition between political ideas is iterative; however, these Information Operations promise to align large swaths of people and communities with a specific political theory of action. In the military context, successfully constructed narratives can shift actors from adversaries to allies or transform cultures.[22]

How to Plan - Ask Questions

- What types of information do you want to communicate and how will this help in achieving the goals you have aimed for?
- What categories of target audiences will it help you the most to influence in your intended ways?
- What do you know about the target audiences? What do those audiences want, value, need, fear and so on?

- What are the favourite means of information sharing and communication among the target audiences?
- How do the target audiences perceive the influencer now? What are those views based on?
- While pursuing your influence campaign objectives, what peer competition, potential allies and enemies should you keep in mind?
- How will you know which types of information resonate with your target audience and how will you adjust your efforts according to that analysis?
- Will you need to disguise the origins of the influence campaign using deception, proxies and digital influence mercenaries?
- How will you recognise that you have achieved your influence goals? What data will you analyse and when will you assess this?

A typical offensive strategy against a target population may consist of following steps

- Break down the population into communities based on various criteria, such as, hobbies, politics, interests, concerns and needs. Find the social dynamics of communication and the flow of ideas within each community.
- Locate who in each community is most susceptible to given types of messages. Discover the narratives that lead the discussion in each community, categorised by type.
- Using all of the above design and pushing a narrative likely to succeed in displacing an unfavourable narrative with one that is more favourable.
- Utilise continuous monitoring and interaction to assess the success of your effort and make adjustments in real-time.

The evolution of the concept of Information Operations and its components has been covered in the chapter on the components of Information Operations. The dichotomies between various terms and specific relevant terms, such as, Public Field Diplomacy and Strategic Communication, are discussed there.

CONCLUSION

Key takeaways from Adm. Mike Mullen, former Chairman of the Joint Chiefs of Staff, in an August 2009 article in *Joint Forces Quarterly.*[23]

- We need to worry a lot less about how to communicate our actions and much more about what our actions communicate.
- Our adversaries monitor the news to discern coalition and US intent as weighed against the efforts of our forces. When they find a say-do gap...they drive a truck right through it.
- We must be vigilant about holding ourselves accountable to higher standards of conduct and closing any gaps, real or perceived, between what we say about ourselves and what we do to back it up.
- Our messages lack credibility when we haven't invested enough in building trust and relationships and when we fail to deliver on our promises.
- Our adversaries intimidate, control and communicate from within. They aren't just out there shooting videos; they deliver. Each beheading, each bombing and each beating sends a powerful message or, rather, is a powerful message.
- Most Strategic Communication problems are not communication problems at all. There are policy and execution problems. Each time we fail to live up to our values or don't follow up on a promise, we look more and more like the "arrogant Americans" the enemy claims we are.
- Messages are not something we can launch downrange like a rocket; they are something we can fire for effect. Good communication runs both ways. It's not about telling our story. We must also be better listeners.
- We need to appreciate cultural differences and people's needs better and hopes for the future to supplant the extremist narrative. We cannot capture hearts and minds; we must engage them; we must listen to them, one heart and one mind at a time—over time.

Chapter IV

Psychological Warfare

> *"I began to understand that I was caught up in two wars: one fought on the ground with tanks and artillery and an information war fought largely, though not exclusively, through social media. And, perhaps counter-intuitively, it mattered who won the war of words and narratives (rather) than who had the most potent weaponry."*
>
> —**David Patrikarakos**, ***War in 140 Characters***

In the complex landscape of modern warfare, controlling the narrative is as crucial as physical dominance. The ability to influence the thoughts, emotions and behaviours of target audiences can determine the outcome of conflicts and shape geopolitical dynamics. Psychological Operations offer a means to achieve these ends by manipulating information to create desired psychological effects.

Psychological Operations represent a powerful tool in the modern military strategy arsenal. By leveraging information to influence perceptions and shape behaviour, Psychological Operations can achieve strategic objectives without resorting to conventional force.

Psychological Operations can be defined as the planned use of propaganda and other psychological actions to influence the opinions, emotions, attitudes and behaviour of hostile, neutral or friendly groups to support the achievement of national objectives. Psychological Operations utilise information to evoke specific responses that will ultimately benefit the mission's goals.

One of the crucial characteristics of Psychological Operations is their continuous nature. Unlike traditional military engagements, which are often confined to specific battles or campaigns, Psychological Operations are ongoing processes. They begin well before hostilities commence and continue long after the cessation of direct conflict. This continuity ensures that the desired psychological effects are sustained, gradually shaping the perceptions and behaviours of target audiences over time. The true impact of these operations may only become apparent months or years after their execution.

The ability to shape and direct the flow of information can determine the outcome of both conventional and unconventional conflicts. Several key factors highlight this strategic importance.

Influence on Public Opinion and Morale

Psychological Operations aim to influence the beliefs, emotions and behaviours of target audiences, including civilian populations and enemy forces. By shaping public opinion, these operations can bolster support for military actions, undermine the morale of adversaries and create favourable conditions for achieving strategic objectives.

Disruption of Enemy Decision-Making

Effective Perception Management can sow confusion and doubt within enemy ranks, disrupting their decision-making processes. By disseminating misleading or false information, military strategists can manipulate enemy perceptions, leading to miscalculations and errors.

Building and Maintaining Alliances

Psychological Operations are not solely directed at adversaries; they also play a crucial role in building and maintaining alliances. By promoting narratives that emphasise shared values, mutual benefits and common goals, military strategists can strengthen ties with allies and partner nations.

Countering Adversary Propaganda

Adversaries, including State and non-State actors, leverage propaganda and disinformation to achieve their objectives. Effective Psychological Information Warfare strategies are necessary to counter these efforts, exposing falsehoods and promoting truthful narratives.

PRINCIPLES OF PSYCHOLOGICAL OPERATIONS

The effectiveness of Psychological Operations depends on several key principles:

Credibility. The messages conveyed in Psychological Operations must be credible to the target audience. This involves using accurate information and trustworthy sources to búild legitimacy. Credibility enhances the persuasiveness of the message and increases the likelihood of achieving the desired psychological effect.

Relevance. Psychological Operations messages must be relevant to the target audience's beliefs, values and cultural context. Understanding the audience's motivations, fears and aspirations is essential for crafting messages that resonate and prompt the intended response.

Consistency. Consistent messaging across different channels and over time reinforces the intended narrative and prevents confusion. Inconsistent or contradictory messages can undermine the credibility and effectiveness of the Psychological Operation.

Timeliness. The timing of Psychological Operations is crucial. Messages must be delivered at the right moment to maximise their impact. This involves understanding the situational context and capitalising on opportunities to influence the target audience effectively.

Adaptability. Psychological Operations must be adaptable to changing circumstances and feedback. Continuous monitoring and assessment of the operation's impact allow for adjustments to the strategy, ensuring that the messages remain effective and responsive to the evolving situation.

Integration. Effective PSYOPS require integration with other elements of military strategy and national policy. Coordinating Psychological Operations with kinetic actions, diplomatic efforts and economic measures creates a synergistic effect that enhances overall mission success.

Security. Protecting the integrity and confidentiality of Psychological Operations is vital to prevent adversaries from countering or exploiting them. This involves safeguarding sensitive information and employing counter-intelligence measures to detect and mitigate threats. Maintaining the operational security of the campaign, especially in covert operations, is crucial.[24]

Tools and Techniques for Implementing Psychological Operations

In the sophisticated realm of Influence Operations, a plethora of tools and techniques are employed to implement Psychological Operations effectively. These methodologies span from traditional media channels to advanced digital platforms, leveraging both psychological insight and technological advancements to strategically shape perceptions and behaviours.

Media and Communication Tools

Traditional media channels, such as, television, radio and newspapers, have been used for Psychological Operations for a long time. These media are utilised to disseminate targeted messages that can reach a broad audience quickly and effectively. Television and radio are particularly potent due to their ability to convey messages through both visual and auditory means, which can enhance the emotional impact of the content.

Along with traditional media, digital communication tools have revolutionised the way Psychological Operations are conducted. Social media platforms like Facebook, Twitter (now X) and Instagram allow for rapid dissemination of information and enable the micro-targeting of specific demographics with tailored content. These platforms also facilitate the rapid spread of information, where messages can be amplified exponentially within a short period.

Psychological Techniques

To maximise the impact of media and communication tools, sophisticated psychological techniques are often integrated into Psychological Operations. These include:

- **Narrative Construction**. Crafting engaging stories that connect with audiences is essential. Stories offer a way for people to understand information and a well-built story can be very convincing.

- **Emotional Appeals.** Messages that aim to stir strong feelings can be very effective in changing behaviour. Fear, pride, anger and hope are common emotions that campaigns often focus on to get particular responses.
- **Authority Appeals.** Using trusted sources or respected individuals to convey messages can enhance the credibility of the information and influence how the audience perceives it.
- **Reciprocity and Conformity.** These principles from social psychology are often leveraged to encourage target behaviours. For example, showing that many others have adopted a position can drive individuals towards conformity.

INTEGRATION ACROSS PLATFORMS

The effectiveness of these tools and techniques often depends on how well they work together across different platforms and media. A coordinated multi-channel approach makes sure that messages are reinforced and more likely to be understood by the target audience.

PLANNING AND EXECUTION OF PSYCHOLOGICAL WARFARE OPERATIONS

The planning stage is foundational to the success of any PSYOPS campaign. It involves defining clear objectives, understanding the target audience, developing a compelling message and choosing the appropriate channels for message dissemination.

Objective Definition

Every PSYOPS campaign must start with a clear definition of its objectives. These should be Specific, Measurable, Achievable, Relevant and Time-Bound (SMART). Whether the goal is to change public opinion, influence political decisions, or undermine enemy morale, the objectives should align with broader strategic goals.

Audience Analysis

Knowing the target audience intimately is crucial. This involves understanding their demographics, psychographics, cultural details, media use and possible weaknesses. The success of the campaign depends on how well the message connects with this audience. This analysis is a key part of the planning process.

Message Development

The message must be tailored to the audience's values and beliefs. It should be compelling, credible and clear. Crafting a narrative that appeals both emotionally and logically to the audience can significantly enhance the campaign's impact.

Channel Selection

Selecting the right channels to reach your target audience is crucial. This could involve a mix of traditional media, social media, direct communication and even covert methods, depending on the audience and the objectives. Each channel offers different strengths and reaches different segments of the audience.

Resource Allocation

Effective campaigns require the right resources. This includes financial resources, people and technology. Using these resources wisely means budgeting for current needs and predicting future requirements as the campaign changes.

The planning, execution and management of Psychological Warfare operations require close attention to detail, strategic thinking and coordination across different military and non-military areas. These operations aim to mislead or demoralise the enemy while maintaining high morale among one's own forces and shaping the broader narrative favourably.

The planning phase is crucial. It involves a detailed examination of the enemy's psychological profile, cultural values, social norms and communication networks. This phase sets the goals of the Psychological Operations and identifies specific psychological weaknesses that can be targeted. Planners must consider the desired outcome of the operation and how it aligns with overall military objectives. Effective planning requires an understanding of the available tools and methods, including media channels, digital platforms and local influencers who can effectively amplify the intended message. It also requires planning to ensure that resources, such as broadcasting equipment, Internet access and trained staff, are ready to carry out the operation.

Executing Psychological Warfare Operations

Execution requires dynamic coordination among various elements involved in the operation. This may include the deployment of leaflets, the broadcasting of targeted radio programmes, social media campaigns and even face-to-face interactions with the local population or enemy prisoners. During this phase, the Psychological Operations teams work closely with intelligence units to monitor the effectiveness of the operations in real-time and adjust tactics accordingly.

Managing Psychological Warfare Operations

Management involves ongoing assessment, adaptation and control of Psychological Operations to ensure they remain effective and relevant to the changing battlefield dynamics. Managers of these operations must maintain a steady flow of feedback from intelligence sources and frontline observations to measure the performance of the operations. This feedback helps refine strategies and messages, ensuring they connect with the target audience and effectively counter enemy propaganda.

Integration with Kinetic Operations

Integrating psychological strategies with kinetic operations enhances overall military effectiveness by ensuring that both components support and reinforce each other. For example, if a kinetic operation aims to capture a strategic location, conducting Psychological Operations first to lower enemy morale and combat readiness can significantly increase the chances of success.

The seamless integration of psychological and kinetic operations requires commanders and their staff to think strategically about the use of information as a force multiplier. The success of these combined operations relies on more than just defeating the enemy physically. It also requires dominating the information space. This allows for shaping the narrative and influencing the beliefs that motivate both enemy and civilian actions. This comprehensive approach to warfare, where mental and physical efforts work in tandem, is crucial to modern military strategy and its effective implementation on the battlefield.

Psychological Operations can continue post the kinetic action to consolidate gains and stabilise the region. For example, after a successful military operation, PSYOPS teams can work to win the hearts and minds of the local population by communicating the benefits of peace, the return of normalcy and support for rebuilding efforts, thereby reducing the likelihood of insurgency or continued resistance.

The combination of psychological strategies with kinetic operations is a complex approach that requires careful planning and precise execution to enhance military effectiveness. This integration is seen not just as a parallel coordination of efforts but as a strategic interweaving of psychological impacts with physical actions on the battlefield. By doing this, military forces can achieve tactical victories and secure strategic success. They can also influence the wider socio-political landscape.

Enhancing Initial Strike Capabilities

Integrating Psychological Operations with initial kinetic strikes can demoralise the enemy and reduce their willingness to fight. For example, before a planned offensive, Psychological Operations can disseminate misinformation about the size and strength of the attacking force, leading the enemy to overestimate the opposition and potentially surrender or retreat without engaging in actual conflict.

INTEGRATED PSYOPS

Integrated PSYOPS represents a sophisticated confluence of various strategic efforts aimed at achieving specific psychological impacts and operational goals across different spectra of conflict and peacetime activities. These operations are carefully designed to connect elements of Psychological Operations, Cyber Warfare and traditional military actions. This ensures that each part improves the others, creating a clear and persuasive narrative that influences target populations and decision-makers.

The essence of integrated PSYOPS is their ability to function smoothly across different domains and environments. Whether shaping the views of a local population in a conflict zone, deterring potential adversaries in a geopolitical hotspot, or reinforcing alliances with key partners, these operations utilise a variety of tools and techniques to manipulate information, perceptions and ultimately, behaviours.

STRATEGIC SYNERGY

One of the main strengths of integrated PSYOPS is their ability to synchronise activities across various domains to achieve a combined effect. For instance, a cyber operation that disrupts an adversary's communication infrastructure can be synchronised with Psychological Operations that spread disinformation or confusion among the adversary's military ranks and civilian population. Similarly, kinetic military actions can be enhanced with real-time Psychological Operations that mislead or deceive the enemy about the true intentions and capabilities of friendly forces.

MULTI DOMAIN OPERATIONS (MDO)

The modern battlefield is characterised by the convergence of multiple domains: land, air, sea, space and cyberspace. Integrated PSYOPS are crafted to operate fluidly across these domains, utilising the unique capabilities and effects available in each to influence outcomes in others. For example, space-based assets can be utilised to gather intelligence that informs cyber and Psychological Operations, while activities in the cyber realm can protect or enhance the capabilities of assets in other physical domains.

EVALUATING PSYOPS CAMPAIGNS

Post-execution evaluation is crucial for understanding how well the campaign performed and for learning lessons for future efforts. This includes a close examination of whether the campaign achieved its goals, how efficiently resources were utilised and the overall impact on the target audience. Feedback loops and post-action reviews are key to this process. They provide information that can improve tactics and strategies for future Influence Operations. The lessons learned guide the next round of planning, making sure each version is more focused and precise than the previous one.

INTER-AGENCY COORDINATION

Inter-agency coordination is a critical element in the successful implementation of PSYOPS, which often span multiple sectors of government and the military. The effective coordination of such diverse agencies ensures that efforts are not duplicated, resources are used efficiently and, most importantly, that the actions of one agency do not inadvertently undermine those of another.

PSYOPS typically involve inputs from intelligence agencies, military units, diplomatic departments and sometimes other governmental bodies, such as, economic and cultural departments, depending on the nature and scope of the campaign. Each of these entities may have different cultures, priorities and methodologies, making coordination both essential and challenging.

The process usually begins with clear communication of the strategic goals from the highest levels of government. A unified command structure or a designated lead agency can effectively manage the inter-agency process. This approach ensures that each entity understands its role and how it contributes to the overall campaign goals. For example, the intelligence community provides essential background information and ongoing situational awareness. The military is responsible for the tactical deployment of assets, while the foreign affairs department handles diplomatic issues and messaging.

Mechanisms for regular inter-agency meetings and briefings can facilitate the exchange of information, enabling agencies to align their activities and adjust to new developments in real-time. These meetings should be structured to encourage open dialogue and information sharing within the confines of operational security.

Technology plays a crucial role in facilitating the coordination of various agencies. Communication and data-sharing platforms allow real-time collaboration and decision-making. This ensures that everyone has access to the latest intelligence and operational updates. These tools must be secure to protect sensitive information from adversaries.

Training and joint exercises that include multiple agencies help remove institutional barriers. They also foster a culture of collaboration, preparing teams to work together effectively in real-world operations.

Adaptability and Responsiveness

The rapidly evolving nature of modern conflicts and the rapid dissemination of information require operations that are both proactive and adaptable to changing situations. Integrated PSYOPS are designed with flexibility in mind, allowing military strategists to quickly alter or scale their tactics based on real-time battlefield dynamics and emerging opportunities.

Ethical and Legal Issues

The conduct of integrated PSYOPS must follow strict ethical and legal standards. Manipulating information, particularly in ways that could harm civilian populations or violate international laws, poses significant ethical challenges. People engaged in these operations are bound by codes of conduct that emphasise the lawful and ethical use of information as a tool of warfare. Ensuring these standards are followed is crucial for maintaining the trust and support of international communities and domestic groups.

The future may bring more integration of Artificial Intelligence and machine learning in creating and delivering PSYOPS. This will allow for more personalised and contextually relevant messages. The increasing significance of space and cyber as operational areas will also improve the capabilities of integrated PSYOPS. As a result, they will become an even more vital part of national security strategies.

Integrated PSYOPS represent a critical aspect of modern military strategy, combining the art of influence with the science of warfare. This comprehensive approach not only secures tactical advantages but also safeguards the principles on which democratic societies are based.

COUNTER PSYOPS MEASURES

PSYOPS also involve defensive strategies designed to protect one's own public from the adversary's influence efforts. These include:

- **Media Literacy Programmes.** Educating the public on how to assess information sources and recognise disinformation campaigns critically.
- **Rapid Response Teams.** Units dedicated to identifying and countering disinformation in real-time, often through direct refutations or the provision of accurate information.

Professional Skill Sets that have Direct Relevance to Psychological Operations

The skill sets needed to perform Psychological Operations are:

- Communications technologists provide insight into methodologies that maximise the utility of existing communication modalities and identify emerging technical capabilities.
- Behavioural scientists and cultural anthropologists provide a deep understanding of human cultures, identities, attitudes and behaviours.
- Educators with knowledge of culturally relevant teachings offer valuable perspectives.
- Historians are knowledgeable in cultural viewpoints and can perform as interpreters of current and future events.
- Religious scholars and leaders offer valuable insights into the fundamental aspects of cultural life.
- Economists provide data models to know and forecast financial events.
- Linguists and translators develop cultural sensitivities of great value in selecting keywords, messages and communication formats that resonate with intended audiences.
- Librarians and researchers offer expert information access and data management skills, as well as country and culture-specific knowledge, contacts and capabilities.
- Political scientists provide an understanding of power and influence in modern societies.
- Corporate entrepreneurs and business managers have experience with country and regional cultures, as well as relationships with international audiences, government leaders and non-governmental voluntary organisations.
- Marketing managers of products and services are used to leading the complex and interdisciplinary management process associated with building and maintaining brand equity.
- Market researchers who advise global brand management teams have a wide range of measurement techniques to study and monitor international consumer interests, attitudes and preferences.

- Producers and directors of films, television programming, advertising commercials, radio and video games are experts in crafting compelling and persuasive storylines and images.
- Advertising art directors, copywriters and media planners have proven abilities to transform copy and media strategies into compelling messages, events and programmes and identify media vehicles that attract target audiences.
- Retired government officials can offer a historical perspective as well as continuity of programmes.
- Authors, artists and musicians live a life of demonstrated creativity that transcends national boundaries and their personal stories offer windows into the broader population.

Ethnography

For Psychological Operations, professional ethnographers are needed. A typical ethnographer does the following:

- Learns the local language.
- Works to build a rapport with key members of the local community and gains access into that community.
- Spends multiple hours per day, for months or even years, observing how people conduct their everyday business and recording these observations.
- Transcribes and codes these observations into field journals to be used as primary source materials.
- Analyses this data to assess patterns of behaviour.
- Conducts formal and informal interviews with key informants, focus groups or target populations to cross-reference different interpretations and learn the underlying meaning.

These practices enable the ethnographer to develop an understanding of underlying meanings, a shared worldview and ultimately a tacit knowledge of "what makes that group of people tick."[25]

Today, technologies exist that can perform each of these steps continuously and at a large scale. However, while current technologies support the manual application of the results of psychological research, they do not fully automate it. This would be the next stage in technology development.[26]

US EXAMPLE

Roles and Responsibilities of various agencies for carrying out Information Warfare

- The United States Agency for International Development (USAID) works to inform recipients and partners of US humanitarian and development aid initiatives. Presently, USAID is under drastic reduction.
- The Office of the Director of National Intelligence (ODNI) is responsible for coordinating the efforts of intelligence agencies to conduct research and analysis on foreign public opinion, communication modes and mechanisms and violent extremist communication.
- The National Counterterrorism Centre coordinates, integrates and synchronises US government efforts to counter violent extremism and deny terrorists the next generation of recruits.
- Other departments and agencies with specific subject matter expertise and related communication and engagement capabilities, may be asked to participate in the development and implementation of communication and engagement strategies as needed.
- The Department of State carries out Public Diplomacy as an essential part of foreign policy.
- The Department of State distinguishes between Public Affairs, which includes outreach to the domestic population and Public Diplomacy (PD) which seeks to promote the national interest of the United States through understanding, informing and influencing foreign populations/and by promoting mutual understanding between the people of the United States and people from other nations around the world.
- The Department of Defense (DOD) is a key contributor to communication and engagement efforts. The key elements of the

DOD include, but are not limited to, Information Operations (IO), Defense Support to Public Diplomacy (DSPD), Public Affairs (PA) and Civil Affairs (CA), all working together to accomplish military objectives that support national objectives.

- The Broadcasting Board of Governors (BBG) is responsible for non-military, international broadcasting sponsored by the US government, including the Voice of America (VOA). Radio Free Europe/Radio Liberty (RFE/RL), Radio Free Asia (RFA), Radio and TV Marti and the Middle East Broadcasting Networks (MBN)—Radio Sawa and Alhurra Television. These organisations are also being disbanded or trimmed down.

An example of the organisation of PSYOPS in the US Armed Forces is given below.

PSYCHOLOGICAL OPERATIONS GROUP

- One Active Component PSYOPS Group (approx. 1300 personnel with elements deployed globally).
- Two Reserve Component PSYOPS Groups (approx. 2600 personnel with elements deployed in Iraq, Afghanistan and the Balkans).
- One Special Operations Wing (six aircraft and the US government's sole capability to rapidly broadcast deeply into denied areas).

4th PSYOPS Group

- Only active duty Army PSYOPS unit.
- Part of the US Army Special Operations Command (USASOC).
- Strategic Studies Detachment (SSD).
  - About 40 total analysts; Most have PhDs or are Masters degree holders.
  - The majority are historians, though some are anthropologists and political scientists. All have extensive experience in the regions they cover.
- Additionally, the Marine Corps Intelligence Activity (MCIA) and the Defense Intelligence Agency (DIA) Human Factors Group.

- Current Challenge. Balance between operational support and analytic production.

The US Army established its first **Information Operations Command** in 2002.

Mission. The 1st IO provides forces to synchronise information capabilities and prepare forces to resist adversarial Information Warfare while providing Specialised IO training to enable Army and Joint forces to achieve information advantage.

Mission

1st Information Operations (IO) Command (Land) provides IO support to the Army and other Military Forces through deployable IO support teams, IO reach back planning and analysis, and the synchronization and conduct of Army Computer Network Operations (CNO) in coordination with other CNO and Network Operations stakeholders, to operationally integrate IO, reinforce forward IO capabilities, and to defend Cyberspace in order to enable IO throughout the Information Environment

The key functions of the 1st Information Operations Command (Land) are:[27]

- Info Environment Analysis.
- Social Media Overwatch.
- Open Source Intelligence.
- Planning & Targeting Support.
- Vulnerability Assessment.
- Specialised IO Training.
- IO Culminating Training Event.
- OPSEC Assessments.
- Expeditionary Teams.

The Command consists of a Brigade Headquarters and two subordinate IO battalions, each with both active duty and Army Reserve detachments.

The 1st Information Operations Command (Land) has been officially deactivated as of 8 May 2025. Its functions are being transitioned to newly established Theatre Information Advantage Detachments (TIADs) and other Army information advantage forces. It was slated for deactivation in the Army Force Structure Transformation (ARSTRUC) Plan, released in February 2024. The decision to deactivate the 1st IO was part of a broader restructuring effort to create Theatre Information Advantage Detachments (TIADs). These new 65-person teams will focus on synchronising information capabilities at the Theatre level: one in the Pacific, one in Europe and another that Army Cyber is orienting towards trans-regional threats.

Those organisations will be doing the day-to-day business of setting the conditions and informing commanders of the Information Environment.

Col. Willie Rodney, who commanded the organisation, said at the deactivation ceremony, according to the Army: "The rise of multi-domain operations demands the Army integrate the capabilities that are executed in domains other than air, land and sea are incorporated in the scheme of maneuver and the overall operations process. The need for IO is not going away with the command; rather, the Army is forcing it to be integrated throughout the service and its forces. Overall, it's a step towards where we've always wanted/needed to go."

Lt. Gen. Maria Barrett, Commander of Army Cyber Command, said at the deactivation ceremony: "As we transition into the next era of Multi-Domain Operations, we carry forward the lessons learned and the expertise honed by 1st IO, ensuring that our cyber forces remain agile, resilient and ready for the challenges ahead."[28]

PSYCHOLOGICAL WARFARE BY TERRORISTS AND VIOLENT NON-STATE ACTORS (VNSAS)

> *"We typically design physical operations first, then craft supporting Information Operations to explain our actions. This is the reverse of Al-Qaeda's approach. Despite our professionalism, compared to the enemy's, our public information is often an afterthought. In military terms, for Al-Qaeda, the 'main effort' is information; for us, information is a 'supporting effort."*
>
> —**David Kilcullen, *Countering the Terrorist Mentality, New Paradigms for 21st Century Conflict.***

While nation-states have long employed Psychological Operations (PSYOPS) as part of their military strategy, the rise of Terrorists and Violent Non-State Actors (VNSAs) has dramatically expanded the scope, methods and impact of Psychological Warfare. Terrorists and VNSA groups leverage psychological tactics to instil fear, manipulate public opinion, recruit sympathisers and destabilise societies.

Tactics

Their psychological tactics serve the following strategic goals:

- **Intimidation.** Create widespread fear to paralyse civilian life and coerce political response.
- **Mobilisation.** Use emotive propaganda to recruit and radicalise.
- **Polarisation.** Amplify social, ethnic or religious fault lines.
- **Delegitimisation.** Undermine trust in governments, international institutions and law enforcement.
- **Manipulate** media narratives and public opinion.

KEY TACTICS AND METHODS

Propaganda and Media Warfare

- **Social Media and Online Radicalisation.** Groups like ISIS and Al-Qaeda use platforms like Telegram, Twitter (now X) and encrypted apps to disseminate propaganda, glorify violence and recruit globally.
- **Videos of Executions.** Beheading videos (e.g., ISIS's executions of journalists) are designed to shock, demoralise enemies and attract attention.
- **Symbolism and Branding.** Flags, anthems and logos (e.g., ISIS's black flag) create a sense of identity and omnipresence.

PSYCHOLOGICAL TARGETING TECHNIQUES

Fear Engineering. Shock tactics like beheadings, suicide bombings and mass hostage events are not just operational acts, but psychological spectacles. They create trauma, embedding the VNSA's brand in public consciousness.

Symbolic Violence. Locations chosen for attack often carry symbolic weight, such as, airports (representing mobility), schools (symbolising the future) and religious sites (embodying identity). These choices reinforce feelings of vulnerability and disrupt societal symbols of safety and continuity.

Information Saturation. VNSAs flood digital spaces with hashtags, fake news and anonymous manifestos. Quantity often outweighs quality, repetition builds believability and sustains the attacker's visibility.

Memetic Warfare. The use of memes and viral content to normalise extremism or ridicule counter-narratives is an emerging trend. It blends irony, humour and hate into psychologically sticky formats.

USE OF TECHNOLOGY

The digital age has transformed the reach and effectiveness of terrorist PSYOPS. Key technological enablers include:

- **Social Media and Viral Content.** Platforms like YouTube and X allow rapid dissemination of propaganda. ISIS's slickly produced videos, featuring drone footage and cinematic editing, rival professional media productions, enhancing their appeal to younger audiences.
- **Encrypted Communication.** Tools like Telegram and WhatsApp enable secure coordination and the sharing of propaganda, evading law enforcement agencies.
- **Deepfakes and AI.** Emerging technologies, such as, deepfake videos, pose new threats. While not yet widely used by VNSAs, the potential to create convincing disinformation campaigns is significant.
- **Dark Web and Decentralised Platforms.** The dark web provides anonymity for hosting propaganda and recruiting, while decentralised platforms resist takedown efforts by authorities.
- **Gamification of violence.** Turning radicalisation into an interactive experience.

These technologies enable VNSAs to operate globally, bypassing traditional media gatekeepers and directly reaching diverse audiences.

PSYCHOLOGICAL IMPACT ON SOCIETIES

The effects of terrorist PSYOPS are profound and far-reaching:

- **Widespread fear and anxiety.** Even in the absence of direct attacks, the persistent threat of terrorism can lead to chronic societal anxiety.
- **Erosion of trust.** Confidence in government, law enforcement and social institutions may be undermined.
- **Social polarisation.** Terrorist acts can deepen divisions along ethnic, religious or political lines, leading to scapegoating and social unrest.

Economic disruption. Fear-induced changes in behaviour, like avoiding public spaces and travel, can have significant economic consequences.

Narratives as Weapons. Narrative is the spine of Psychological Warfare. VNSAs create self-reinforcing myths like martyrdom, resistance and apocalypse that sustain organisational identity and justify violence. These stories are calibrated to exploit collective grievances, historical trauma and socio-political vacuums.

Narrative Control and Misinformation. Terrorist groups use social media to shape public perception during and after attacks, often hijacking trending hashtags or flooding platforms with their version of events. This can sow confusion, panic and mistrust in official sources.

Example: The Islamic State of Iraq and Syria (ISIS)

The ISIS represents the most sophisticated example of Psychological Warfare by a VNSA. The ISIS's ability to attract thousands of foreign fighters is a testament to its psychological and ideological appeal, packaged in modern formats. The ISIS masterfully used online platforms to promote the utopian vision of an Islamic Caliphate. Its media wing, al-Hayat, produced high-quality videos, magazines such as Dabiq and social media content that blended religious propaganda with action-oriented messaging.

ISIL's Online Output. It is interesting to see ISIL's organisation for Psychological Operations.

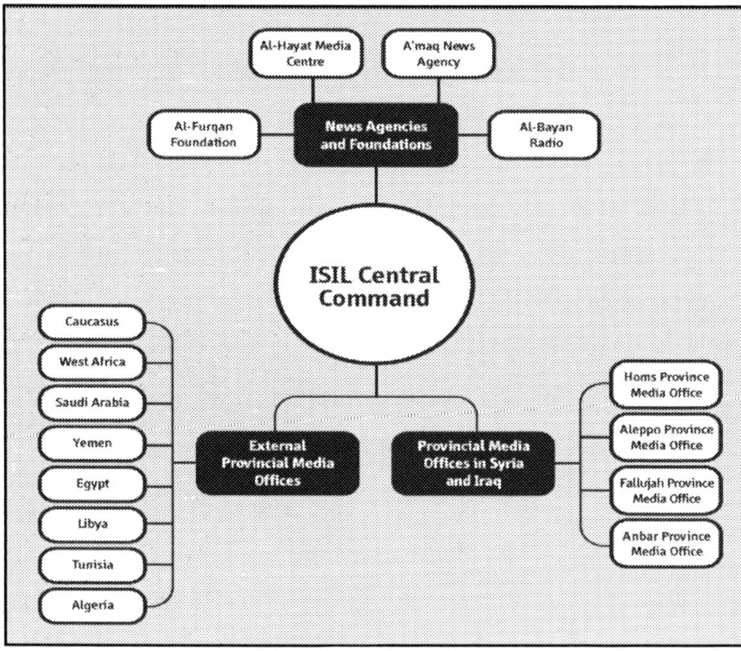

CONCLUSION

The PSYOPS capabilities of terrorist organisations and violent non-State actors have evolved dramatically over recent decades, reflecting broader changes in technology, media and social dynamics. These operations represent sophisticated applications of psychological principles designed to achieve strategic objectives through fear, polarisation and manipulation of the narrative.

Understanding these operations requires recognition of their strategic logic, tactical sophistication and psychological foundations. As technology continues to evolve and social media platforms proliferate, the importance of Psychological Operations will continue to grow.

Effective responses to terrorist PSYOPS must combine technical countermeasures with psychological resilience-building, media literacy education and the development of alternative narratives. The battle for hearts and minds remains as crucial as ever in contemporary security environments, requiring sustained attention from policy makers, researchers and practitioners alike.

EXAMPLES OF HOW PSYOPS IS CONDUCTED

The ISIS in Iraq

Abu Musab al-Zarqawi became the "Bin Laden of the Internet". It is an example of the weaponisation of social media by non-State actors. Zarqawi's jihadist network, al Qaeda in Iraq (AQI), weaponised YouTube by creating content depicting their successes in killing US soldiers and civilians to a musical soundtrack. By 2006, AQI named itself as the Islamic State of Iraq with its own IW/media arm tasked with professionalising the development of the content with a message of fear, action and blood to recruit and shape public opinion.

The ISIS used the Internet successfully to convince numerically superior Iraqi forces to abandon posts and weapons out of fear. This resulted in the rapid conquest of Mosul and large swaths of territory in Iraq and Syria. In addition, the ISIS carried out its military offensive like a virtual marketing tour that recruited over 30,000 people from nearly a hundred countries to join its cause.

A column of approximately 1,500 ISIS fighters rolled into northern Iraq. They were equipped with dirty pickup trucks and second-hand AK-47s. They also broadcasted their offensive. If you're launching an invasion in conventional military operations, you don't want the enemy to know about it. They wanted everyone to be aware of it. So they had countless fans and botnets on Twitter that converged around a hashtag, #AllEyesOnISIS.

The effect on Iraqi soldiers was devastating. The Iraqi Army was significantly larger, better equipped with tanks and helicopters and more trained, backed by the US with the most powerful military in the world. They were looking down at their smartphones and seeing what seemed like an ISIS victory playing out. It made 30,000 defenders run away, leaving much of their equipment for ISIS to claim and later broadcast, using all the American equipment. The unfolding events on social media altered the dynamics of the battlefield.

Eventually though, things were reversed. By 2016, Iraqi forces understood the weaponisation of SMPs. They used ISIS Tactics, Techniques, Procedures

(TTPs) against them in its SMP-enabled IW efforts using portable cellphone towers and its own #FreeMosul tag. The US Departments of State and Defense joined the Iraqi forces in the cyber and social media offensive. The result was there for all to see.

Syria

In 2015, after an Iran-backed offensive by the beleaguered Syrian regime failed to regain control of the city of Aleppo, members of the Islamic Revolutionary Guard Corps-trained brigades started posting photos of the experience on Facebook, Twitter and Instagram. These photos divulged the aircrafts they boarded, the geo-location of fighters, the identity of their comrades and commanders, the weapons they carried and the airports the Iranian regime used for its logistical efforts.

When fighters died, militias took to social media to create remembrance pages and posted photos of funerals and martyrdom videos. Their friends responded with likes and comments, in the process revealing their identities. This wealth of open-source information helped real-time intelligence gathering. For example, selfies taken onboard Iran Air aircraft proved that the Iranian commercial carrier was being employed to support the fighting. As a result, it helped the US to sanction Iran Air.

The same technologies can be used for defensive purposes. For example, one can use these techniques to break down the communities described above and detect adversary efforts to push a narrative, as well as examine the content of that narrative. The technology can help researchers concentrate while searching through massive amounts of social media data.[29]

Today, technologies exist that can perform each of these steps continuously and at a large scale. However, while current technologies support the manual application of psychological research results, they do not fully automate it. This would be the next stage in the development of technology.

PROBLEMS OF CONDUCTING PSYOPS

The conduct of Psychological Operations requires sanction from higher authorities than kinetic operations. During Operation Inherent Resolve, the authority to attack the ISIS kinetically required a Brigadier rank officer or even below. For an information operation, approval of at least a Major General or above was required. Any operation conducted via the Internet or social media requires approval at the Pentagon level. These constraints led to an often expressed sentiment that "it is easier to get permission to kill terrorists than it is to lie to them."[30]

The armed forces worldwide generally consider kinetic military specialisations, such as armour, infantry and artillery, as worthy of a higher degree of respect than non-kinetic specialisations. Everyone is busy and incentives to familiarise oneself with matters deemed of lesser importance are likely to be scarce. Military specialities in Information Operations rank lower in the military pecking order and are accorded less respect than those specialising in traditional combat arts.

Despite the rhetoric and doctrinal statements, military culture is oriented towards the operational environment where battles are won. Mass, firepower and technology have been regarded as tools to win battles.

Initially, in the US, the initiative for Psychological Operations or Strategic Communications was with the DOD due to the availability of funds. The Department of State was unable to secure adequate funding.

PSYOPS have often been singled out for unfavourable comparisons among non-kinetic combat capabilities. In 2011, the then-US Secretary of Defense, Robert Gates, directed that the term "Psychological Operations" (PSYOPS) be replaced by "military information support operations." The explanation for the name change was that "although PSYOPS activities rely on truthful information, credibly conveyed, the term PSYOPS tends to connote propaganda, brainwashing, manipulation and deceit."[31]

The widespread loss of information gatekeepers is unprecedented and has contributed to the scope and effectiveness of modern PSYOPS campaigns. Even the reputed media houses like BBC's reputation has suffered. A recent poll showed that a fifth of Britons had no trust in the BBC, to put it bluntly.

There has been a general decline in faith in government, mainstream media and other traditional institutions. People are assisted by algorithms that push information that data indicates will be of interest to them. This fragmented Information Environment makes it challenging to establish a shared national narrative that protects society against hostile influences.

Chapter V

Artificial Intelligence as a Tool for Online Radicalisation: Mechanisms, Risks and Mitigation Strategies

INTRODUCTION

The rapid evolution of Artificial Intelligence (AI) has transformed nearly every sector of society. While AI promises immense benefits, it also presents significant risks, particularly in the hands of malicious actors like terrorists and violent non-State actors. The exploitation of AI by terrorist organisations, especially generative AI and Large Language Models (LLMs) has revolutionised information creation and dissemination to facilitate radicalisation, recruitment and propaganda dissemination on a global scale, is a cause of concern for all governments.

Unlike traditional weapons systems, which require significant resources and expertise to develop, many AI tools are becoming increasingly accessible, open-source and user-friendly. Generative AI, chatbots and algorithmic targeting have enabled extremists to automate, personalise and scale radicalisation efforts with unprecedented efficiency and reach.

Terrorist groups operate like networked, agile and smart organisations, quickly adapting emerging technologies from social media to drones faster than formal, conventional organisations and AI is no exception. The Islamic State (IS) exemplified this adaptability, using high-production videos and multilingual content to attract global recruits. While the Internet has long served as a platform for extremist recruitment and propaganda, the integration of Artificial Intelligence into these processes represents a qualitative shift both in the scale and sophistication of radicalisation efforts. Terrorist organisations and violent non-State actors are increasingly leveraging AI technologies to create more personalised, persuasive and persistent radicalisation campaigns that can operate with unprecedented efficiency and reach.

We need to understand a couple of terms that will be used extensively in this chapter.

Artificial Intelligence (**AI**) refers to "the ability of a machine to learn from experience, adjust to new inputs and perform humanlike tasks."[32]

Big Data. Much of AI's appeal lies in its ability to analyse vast amounts of data, also referred to as "big data", faster and with greater ease than a human analyst or even a team of analysts can do. In doing so, AI discovers patterns and correlations unseen to the human eye. AI can extrapolate the likely outcomes of a given scenario based on available big data.[33]

Generative AI utilises machine learning to generate new content, including text, images, audio, video and multifunctional simulations. It works by utilising large datasets and parameters inspired by connections within the human brain. The main difference between generative AI and other forms of AI is that, generative AI systems can develop new outputs, rather than just predicting and categorising, like other machine learning systems. Some examples of generative AI applications include ChatGPT, Bing Chat, Google Gemini and Llama 2.

Terrorist and Violent Extremist Actors (TVEs) have already started using Generative AI tools to enhance their existing methods of producing and spreading propaganda, distorting narratives and influencing public opinion, as part of their Information Operations.

AI programmes are unintentionally accelerating the radicalisation of vulnerable individuals through the ELIZA effect, which is the tendency to ascribe human traits, such as empathy, motive and experience, to computer programmes. AI chatbots can successfully identify our biases and in turn, feed our desires.

MECHANISMS OF AI-ENABLED RADICALISATION

The Psychology of Digital Radicalisation. The radicalisation process involves quite a few psychological stages, including initial exposure to extremist content, gradual acceptance of radical narratives, adoption of extremist identity and potential progression to violent action. AI technologies augment each of these stages by leveraging sophisticated understanding of human psychology and behaviour to create more effective persuasion mechanisms.

Machine learning algorithms can analyse vast amounts of data about individual users, including their online behaviour, social connections, emotional states and personal vulnerabilities, to create detailed psychological profiles. These profiles enable extremist groups to create highly personalised radicalisation campaigns that target specific cognitive biases, emotional triggers and psychological needs that make individuals susceptible to extremist messaging. These AI-generated texts can adopt different writing styles, reference local events and include personal details to create the impression of authentic, relevant communication.

These systems can determine which narratives resonate most strongly with specific users, what types of evidence they find most convincing and which emotional appeals are most likely to motivate further engagement with extremist materials.

Unlike traditional radicalisation methods that rely on dramatic ideological shifts, AI-enabled approaches can implement subtle, incremental changes that feel natural and voluntary to the target individual, making them more effective and harder to detect.

Generative AI for Propaganda and Disinformation. Generative AI models, such as Large Language Models (LLMs), text-to-image generators and deepfake technologies, are now routinely exploited by terrorist groups to create and disseminate propaganda.

- **Synthetic Media.** Software tools like DALL-E, Midjourney, Stable Diffusion and Bing Image Creator can produce highly realistic images and videos that represent fictitious events. These synthetic media assets are used to manipulate public sentiment, incite violence and spread disinformation. These tools require minimal technical expertise; users input descriptive prompts and AI generates images or video clips that match the description, often within seconds.

- **Deepfakes.** AI-generated deepfakes enable the creation of videos in which public figures or adversaries appear to say or do things they never actually said or did. This technology is used to undermine trust in institutions, discredit opponents and fuel conspiracy theories. These deepfakes are often indistinguishable from genuine footage, especially when viewed quickly or shared on social media platforms.
- **Automated Content Generation.** LLMs can rapidly produce manifestos, social media posts and recruitment materials in multiple languages, enabling terrorist groups to reach diverse audiences with minimal human effort.
- **Games.** VNSAs have also been found modifying existing games online or creating their own online game-play spaces, with concerns that game creation engines could be used to make increasingly compelling propaganda.

Some terrorist organisations released guidelines on how to use AI to develop propaganda and disinformation. The Islamic State published a technology support guide on how to use generative AI tools securely in the summer of 2023.

Through all these methods, terrorists could use generative AI to create hallucinations through diverse strategies, like Psychological Warfare, false flag operations or propaganda to influence people's behaviour. Hallucinations mainly refer to situations where the AI system generates unexpected, unusual or nonsensical outputs.

AI-Driven Recruitment and Interactive Radicalisation. AI is not only enhancing propaganda but also revolutionising recruitment strategies. Chatbots and virtual agents powered by AI can engage in personalised, interactive conversations with potential recruits, mimicking human empathy and understanding. Later, a human being might take over the conversation to engage more personally. LLMs like ChatGPT, enable terrorist groups to provide a human-like experience even without the interference of humans.

A UN study reported that concerns have been raised about OpenAI's tools in terms of their capabilities in "micro-profiling and micro-targeting, generating automatic text for recruitment purposes".

Case Study: Islamic State Khorasan Province (ISKP)

The Islamic State of Iraq and Syria (ISIS) was among the first terrorist organisations to systematically exploit AI technologies for radicalisation purposes. The group developed sophisticated social media strategies that used algorithmic analysis to identify potential recruits and deliver personalised extremist content designed to facilitate ideological conversion.

The ISKP uses generative AI to produce multilingual propaganda, breaking down language barriers and expanding its recruitment pool across Russian, Pashto-speaking people and European communities.

The ISIS operatives used AI-powered tools to analyse social media profiles and identify individuals expressing anger, frustration or alienation that could be channelled towards extremist purposes. The group created automated systems that could initiate contact with these individuals through seemingly organic social media interactions, gradually introducing extremist narratives while building personal relationships.

The organisation also employed AI technologies to optimise the timing and delivery of radical content, using machine learning algorithms to determine when individuals were most likely to be receptive to extremist messaging. This approach significantly increased the effectiveness of their recruitment efforts while reducing the risk of detection by platform moderation systems. The ISKP employs keywords, hashtags and engagement mechanisms, further refined by AI, to optimise the visibility and impact of its content.

CHALLENGES IN COUNTERING AI-ENABLED RADICALISATION

The Evolving Threat Landscape. As generative AI becomes more advanced and accessible, the risk of its misuse by terrorists and VNSAs will only increase. Groups such as, the ISIS, Al-Qaeda and Hezbollah are already exploring these technologies and their tactics are likely to become more sophisticated over time.

CHALLENGES IN DETECTION AND PREVENTION

Technical Challenges. Detection of AI-enabled terrorist activities poses significant challenges for security agencies. Traditional surveillance methods are less effective against AI-enhanced operational security, which allows terrorist activities to persist with minimal human involvement, complicating human intelligence efforts. The rapid evolution of AI outpaces the development of defensive measures, creating a technological arms race that demands constant vigilance from security professionals. Additionally, the dual-use nature of AI technologies blurs the line between legitimate and malicious applications, making regulation difficult without stifling innovation. Security agencies must adapt swiftly to counter these sophisticated threats while navigating the complexities of AI's widespread accessibility.

Legal and Ethical Considerations. Addressing AI-enabled terrorism raises complex legal and ethical issues. Adapting traditional counterterrorism measures to counter AI-driven threats may infringe on privacy and civil liberties, requiring a careful balance between security and individual rights. The global nature of AI platforms complicates regulation, as terrorists can exploit tools across jurisdictions with differing legal frameworks, hindering comprehensive responses. Additionally, the use of AI by security agencies to detect and prevent terrorism, while effective, demands strict oversight to prevent abuse and safeguard civil liberties. These challenges necessitate nuanced policies to regulate AI use while effectively addressing the evolving threat of terrorism.

AI could also play a significant role in helping counter-terrorism efforts in various ways:

- **Surveillance and monitoring.** AI can analyse live videos to spot suspicious behaviour or objects in public, helping authorities respond quickly to potential threats. For counter-propaganda and de-radicalisation, AI's tools could support de-radicalisation programmes by identifying at-risk individuals and analysing their online behaviour.
- **Predictive analytics.** By analysing patterns in historical data, social media activity and other intelligence sources, AI could predict potential terrorist attacks. It can assess the behaviour of individuals or groups to identify signs of radicalisation and intervene before attacks happen.

- **Data analysis and intelligence gathering.** AI integrates large datasets from various sources, including surveillance footage, digital platforms and financial transactions, to provide comprehensive insights. It uses language processing to understand and analyse communication intercepts and online content for potential threats.
- **Improve operational efficiency in counter-terrorism.** It can optimise resource allocation for operations, ensuring personnel and equipment are effectively deployed. AI can provide decision-makers with real-time data and recommendations, enhancing the effectiveness of counter-terrorism strategies.
- **AI Chatbots.** Counter-terrorism practitioners can develop AI chatbots trained to 'think' like radicalised individuals by training them on large amounts of data that reflects the worldview of a particular terrorist group, such as, writings, social media posts and videos promoted by terrorist groups. Practitioners can then expose the chatbots to different counter-narratives and based on the chatbots' reactions, assess which counter-narratives are most effective at 'de-radicalising' the chatbots. This is a risk-free way to test and refine counter-messaging without exposing humans to any risk of blowback.[34]

Collaboration and Policy Innovation. Effective counter-measures require collaboration between governments, technology companies and civil society. Policies must strike a balance between the need for security and the protection of fundamental rights, ensuring that counter-terrorism efforts do not infringe upon privacy or freedom of expression.

- **International Cooperation.** Terrorism is a global threat that transcends borders. International collaboration is essential for sharing intelligence, harmonising regulations and coordinating responses to AI-enabled radicalisation.
- **Public-Private Partnerships.** Technology companies play a critical role in detecting and removing extremist content. Partnerships between public and private sectors can accelerate the development and deployment of effective counter-measures.

Education and Digital Literacy. Building resilience to AI-enabled radicalisation requires investment in education and digital literacy. Empowering individuals to evaluate online content and recognise manipulation tactics critically can reduce the effectiveness of extremist propaganda.

- **Media Literacy Programmes.** Teaching individuals to identify deepfakes, synthetic media and disinformation can inoculate them against radicalisation efforts.
- **Community Engagement.** Engaging local communities in prevention efforts can help identify at-risk individuals and provide support before they are fully radicalised.

RECOMMENDATIONS

To address the malicious use of AI for radicalisation, the following strategies are proposed:

Develop Advanced Detection Technologies. Governments and technology companies should collaborate to create AI-driven tools for detecting deepfakes and extremist content. These tools must be regularly updated to counter evolving AI technologies.

Strengthen International Cooperation. Establish global standards for AI governance to close regulatory gaps and prevent terrorists from exploiting jurisdictional differences.

Enhance Counter-Narratives. Invest in AI-driven counter-messaging campaigns that target at-risk groups with tailored, culturally relevant content.

Promote Ethical AI Design. Ensure AI systems are trained on diverse, unbiased datasets to prevent amplification of divisive narratives. Transparency in AI development is critical.

Balance Security and Rights. Implement oversight mechanisms to prevent AI-based surveillance from infringing on privacy and freedom of expression. Clear definitions of "violent extremism" are essential.

Public Awareness and Education. Educate vulnerable populations about the risks of AI-driven radicalisation to build resilience against manipulative technologies.[35]

NEWS MEDIA

The Reuters Institute Digital News Report 2025 highlights the following developments in the field of news media.

- An accelerating shift towards consumption via social media and video platforms is diminishing the influence of 'institutional journalism' and supercharging a fragmented alternative media environment, which encompasses a diverse array of podcasters, YouTubers and TikTokers.
- In most countries, traditional news media are struggling to connect with the public, experiencing declining engagement, low level of trust and stagnating digital subscriptions.
- Engagement with traditional media sources, such as, TV, print and news websites, continues to decline, while dependence on social media, video platforms and online aggregators increases.
- Personalities and influencers play a significant role in shaping public debates in some countries.
- Usage of X for news is stable or increasing across many markets.
- Video continues to grow in importance as a source of news. More people now say they prefer to watch the news rather than read it, further encouraging the shift to personality-led news creators.
- The importance of news podcasting in reaching younger, better-educated audiences. The United States has one of the highest proportions (15 percent) of people accessing one or more podcasts, with many of these now being filmed and distributed via video platforms, such as, YouTube and TikTok.
- TikTok is the fastest growing social and video network.
- AI chatbots and interfaces are emerging as a source of news as search engines and other platforms integrate real-time news. The numbers are still relatively small overall.
- Younger people are proportionately more likely than older groups to use social media to check information, as well as AI chatbots.
- Audiences in most countries remain sceptical about the use of AI in the news and are more comfortable with use cases where humans remain in the loop. Across countries, they expect that AI will make

> news cheaper to produce and more up-to-date, but less transparent, less accurate and less trustworthy.

As the largest technology platforms integrate AI summaries and other news-related features, publishers worry that these developments could further reduce traffic to their websites and applications. But in a world increasingly populated by synthetic content and misinformation, all generations still prize trusted brands with a track record for accuracy, even if they do not use them as often as they once did.[36]

Chapter VI

Social Media

In a remarkable book on social media, P.W. Singer and Emerson T. Brooking have brought out the essence of the weaponisation of social media. The following quotes from the book are apt:

> "The modern internet is not just a network, but an ecosystem of 4 billion souls.... Those who can manipulate this swirling tide, steer its direction and flow, can.... accomplish astonishing evil. They can foment violence, stoke hate, sow falsehoods, incite wars and even erode the pillars of democracy itself."

> "Attacking an adversary's most important centre of gravity—the spirit of its people—no longer requires massive bombing runs or reams of propaganda. All it takes is a smartphone and a few idle seconds. And anyone can do it."

> "Whether the cause is dangerous (support for a terrorist group), mundane (support for a political party) or inane (belief that the earth is flat), social media guarantees that you can find others who share your views and even be steered to them by the platforms' own algorithms... As groups of like-minded people clump together, they grow to resemble fanatical tribes, trapped in echo chambers of their own design."

Social Media Platforms (SMPs) are websites, tools, applications and gadgets that provide social media services. Any social media service like Facebook, Twitter(X), YouTube, Instagram, WhatsApp is a social media platform. The SMP industry connected the world, enabling the dissemination of information to millions with a single click. It has created an addiction. At the same time, it has had a damaging side effect on democracy. Critical thinking has taken a back seat. The average human's attention span has fallen to eight seconds, hindering critical thinking skills. As the use of mobile devices and SMPs increases, users' attention span and critical thinking decrease. This cognitive environment is ripe for social manipulation and gave birth to 21st Century Information Warfare.

Information Warfare strategies have been employed in various contemporary conflicts. During the Arab Spring, social media played a crucial role in mobilising protesters and disseminating information, both supporting and undermining different regimes. In the conflict between Russia and Ukraine, cyber attacks and Information Operations have been used extensively to influence perceptions and disrupt military operations. These examples illustrate the critical role of Information Warfare in modern conflict and the necessity for military professionals to understand and counter these tactics.

Social media is not just a communication space but a new kind of battle space. The boundaries between foreign and domestic sources of information chaos and dysfunction are blurring. Nation-states and non-State actors alike are leveraging social media to manipulate the cognitive biases of like-minded populations, influencing conflict dynamics.

Responding to these challenges will not be easy. It will involve taking complex and controversial decisions about the private sector's responsibility, restrictions on speech and national security issues.

Since most Psychological Warfare campaigns are waged on social media platforms today, this particular issue has been deliberated in detail.

Psychological Warfare operators leverage these mechanisms by creating content designed to trigger strong emotional reactions, such as, fear, anger, outrage or tribal loyalty. Content that resonates emotionally or psychologically with users spreads organically through social networks, creating a force-multiplication effect that would be impossible to achieve through traditional means.

Psychological Warfare campaigns can now target individuals based on their political affiliations, emotional states, personal insecurities, social relationships, geographic location and many other variables.

Social media has transformed Psychological Warfare into a high-speed, low-cost, deniable and persistent instrument of strategic influence. While it offers powerful tools for both persuasion and manipulation, its misuse threatens democratic institutions, social stability and cognitive liberty. Understanding these dynamics and building societal resilience is essential to countering this evolving form of conflict.

WEAPONISATION OF INFORMATION

The advent of social media has changed how we wage war. Both nation-states and non-State actors are leveraging social media to manipulate the cognitive biases of like-minded populations, influencing conflict dynamics. The social media battlefield has evolved into an inevitable component of every international conflict.

Information as a Weapon. Information, whether factual, misleading or outright false, becomes the primary tool. Social media platforms, with their rapid dissemination capabilities and diverse content formats (text, images, video, audio), are ideal for weaponising information.

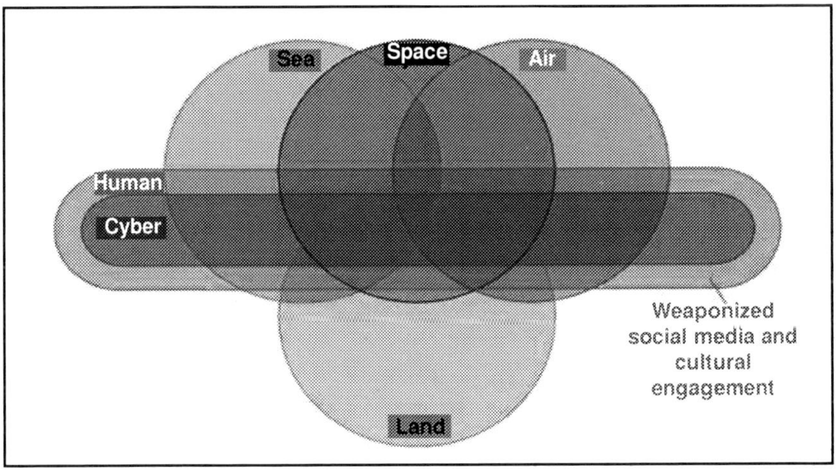

The SMP's efforts to make the world open and connected are financially enormously successful. They also present an opportunity to manipulate national instruments of power. The problem is becoming more complex as SMP use around the world is omnipresent.

The Boundaries of Social Manipulation

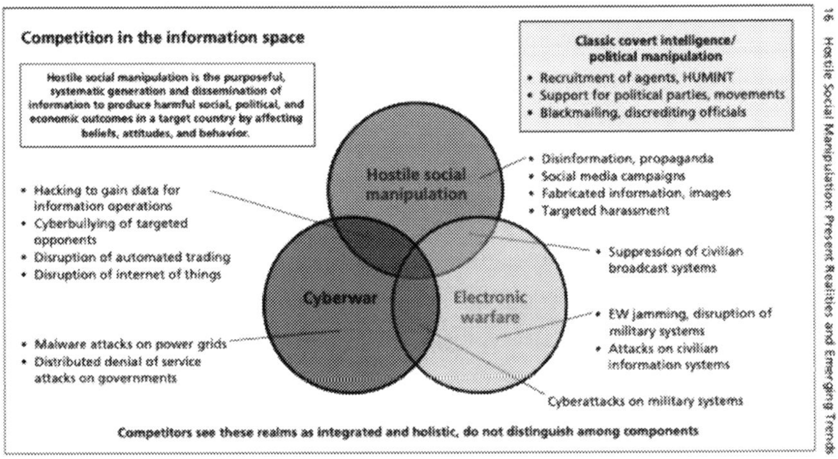

NOTE: HUMINT = human intelligence.

The private sector now owns Facebook, Twitter (now X), YouTube, Instagram and other popular platforms. They shape and influence what we think. Responding to these challenges will not be easy. It will involve making complex and controversial decisions about the private sector's responsibility, restrictions on speech and national security issues.

The manipulation of social media today is explained in the following diagram.

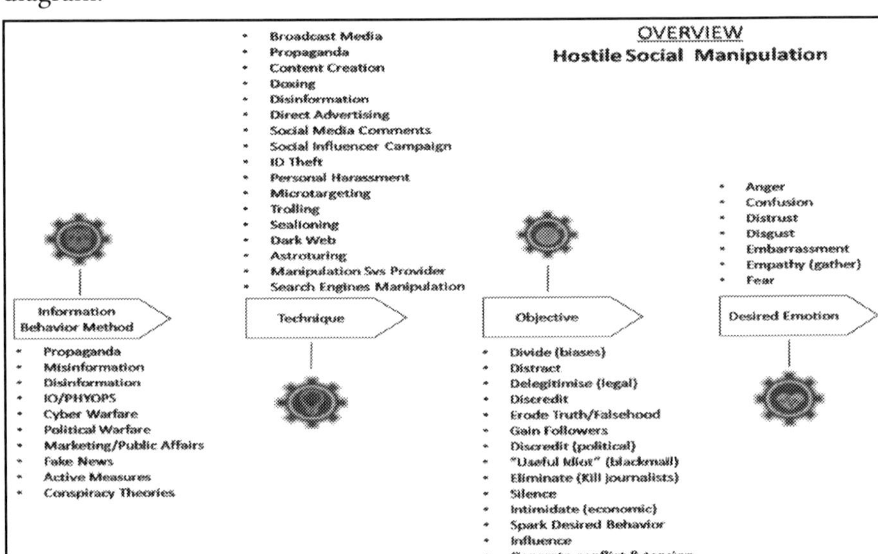

Source: RAND corporation, Hostile Social Manipulation, 2019, https://www.rand.org/content/dam/rand/pubs/research_reports/RR2700/RR2713/RAND_RR2713.pdf

ROLE OF SOCIAL MEDIA COMPANIES

The sophisticated algorithms that social media companies like Facebook, TikTok, Twitter and Instagram employ ensure that users see only the kind of content they want to see. The objective on both sides is not to change people's minds, but to reinforce the views of those whose minds are already made up and provide them with talking points and content that they can share among their own networks. The power of this tool is so immense that it cannot be wished away or characterised just as a facilitator.

Social media platforms maintain that they have been vigilant in policing inaccurate content and incitements to violence. Policing misinformation can be a double-edged sword, particularly in political conflicts where the truth is sometimes subjective. Even if platforms have the best intentions, being too heavy-handed in flagging and correcting information might have the opposite of the intended effect. Applying moderation policies consistently and efficiently poses enormous logistical challenges. Few users on either side of the conflict appear to be satisfied with the results.

Efforts to remove inflammatory content have also spurred allegations of prejudice and overreach. Instagram and Twitter (X) blamed technical faults, after posts mentioning the eviction of Palestinians from the Sheikh Jarrah neighbourhood, were wrongly deleted.

The Dichotomy between Freedom of Speech in Social Media and National Security Concerns

Social media platforms are private players. The largest actors, like Facebook, Google, Twitter and Microsoft are global conglomerates. They have no public accountability. There is no regulatory oversight. Social media platforms are the vehicle. They are not the wrongdoers who are creating false narratives. They hold data that could aid in uncovering the perpetrators. However, they are not law enforcers. They do not have the mandate to address issues of national security.

This is the sheer scale of the challenge. On any given day, between 0.5 percent to 1.5 percent of all tweets qualify as violent or hate speech. This means hundreds of millions of posts a year that are encountered by the same number of users. Problems on the other platforms are similar. For example, on Facebook, websites promoting coronavirus conspiracy theories have more than ten times the engagement of public health organisations.

According to the law, they do not police their platforms. They do it as per their internal policies. Identifying disinformation material is problematic. It is usually context-sensitive and it is not always clear what is and what is not in the category to be taken down. It is challenging for a platform to discern what is intentionally false, with the aim of either directly influencing a country's politics or sowing discord and division within that country. Figuring that out needs a complex understanding of the political, social and cultural context. A platform requires a definition to know what to seek out and take down. Social media platforms make decisions about content take-downs according to criteria that include corporate risk factors.

Recently, platforms like Facebook and Twitter (X) have taken action to ban political advertisements, hateful content and disclaimers on some types of content that are far-reaching and verifiably false. This demonstrates that social media companies can implement positive changes.

Social media companies are reluctant to let intelligence and law enforcement agencies look behind the privacy walls of active accounts. This would cause a public outcry as user privacy is at stake. However, making those walls impenetrable prevents those same agencies responsible for keeping us safe from doing their job.

National Security Concerns

Due to the very structure of the Internet, no Western nation has yet found a solution to stop or deter malicious foreign cyber activity. It is nearly impossible to quickly and with certainty determine if a foreign government is behind a disinformation campaign, ransomware implant, or data theft. With uncertain attribution, the government's hands are tied.

The design of the platforms is to tie their profit to our psychology. In a system that monetises clicks, hate speech fueled by disinformation can quickly gain attention and engagement. It confirms pre-existing biases and operates within a structure that rewards trends. The harmful and conspiratorial beliefs are spread via the proliferation of disinformation on social media by adversarial foreign actors seeking to harm national security.

The approach of social media platforms to curb this menace is not encouraging for security professionals. An ex-post response, lack of sustained action and an inadequate sense of urgency usually characterise it. Moreover, the mechanisms implemented by the platforms to identify what is termed "fake news" are unsuitable for this task. They rely on an obscure fact-checking exercise, whereas hostile States use highly sophisticated techniques.

For greater transparency, security agencies should be informed about how such decisions are made and how a platform's algorithm generates recommendations and curate what we see and hear.

There is the sensitive issue of the State demanding to see data, without being intrusive into individual rights. However, one must understand Big Brother is no longer the State. The technology giants have taken that position, who misuse privacy protections based on their own politically driven algorithms rather than submitting themselves to the government's due process. Recent data show that requests by governments to access user data are growing.

The challenge for both social media platforms and government agencies is to devise mechanisms and implement regulations that enable law enforcement agencies to access accounts linked to terrorist groups in real-time. Protecting communications between traffickers and terrorists should not be taken as privacy. Platforms know who these people are and can see what they are posting, even if it lies behind privacy settings.

Owners of social media must understand that freedom and privacy are not all-or-nothing propositions. A balance has to be struck as our safety depends on it.[37]

Social Media has transformed Psychological Warfare into a highly efficient, pervasive and often subtle means of influencing populations. Social media enables State and non-State actors to manipulate perceptions, spread disinformation, destabilise target populations and exploit human psychology at an unprecedented speed and scale. The dynamic nature of social media demands constant vigilance, technological innovation and public awareness to mitigate its weaponisation.

The integration of social media platforms into Psychological Warfare represents a paradigm shift that leverages the intimate, pervasive and interactive nature of digital communication to achieve strategic objectives through manipulation of human psychology on a massive scale.

The foundational advantage of social media in Psychological Warfare lies in its direct access to target populations. Unlike traditional media channels, which require significant infrastructure or cooperation from media organisations, social media platforms allow operators to bypass intermediaries and communicate directly with their target audiences.

Impact of Social Media on Psychological Warfare

- **Scale and Speed.** Social media allows PSYWAR campaigns to reach billions of users almost instantaneously, across geographical boundaries. A single piece of disinformation can go viral globally within hours.
- **Low Cost and Accessibility.** Compared to traditional propaganda methods (e.g., printing leaflets, setting up radio stations), running a social media influence campaign can be relatively inexpensive, lowering the barrier to entry for various actors.
- **Anonymity and Plausible Deniability.** The nature of social media, with its ease of creating fake accounts and operating across borders, makes it challenging to attribute PSYWAR operations definitively. This provides plausible deniability for State actors.
- **Personalisation and Engagement.** Social media platforms are designed for engagement, making users more receptive to content. The ability to personalise messages increases their persuasive power.
- **Erosion of Trust.** The constant bombardment of manipulated content, fake news and conflicting narratives on social media erodes public trust in traditional media, governments and even facts themselves, leading to a more fractured and vulnerable society.
- **Amplification of Extremism.** Social media algorithms often favour engaging, emotionally charged content, inadvertently boosting extremist views and making radicalisation easier.
- **Challenges to Detection and Moderation.** The sheer volume of content and the sophistication of PSYWAR tactics make it incredibly

challenging for social media platforms to detect and remove all malicious content, resulting in a constant cat-and-mouse game.

- **Microtargeting.** It is based on user data and psychographics.
- **Interactive feedback loops.** It allows for campaign adjustments in real-time.

CORE PRINCIPLES OF PSYCHOLOGICAL WARFARE IN A SOCIAL MEDIA CONTEXT

Targeting Perception and Behaviour. Social media PSYWAR aims to manipulate how target audiences perceive reality, influencing their beliefs, emotions and ultimately, their actions. This could range from inciting panic, fuelling dissent, spreading specific political narratives or eroding trust in institutions.

Exploiting Cognitive Biases

PSYWAR leverages inherent human psychological vulnerabilities. Social media's design often amplifies these biases:

- **Confirmation Bias.** Users tend to seek out and believe information that confirms their existing beliefs, leading to echo chambers. PSYWAR exploits this by feeding narratives that resonate with pre-existing biases.
- **Emotional Contagion.** Emotionally charged content (fear, anger, outrage) spreads rapidly on social media, often bypassing critical thinking. PSYWAR crafts content designed to elicit strong emotional responses.
- **Mere Exposure Effect.** Repeated exposure to a message, even if false, can increase its perceived truthfulness. Social media's amplification mechanisms (bots, shares) facilitate this.
- **Bandwagon Effect.** People are more likely to adopt a belief or behaviour if they see others doing it. PSYWAR creates the illusion of widespread support through fake accounts and manufactured trends.

KEY TACTICS AND TECHNIQUES EMPLOYED ON SOCIAL MEDIA

Disinformation and Misinformation Campaigns

- **Fake News Articles.** Creating entirely fabricated news stories designed to appear legitimate and spreading them through social media shares. These often mimic the style of reputable news outlets.
- **Doctored Media (Deepfakes, Shallowfakes).** Manipulating images, audio or video to create convincing but false content. Deepfakes, generated by AI, are particularly powerful in fabricating speeches or events that never happened. Shallowfakes are simpler manipulations, like altered photos or videos taken out of context.
- **Decontextualisation.** Taking genuine information (photos, videos, quotes) and presenting it out of its original context to create a misleading narrative.
- **Conspiracy Theories.** Spreading elaborate, unsubstantiated theories that often tap into public distrust of authority, providing alternative explanations for events that are difficult to debunk.
- **Information Laundering.** Introducing false or misleading information on fringe platforms, then amplifying it through more mainstream social media channels or seemingly legitimate influencers to give it credibility.

SOCIAL MEDIA ACCOUNT MANIPULATION

- **Fake Accounts/Sock Puppets.** Creating fictitious online personas (often with stolen photos and fabricated backstories) to interact with real users, spread narratives and appear as genuine individuals.
- **Bot Networks (Botnets).** Automated accounts that can rapidly amplify messages, artificially inflate engagement metrics (likes, shares, comments), create trending topics or flood discussions to drown out opposing views.
- **Cyborg Accounts.** Accounts managed by a combination of human operators and automation, making them harder to detect than pure bots.

- **Stolen/Hacked Accounts.** Compromising legitimate user accounts to post propaganda, spread disinformation or gain access to networks.
- **Troll Farms.** Organised groups of individuals paid to engage in online harassment, spread propaganda and sow discord, often operating from specific locations.

Narrative Shaping and Framing

- **Hashtag Hijacking and Trend Manipulation.** Attackers hijack popular hashtags or manipulate trending topics to spread their content, drown out genuine discourse and ensure their narratives reach a wider audience.
- **Agenda-Setting.** Deliberately pushing certain topics or narratives into public discourse to shift attention or frame an issue in a desired light.
- **Polarisation.** Amplifying existing societal divisions (e.g., political, ethnic, religious) by creating content that demonises opposing groups, fosters "us vs. them" mentalities and reduces opportunities for common ground.
- **Astroturfing.** Creating the deceptive appearance of spontaneous grassroots support for a policy, cause or candidate when it is, in fact orchestrated by a hidden entity.

Targeted Influence and Personalisation

- **Data harvesting and Micro targeting.** Using vast amounts of user data (demographics, interests, online behaviour) to tailor messages to specific individuals or small groups, exploiting their vulnerabilities, biases and emotional triggers. This makes the propaganda more effective and harder to recognise.
- **Psychographic Profiling.** Analysing psychological traits of individuals or groups to craft highly persuasive messages.
- **Influencer Marketing (Malicious).** Paying or co-opting seemingly independent social media influencers to spread specific narratives, often without disclosing their true affiliation or agenda.
- **Viral Memes and Visual Propaganda.** Memes and visual content are easily shareable and can quickly shape perceptions, reinforce

stereotypes or spread disinformation in a format that is accessible and emotionally resonant.

Cyber-Enabled Harassment and Intimidation

- **Doxing.** Publishing private or identifying information about an individual online without their consent, often with malicious intent (e.g., to incite harassment or violence).
- **Cyberbullying/Trolling.** Coordinated harassment campaigns aimed at silencing dissent, intimidating journalists, activists or political opponents and creating an unwelcoming environment for certain viewpoints.
- **Threats and Intimidation.** Directly or indirectly issuing threats to induce fear and conformity.

"Hack-and-Leak" Operations. Compromising accounts or systems to steal sensitive, embarrassing or divisive information and then strategically leaking it on social media to damage reputations, discredit individuals or organisations or influence political events.

Social Engineering and Honey Trapping. Fake profiles or impersonation are used to build trust with targets, extract confidential information or manipulate behaviour through social engineering tactics.

Mobilisation and Behavioural Manipulation

- Social media campaigns can move beyond perception to influence real-world behaviour, such as mobilising protests, boycotts or even inciting violence.
- Swarming tactics and astroturfing (fake grassroots movements) create the impression of mass support, encouraging real users to join in and escalate the campaign.

Countering Social Media PSYWAR

Defensive strategies must address both technological and human factors in social media Psychological Warfare. Platform-level interventions include improved detection algorithms, content moderation policies and transparency measures. Individual resilience building involves media literacy education, critical thinking skills development and awareness of psychological manipulation techniques. Societal responses require policy frameworks, international cooperation and cultural changes that prioritise information integrity and psychological security.

Combating social media-based Psychological Warfare requires a multi-pronged approach:

- **Media Literacy.** Educating the public on how to critically evaluate online information, identify manipulation tactics and verify sources.
- **Platform Accountability.** Pressuring social media companies to invest more in content moderation, transparency (e.g., labeling state-sponsored media) and rapid removal of coordinated inauthentic behaviour.
- **Fact-Checking.** Supporting and promoting independent fact-checking organisations to debunk false narratives quickly.
- **Cyber Threat Intelligence.** Developing capabilities to identify, track and attribute PSYWAR campaigns to their perpetrators.
- **Strategic Communication.** Governments and reputable organisations proactively communicate accurate information to counter false narratives.
- **Building Societal Resilience.** Fostering critical thinking, promoting civil discourse and addressing underlying societal grievances that make populations vulnerable to manipulation.
- **Technological Solutions.** Developing AI and machine learning tools to detect deepfakes, bot networks and manipulative content.

Detection and countermeasures face significant challenges due to the sophisticated nature of social media Psychological Warfare. The blend of authentic and inauthentic content, the exploitation of legitimate platform features and the psychological subtlety of many influence techniques make identification difficult. Platform companies struggle to distinguish between legitimate persuasion and harmful manipulation, while users often lack the awareness or skills to recognise sophisticated psychological influence attempts.

The ethical implications of social media Psychological Warfare raise fundamental questions about consent, autonomy and human dignity. The manipulation of psychological vulnerabilities without explicit consent represents a form of mental violation that challenges basic principles of individual freedom and self-determination. The use of intimate personal data for psychological manipulation raises privacy concerns that extend beyond traditional notions of data protection.

International law and governance frameworks struggle to address social media Psychological Warfare due to jurisdictional complexities, definitional challenges and the rapid pace of technological change. The cross-border nature of social media operations complicates traditional concepts of sovereignty and intervention. In contrast, the subtle nature of psychological influence makes it difficult to establish clear legal standards or thresholds for harmful activity.

Future developments in Artificial Intelligence and Machine Learning will likely enhance the sophistication and effectiveness of social media Psychological Warfare. Advanced natural language processing, predictive analytics and automated content generation will enable more precise targeting, more convincing content and more efficient operations. The integration of emerging technologies, such as, Virtual Reality and Augmented Reality, may create new dimensions for psychological manipulation.

Chapter VII

Psychological Warfare and Various Terms

CONFUSION OF TERMINOLOGIES

Post the Gulf War, the US DOD pioneered all the thinking and doctrines of Information Warfare and later Information Operations. However, various terms used in their doctrines are somehow confusing and lack clarity. It is not surprising that the strategic community and the DOD themselves use the terms Information Warfare, ''Information Operations,' 'Psychological Operations', 'Military Information Support Operations (MISO)', 'Strategic Communication,' 'Influence Operations,' and possibly 'Cyberspace Operations' interchangeably, although they are not synonymous.

These inconsistencies can ultimately lead to conceptual confusion, resulting in the misallocation and misalignment of resources and capabilities. For instance, such confusion will make it challenging to hire and train the right people for cyber and Psychological Operations/MISO positions due to a lack of understanding of the skill sets different missions require.

Various terms are used in the doctrines of Information Warfare and later, Information Operations. The terms used in these doctrines are somehow confusing and lack clarity. The strategic community, as well as Indian experts, use the terms Information Warfare, Information Operations, Psychological Operations, Perception Management, Military Information Support Operations (MISO), Strategic Communication, Influence Operations, Cognitive Warfare, Public Field Diplomacy and Cyberspace Operations interchangeably, though they are not synonymous.[38]

Some of the terminologies used are:

- Psychological Operation
- Strategic Communications
- Influence Operations
- Perception Management
- Cyber-enabled Influence/Information Warfare and Manipulation (IIWAM)
- Cognitive Warfare
- Narrative Warfare
- Sentiment Analysis
- Political Warfare
- Public Information Warfare
- Public Field Diplomacy
- Information Advantage

This author is of the view that all the above terms come under the overall ambit of Psychological Warfare. These can be a subset of Psychological Warfare. Some of these terms are explained subsequently.

PUBLIC AFFAIRS

According to JP 3-61, Public Affairs (PA) provides information to domestic and international audiences, contributing to global influence and the deterrence of attacks. This guidance does not differentiate between adversaries and own audiences. It includes both. The target audiences may differ, but the consistency of messages is essential to credibility. PA focuses on truth and credibility and must be fact-based.[39]

To successfully tell the Army's story, a range of digital communication tools are used. Some of the tools required for the current and emerging demands of the communication environment are:

- Digital Media Management and Media Relations sections.
- Conduct Assessments and Counter Misinformation/Disinformation core tasks.

- Public Affairs Code of Ethics and Commander's Communication Synchronisation concepts.
- Clear guidance on crucial responsibilities.
- Crisis Communication.
- Community Engagements.
- Drone Usage.
- Social Media Management.

The following efforts focus on the future direction of timely and accurate release of information on most platforms:

- **Dissemination.** Impartial and objective dissemination of information about one's own action.
- **Social media.** Army social media platforms are official representations of the Army. The Commanding Officer must grant social media managers on official Army social media accounts the authority to release content. Waiting to get ratification by higher headquarters means loss of precious time.
- **Countering misinformation/disinformation.** A Commander cannot counter false information without being credible. PA can mitigate and counter adversarial disinformation and misinformation with accurate and timely public information and imagery.

Perception Management

Perception Management is undertaken within the country for misinformed citizens. Psychological Warfare is conducted across the boundaries of the country.

Presently, there is a clear dividing line between PA and Psychological Warfare. The main reason for separation is the commitment to use or not use truthful information. You cannot lie to your own population. We do not carry out Psychological Operations against our own countrymen. Truth can become a casualty here, as Yudhistir said in the great battle of the Mahabharata, "Ashwathama Hatha Iti, Narova Kunjarova." This statement was a deliberate half-truth used to trick Dronacharya into believing that his son, Ashwathama, had been killed, allowing Dhrishtadyumna to then strike him down.

Perception Management differs from Psychological Warfare in that, Psychological Warfare conveys its messages through uncontrolled public media, whereas Perception Management uses media controlled by its own forces and agencies. PIO provides accurate and timely information without attempting to influence or sway the audience. PIO and Psychological Warfare products should provide a timely flow of information to the external and internal audience. PIO and Psychological Warfare must be separate and distinct.

INFLUENCE OPERATIONS

According to the RAND Corporation, Influence Operations are the coordinated, integrated and synchronised application of national diplomatic, informational, military, economic and other capabilities in peacetime, crisis, conflict and post-conflict to foster attitudes, behaviours, or decisions by foreign target audiences that further US interests and objectives. This definition has a striking resemblance to the definition of Strategic Communications.

The US DOD defines Strategic Communication as focused US Government efforts to understand and involve key audiences to create, strengthen or keep conditions favourable for the advancement of US Government interests, policies and goals through the use of coordinated programmes, themes, plans, messages and products synchronised with the actions of all instruments of national power.

Thus Influence Operations can be considered synonymous with Strategic Communications.

STRATEGIC COMMUNICATION

The White House National Framework for Strategic Communication (2010) defined Strategic Communication as:

> Strategic Communication is a dynamic process with responsibility held by those at the highest levels of government—the President and senior government leaders. However, to achieve this requires a commitment not yet seen, although some steps have been taken to improve the nation's capability. What is needed is a transformation supported by resources and a strong sense of purpose that matches the nation's commitment to defence, intelligence, law enforcement and homeland security.

Strategic Communication(s) refers to:

- The synchronisation of words and deeds and how they will be perceived by selected audiences.
- Programmes and activities deliberately aimed at communicating and engaging with intended audiences, including those implemented by Public Affairs, Public Diplomacy and Information Operations professionals.[40]

Strategic Communication Relationships

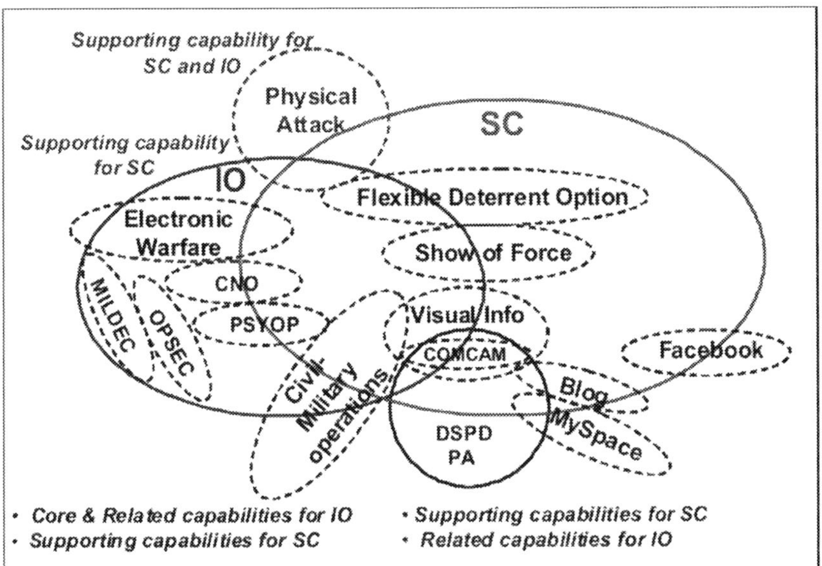

Source: https://www.jstor.org/stable/20007917?seq=3

PUBLIC DIPLOMACY

The concept of "Public Diplomacy" was coined in the United States in the 1960s. In 2016, the US Government made a concerted effort to adjust its resources to counter the growing threat of disinformation. Initially, the response was uncoordinated, with many actors responding independently based on their policy focus. With the creation of the Global Engagement Center (GEC), a coordinated effort to counter the effects of disinformation started taking shape.

Public Diplomacy is defined as the efforts by a country's government to communicate and interact openly and directly with foreign audiences, including academics, NGOs, businesses, institutions and even the general public, to deepen mutual understanding and promote/protect its national interests.

The aim of a country's Public Diplomacy activities is to:

- Influence how foreign citizens perceive the country, correcting misperceptions about its policies and values and battling stereotypes.
- Promote general mutual understanding of people.
- Impact official relations with the foreign government in a way that serves the country's national interests.

PUBLIC DIPLOMACY IN INDIA

- Indian Public Diplomacy dates back to the days of Chanakya, who advocated the importance of listening as one of the most crucial attributes of an ideal king.
- The Public Diplomacy Division of the Ministry of External Affairs was established in May 2006 to "educate and influence global and domestic opinion on key policy issues and project a better image of the country commensurate with its rising international standing."
- The Indian Council for Cultural Relations (ICCR), founded in 1950, is the pre-eminent instrument of cultural diplomacy. It maintains 24 cultural centres outside India to project Indian culture to local people.
- The Ministry of Information and Broadcasting lends support to the Public Diplomacy initiative through the strategic use of the media.
- Other Government agencies carry out programmes that promote the Indian image abroad and engage in Public Diplomacy, both independently and collectively. Campaigns like 'Pravasi Bharatiya Divas' and the 'Know India' programme have met with resounding success.
- The India Perspective magazine is published in 17 languages and distributed in over 150 countries around the world.

- The Public Diplomacy Division also partners with major domestic and international universities, think tanks and research organisations to organise seminars and conferences.

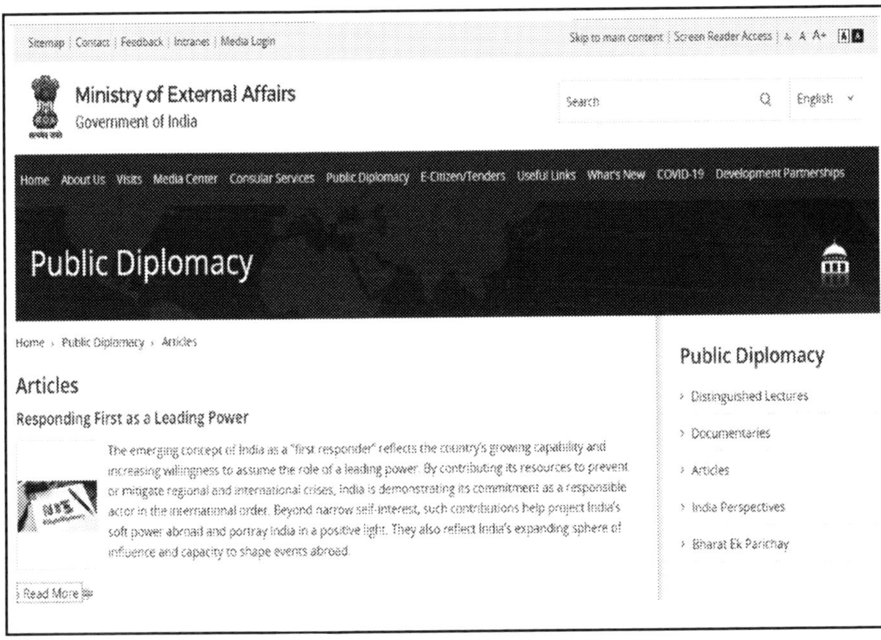

Initially, in the US, the initiative for Psychological Operations or Strategic Communications was with the DOD for the simple reason of availability of funds. The Department of State could not garner adequate finances. That has changed now. In February 2018, the Department of State announced that it had reached an agreement with the DOD to transfer a maximum of $40 million to the Global Engagement Center (GEC) to fund "counter propaganda and disinformation from foreign nations." In FY2018, GEC's Countering State-sponsored Disinformation (CSD) funding totalled $41.1 million, meaning that 49 percent of its CSD operations were dependent on the DOD, but they were wholly GEC-led and added a significant new element to the Department of State programming mix.[41]

Relationship between Strategic Communication, Information Operations, Public Diplomacy and Public Affairs

In the US, the responsibilities are given as under:

ROLES AND RESPONSIBILITIES

- The Department of State carries out Public Diplomacy as an essential part of foreign policy.
- The Department of State distinguishes between Public Affairs, which includes outreach to domestic publics and Public Diplomacy, which seeks to promote the national interest of the United States through understandingly engaging, informing and influencing the foreign public and by promoting mutual understanding between the people of the United States and people from other nations around the world.
- The DOD is a key contributor to communication and engagement efforts. The key elements of the DOD include, but are not limited to, Information Operations, Defense Support to Public Diplomacy (DSPD), Public Affairs and Civil Affairs, all working together to accomplish military objectives that support national objectives.

DEFENCE SUPPORT TO PUBLIC DIPLOMACY

- The DOD is reviewing resources and capabilities that might best be brought to bear in its support of Department of State efforts to advance US Government Public Diplomacy as well as US Embassies' Information Programmes and to support other agencies' Public Diplomacy that directly supports DOD missions.
- The DOD is committed to planning and conducting activities to implement its Security Cooperation Guidance.
- The DOD is working through the Combatant Commands (COCOMs) to collaboratively shape the operational environment in support of USG information objectives through activities that may include, but are not limited to, Humanitarian Mine Action, Humanitarian Relief and Assistance, Counter-Drug Activities and activities supporting global counter-terrorism.

MILITARY DIPLOMACY

The activities and measures US military leaders take to engage military, defence and government officials of another country, involve communicating US Government policies and messages and building defence and coalition relationships.

Since there were a lot of overlapping responsibilities and additional layers being formed, the US DOD decided not to use the term Strategic Communication.

OFFICE OF THE ASSISTANT SECRETARY OF DEFENSE
1400 DEFENSE PENTAGON
WASHINGTON, DC 20301-1400

PUBLIC AFFAIRS

November 28, 2012

MEMORANDUM FOR COMMANDERS OF THE COMBATANT COMMANDS

SUBJECT: Communications Synchronization – A Local Coordination Process

This memorandum is in response to questions from the field about the status of Public Affairs and Strategic Communication (SC) in Office of the Secretary of Defense (OSD). The responsibility for SC in OSD was shared by the Office of the Assistant Secretary of Defense for Public Affairs (OASD-PA) (Communications Planning and Integration) and USD(P) (Global Engagement). COCOMs typically sent SC plans to these organizations for coordination and approval. SC was viewed as a means to synchronize communication efforts across the department, however, over the last six years we learned that it actually added a layer of staffing and planning that blurred the roles and functions of traditional staff elements and resulted in confusion and inefficiencies. As a result, this year we stood down these staff elements. We also realized that these SC plans mostly contained public affairs planning that we once again expect to come through public affairs channels.

We avoid using the term SC to avoid causing confusion. The more accurate terminology, which will be used in future Joint Publications, is communication synchronization. We are continuing our leadership role in communication and reminding those in the communication business that most things previously termed "SC" are in fact Public Affairs responsibilities.

It is the role of the information related community (Information Operations, Legislative Affairs, Public Affairs…) to ensure the leader's intent is reflected in every staff product, and that the various parts of a command are closely synchronized-there should be no difference between what the Public Affairs office is saying, the J5 is planning and the J3 is doing. This process can be accomplished with working groups and steering groups in concert with base planning and don't require the creation of additional staff elements.

Communication goals should be managed by existing staff elements and in most cases this should be the Public Affairs office. The process requires senior leader involvement and dialogue. Without commander engagement, communication synchronization cannot work.

Thank you for your efforts to ensure this important function is accomplished. These efforts will be formalized as joint doctrine in future versions of the joint publication series

George E. Little
Assistant to the Secretary of Defense
for Public Affairs

Source: https://foreignpolicy.com/wp-content/uploads/2015/01/121206_brooksmemo.pdf

Chapter VIII

Narrative Warfare

The "War of Narratives" is a central front in modern Information Warfare, where controlling the narrative is as crucial as physical dominance. The ability to influence the thoughts, emotions and behaviours of target audiences can determine the outcome of conflicts and is employed to demoralise enemy troops, win the hearts and minds of civilian populations and undermine the credibility and morale of adversaries. Unlike traditional battles over territory or resources, Narrative Warfare is a contest over perception, interpretation and cultural resonance. In Information Warfare, narratives are not mere stories but strategic tools that exploit human cognitive biases, emotions and cultural contexts to achieve their objectives.

THE NARRATIVE IS THE BATTLEFIELD

Defining the War of Narratives. Narrative Warfare refers to the strategic creation, dissemination and contestation of stories that frame events, issues or actors in a way that advances a particular agenda and achieves psychological dominance over adversaries. It is not just about spreading facts or misinformation. It is about crafting compelling stories that resonate emotionally and psychologically with audiences.

Unlike traditional propaganda, which often uses direct messaging, Narrative Warfare creates consistent and emotionally engaging storylines that support the goals of the person using them.

Narrative construction is a series of directed persuasion Information Operations that, when combined, form a coherent perspective about policy in wartime. Narrative construction can be one of the most challenging forms of Information Operations to implement, track, or measure, but it can also be very powerful. Such campaigns incorporate passive and active operations to shape discourse within and between societies.

Narrative Warfare underscores a fundamental truth about modern conflict: wars are no longer won solely by bullets and bombs but also by beliefs and stories. It is warfare in the cognitive domain, where controlling the story can be more potent than controlling territory.

Narratives are deliberately crafted messages, often blending truth, half-truths and falsehoods, designed to control the Information Environment, sway public opinion and achieve strategic objectives without necessarily resorting to kinetic force.

Narrative Warfare shapes not just what people feel but what they believe is true. In the emerging battlespace of ideas, those who craft compelling, credible and consistent narratives will hold the high ground.

The war of narratives unfolds in various areas, including mainstream media, social media platforms, diplomatic communications, cultural outputs, entertainment and personal communication networks. Adversaries in this domain seek to influence domestic and international audiences, erode trust in institutions, provoke societal divisions and discredit leadership. Social media serves as the primary battleground due to its wide reach and rapid pace.

Social media is the primary battleground due to its reach and speed. Actors State, non-State or hybrid, use platforms like X, Facebook or TikTok to disseminate tailored content, often amplified by bots, trolls or algorithms.

Today, skilled players can share multiple versions of their narratives with different audiences simultaneously. They use data analysis to determine which stories resonate best with specific demographic or psychological profiles. Artificial Intelligence amplifies this capability by generating personalised content at scale and identifying optimal timing and channels for narrative deployment.

Deepfakes, AI-generated content and algorithmic amplification can fabricate, distort or flood the Information Environment, making it difficult for truth to emerge. In such an environment, who tells the story and how quickly, is often more important than whether the story is true.

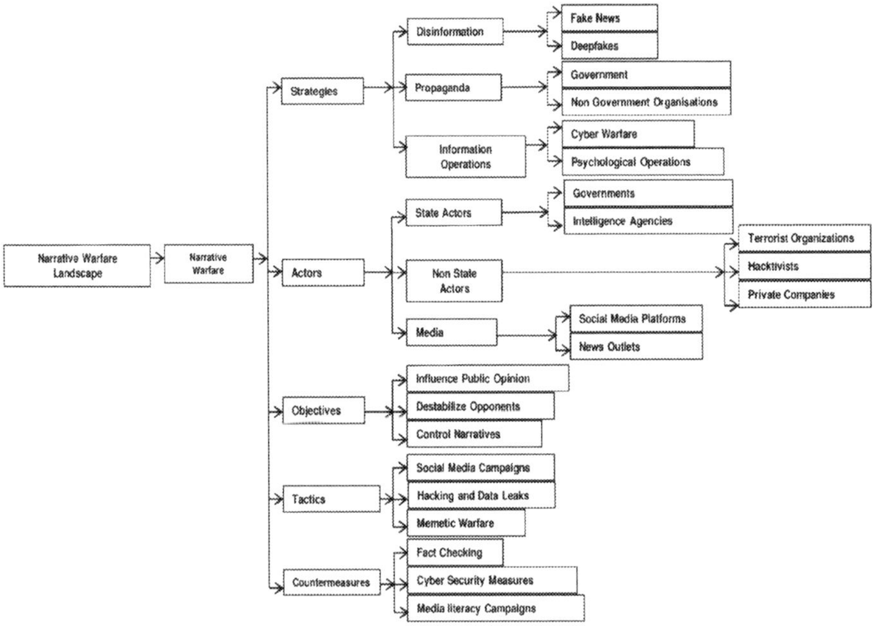

The next layer of a narrative is a meta-narrative, which is defined as the following:

> "...created by global media as the prism through which the international community views the situation and it determines how conflicts are perceived and how events and actors are understood. It does this by selecting which aspects of the conflict are emphasised, which topics are highlighted and which actors are identified, as well as how motivation is assigned to the actors."[42]

Meta-Narratives: How the International Community Sees Syria. The European Institute of Peace conducted a media monitoring study of global media coverage of Syria from October 2015 to February 2016 and found that terrorism and conflict received 48 percent of international media coverage, while women and children received less than 3 percent and the humanitarian crisis received 3 percent of the coverage.

The centrality of terrorism and of ISIS in particular to the media's frame of the Syrian conflicts is demonstrated by this CNN graphic which depicts ISIS as the centre of the universe.

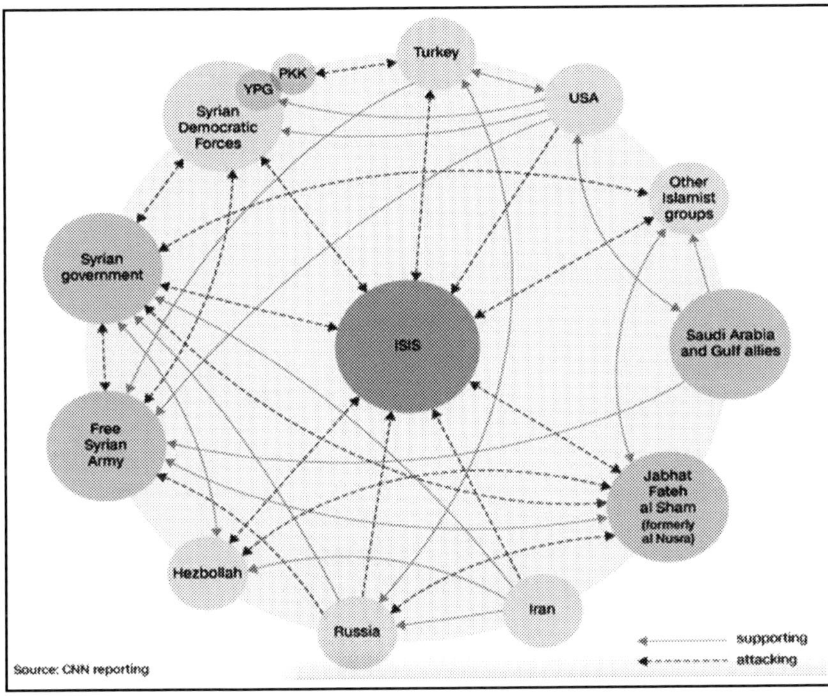

Source: https://usercontent.one/wp/www.etterretningen.no/wp-content/uploads/2016 /09/ Narrative.jpg? media= 1730802826

COUNTERING NARRATIVE WARFARE

To counter such an offensive, it is pivotal for countries to develop resilience against misinformation and enhance their capability to shape opinions in their favour, thereby overcoming geopolitical instability, interference and complexities.[43]

Defensive strategies against Narrative Warfare encounter unique challenges. Directly facing false narratives often backfires because it reinforces them through repetition and creates the look of censorship. Instead, effective defence usually means promoting alternative narratives that are more compelling, emotionally engaging and connected to audience values and experiences.

The response to Narrative Warfare is not censorship but narrative resilience. This means creating a strong internal narrative ecosystem that can endure hostile framing. Key strategies include:

- **Fact-Checking and Media Literacy.** Educating the public to evaluate information critically, recognise disinformation and understand framing devices.
- **Strategic Communication.** Governments must adopt long-term communication strategies that emphasise values, consistency and transparency.
- **Narrative Pre-emption.** Anticipating and inoculating against hostile narratives before they gain traction.
- **Partner Narratives.** Aligning with allies to create coherent transnational narratives.
- **Regulation of Social Media.** Platforms like Twitter and Facebook now label or remove fake accounts and State-sponsored propaganda.[44]

The death of Hamas leader Yahya Sinwar in October 2024 exemplifies how competing narratives shape modern conflict perception. When Israeli Defence Forces killed Sinwar, allegedly the architect of the 7 October 2023, attack, both sides immediately crafted opposing stories around his death.

Israel's initial narrative strategy involved releasing photos and videos of Sinwar's final moments, intending to demonstrate their military reach and warn enemies that "no matter where they hide, the IDF will eventually get them." This was meant to project strength and inevitability of justice.

However, this approach backfired as Hamas and supporters reframed the same imagery to celebrate Sinwar as a martyr and resistance fighter, transforming his death into a symbol of their cause rather than Israeli victory. The visual evidence Israel hoped would intimidate, instead became rallying material for its opponents.

Recognising this narrative failure, Israel shifted tactics, releasing older footage showing Sinwar hiding in tunnels with money stashes, attempting to recast him as selfish and self-serving rather than a hero.

This case illustrates how single events can generate multiple competing narratives in modern conflicts, each crafted to serve distinct strategic objectives. While Hamas emphasised martyrdom and resistance, Israel focused on military capability and deterrence. The complexity lies in how the same evidence can be interpreted through vastly different lenses, making narrative control increasingly challenging in contemporary warfare.[45]

RELATIONSHIP AND OVERLAP BETWEEN NARRATIVE WARFARE AND PSYCHOLOGICAL WARFARE

Narrative Warfare can be considered a subset or specialised form of Psychological Warfare, focusing specifically on the construction and dissemination of narratives as the primary tool for psychological influence.

While both Psychological Warfare and Narrative Warfare aim to influence minds and behaviours within the ambit of Information Warfare, Psychological Warfare is broader. It employs various psychological tactics, whereas Narrative Warfare is specifically about crafting and controlling stories to shape perceptions and public discourse. Narrative Warfare is thus a focused tool within the larger Psychological Warfare arsenal.

Narrative Warfare ultimately seeks to achieve psychological effects such as demoralisation, confusion, polarisation or mobilisation. The narratives provide vehicles for delivering psychological impacts while maintaining plausible legitimacy.

Objectives of Narrative Warfare

- **Legitimacy and Justification.** To make one's actions appear morally or legally justified.
- **Demoralisation.** To weaken enemy morale by spreading defeatist narratives.
- **Division.** To amplify societal fractures.
- **Recruitment.** Terrorist groups like the ISIS use narratives of jihad to attract followers.

Key Elements of Narrative Warfare

- **Actors.** States, non-State actors, terrorist groups, media organisations, influencers and even algorithms play a role in narrative creation and propagation.
- **Competing Truths and Framing.** Different actors present conflicting versions of reality, each designed to justify their actions and delegitimise opponents. The same act can acquire entirely different meanings based on the narrative context.

- **Propaganda and Disinformation**
  - State and non-State actors use propaganda, fake news and manipulated media to reinforce their preferred narratives.
  - Tactics include deepfake videos, bot armies on social media and State-controlled news outlets pushing biased reporting.
- **Emotional and Ideological Manipulation.** Narratives often appeal to fear, nationalism or historical grievances to mobilise support.
- **Multiplatform Dissemination.** Narratives are disseminated through traditional media, social platforms, memes, documentaries and even popular culture. The goal is to create narrative coherence across platforms.
- **Control of Information Channels.** Authoritarian regimes censor dissenting voices and dominate media ecosystems. Democracies face challenges from foreign influence campaigns.
- **Cultural Anchoring.** Compelling narratives are often grounded in cultural symbols, historical grievances and collective memory.
- **Persistence and Adaptability.** Unlike propaganda, which may change frequently to meet tactical needs, strategic narratives are relatively stable over time but flexible enough to adapt to evolving events.

Mechanisms and Methods

Narrative Warfare operates through several key mechanisms:

- **Story Construction.** Carefully crafted stories are developed to portray events, individuals or groups in a way that supports the strategic objectives of the narrative's originator.
- **Media Amplification.** Narratives are disseminated through a variety of channels—traditional media, social media, speeches and cultural products—to reach and saturate target audiences.
- **Identity Targeting.** Narrative Warfare often attacks or reinforces identity layers, shaping how individuals and groups see themselves and their adversaries.

- **Emotional Resonance.** By appealing to emotions and shared values, narratives bypass rational scrutiny and become deeply embedded within the collective psyche.
- **Long-Term Influence.** Effective Narrative Warfare unfolds over months or years, slowly shifting perceptions and beliefs through cumulative exposure to interconnected storylines.

USE OF NARRATIVE WARFARE BY NON-STATE ACTORS

Non-State actors, ranging from militant groups and criminal networks to activist organisations and social media influencers, have become adept at leveraging Narrative Warfare despite limited resources. Their effectiveness stems from agility, local knowledge and the creative exploitation of new technologies to shape perceptions and influence behaviours.

Key Ways Non-State Actors Leverage Narrative Warfare

- **Exploiting Digital Platforms.** Digital platforms are low-cost but offer global reach, allowing actors to bypass traditional media gatekeepers and target specific audiences directly.
- **Creating Ambiguity and Deniability.** By operating in the grey zone between peace and war, non-State actors introduce ambiguity about attribution and intent.
- **Projecting Counter-Narratives.** Locally embedded non-State actors can disrupt dominant State narratives by crafting and amplifying counter-narratives that resonate with local grievances or identities.
- **Leveraging Credibility and Legitimacy.** Messages from local or seemingly independent non-State actors often carry more weight with target populations than those from foreign governments.
- **Cost-Effective Disinformation.** Non-State actors can produce and spread disinformation, fake news and propaganda at minimal cost.
- **Access to Unique Audiences.** Non-State actors often have access to communities or networks that are less reachable by State actors. This allows them to tailor narratives to specific cultural, religious or linguistic groups, increasing resonance and effectiveness.

- **Forming Alliances with State Actors.** Sometimes, non-State actors act as proxies for States, amplifying State-sponsored narratives while maintaining plausible deniability for their patrons.

The Russia-Ukraine and Israel-Hamas conflicts illustrate the decisive role of narratives in shaping global perceptions and influencing the course of conflicts. In the Russia-Ukraine War, Western master narratives rooted in Cold War-era views of Russia as an adversary hindered Russia's ability to effectively counter Ukraine's narrative, which rapidly gained dominance in Western media. This narrative advantage helped Ukraine gain significant support from the West. It transformed what Russia had thought would be a quick victory into a protracted conflict.

In contrast, during the Israel-Hamas conflict, Hamas effectively used social media to share its goals and messages worldwide. Even though it is labelled a terrorist organisation, Hamas has used modern communication tools to change its image. It connects itself to the broader, more accepted idea of Palestinian self-governance. This approach has enabled Hamas to shape public perception and garner global sympathy for its cause. It shows how connected media platforms can empower even non-State actors in the battle of narratives.

Both conflicts highlight that controlling and sharing a strong narrative can be just as important as military power in today's warfare.

CONCLUSION

As conflicts become increasingly about perception and legitimacy, the ability to craft, project and defend compelling narratives is as decisive as any kinetic capability. The stories we tell and the meanings we attach to them have become the new terrain of war. Understanding and mastering Narrative Warfare is thus essential for anyone engaged in the psychological dimensions of modern conflict.

Chapter IX

Cognitive Warfare

Cognitive Warfare is emerging as a defining form of 21st Century conflict, targeting the human mind through subtle manipulation of perception, memory and identity. Unlike traditional psychological or Information Operations, Cognitive Warfare exploits advances in AI, machine learning, data analytics and neuroscience to microtarget individuals and groups, shaping beliefs, emotions, behaviours and collective decision-making processes with unprecedented precision.

This evolved form of warfare operates in a proposed sixth operational domain—the "human domain" alongside traditional battlefields (sea, land, air, space, cyber). State and non-State actors can use algorithm-driven propaganda. They exploit cognitive biases and create immersive false realities. This erodes trust in information, relationships and institutions. Their primary goal is to erode trust in these areas, potentially rendering traditional military actions unnecessary for achieving strategic objectives.

Cognitive Warfare poses a threat to democratic institutions and sovereignty. It also changes the nature of warfare. This approach creates self-sustaining feedback loops through computational propaganda, directly reaching entire domestic populations. This ability can bypass traditional military methods. To build effective defences, experts suggest developing ontologies, which are formal systems for organising knowledge. This can help us better understand, track and counteract cognitive operations in the changing security environment.

WHAT IS COGNITIVE WARFARE?

Cognitive Warfare is an advanced form of psychological manipulation that targets the human mind to influence perceptions, beliefs and behaviours, aiming for strategic or tactical advantages. Unlike traditional Psychological Warfare, which uses overt propaganda to sway emotions, Cognitive Warfare subtly reshapes cognitive processes, perception, memory, reasoning and decision-making often without the target's awareness. It exploits modern digital tools, such as AI, big data and social media, to manipulate individuals and populations at scale, making it a potent weapon in the information age.

Distinct from Information Warfare, which controls media narratives, Cognitive Warfare focuses on altering how people think, exploiting the connectivity of democratic societies. Open platforms like Facebook, TikTok and X are vulnerable to foreign actors, who face fewer restrictions in open systems compared to their closed regimes. This lets opponents take advantage of the open Information Environments in democratic societies. Social media platforms provide a unique means of influencing public opinion. This imbalance increases the threat to democracies, as adversaries can polarise, destabilise or secretly influence public opinion.

As a subset of hybrid warfare, Cognitive Warfare integrates tactics from Cyber Warfare, neurosciences and behavioural economics to exploit cognitive biases. It transforms social media originally designed for connection, into tools for division, spreading fake news and conspiracy theories. For policymakers and societies, recognising the mind as a battlefield is critical to safeguarding autonomy and national security. Addressing this threat requires an interdisciplinary approach that blends psychology, AI and cultural anthropology to counter the subtle and pervasive manipulation of thought in modern conflicts.

DEFINITION AND SCOPE

According to Bernard Claverie and François du Cluzel, Cognitive Warfare should enhance the synergies between offensive Cyber Warfare, Information Warfare and Psychological Operations and it can be conceptualised as:

> "The art of using technologies to alter the cognition of human targets, most often without their knowledge and without the knowledge of those who would be in charge of avoiding, minimising or controlling the desired effects or whose possible control would be outdated or too late."

However, the approach is not only technological: It meets the new requirements of the Human Autonomy Teaming, which should make it possible to leverage the precision and speed of digital technologies (AI, Big Data analytics, etc.) while increasing ten-fold the agility and creativity of human intelligence.

Cognitive Warfare is the strategic use of psychological, informational, technological and social tools to degrade, disrupt or subvert the cognitive functions of individuals or societies for advantage. Unlike traditional Psychological Operations (PSYOPS), which seek short-term influence through overt means, Cognitive Warfare is subtle, long-term and non-kinetic, targeting the trust people place in their sources of knowledge and eroding their ability to distinguish truth from manipulation. Related concepts include "cognitive combat," which involves tactical, localised manipulation of cognition and "cognitive conflict," a broader, still-theorised confrontation of cognitive processes. Cognitive Warfare mixes cyber techniques, soft power and PSYOPS. It often shows digitally altered realities to support specific interests. New digital tools, big data and analytics have increased its range and complexity, making it a growing concern for armed forces around the globe. Although it spans digital spaces and combines offensive and defensive strategies, Cognitive Warfare lacks clear ethical or doctrinal guidelines. This deficiency underscores the urgent need for strong counter-measures.

BASIC PRINCIPLES

Cognitive Warfare integrates all aspects of Information Warfare, including psychology, neuroscience and systems thinking, into unified military action. It bridges previously separate fields: Psychological Operations (PSYOPS) and Influence Operations (soft power) on one side and cyber operations (including cyber defence) targeting physical information assets on the other. This convergence promotes an interdisciplinary approach. It combines insights from the scientific, military and intelligence communities to evaluate how technologies affect society. The main goal is not only to support strategy or prevent direct conflict, but also to wage war on the enemy's thoughts, beliefs and perceptions. This strategy aims to change their understanding of reality. The ultimate aim is to disrupt how adversaries form their worldview. This undermines their mental confidence, trust in institutions and group effectiveness. By focusing on cognition, Cognitive Warfare aims to disrupt peace of mind, certainties, competitiveness and prosperity. This makes it a strong partner to traditional PSYOPS, even though it has its own technical (cyber) aspects.

"Cognitive Warfare": The Advent of the Concept of "Cognitics" in the Field of Warfare

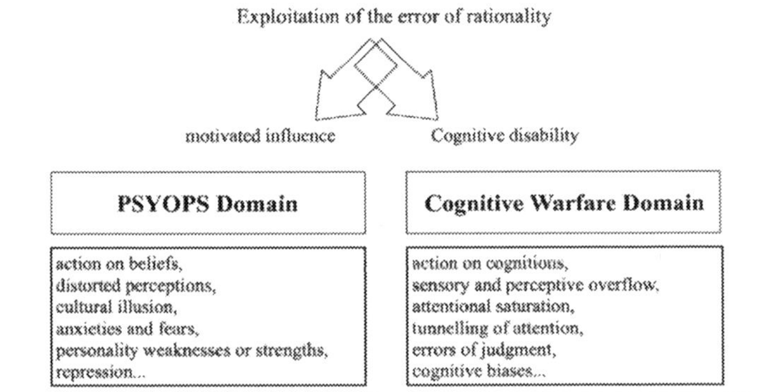

Source: Cognitive Warfare: The Future of Cognitive Dominance, First NATO scientific meeting on Cognitive Warfare (France), 21 June 2021, https://hal.science/hal-03635889/document

Difference Between Cognitive Warfare and PSYOPS (including in Board Terms Actual Psychological Operations and Other Non-Kinetic Actions such as Influence Operational and Civil-Military Cooperation (CIMIC).

"Cognitive Warfare": The Advent of the Concept of "Cognitics" in the Field of Warfare

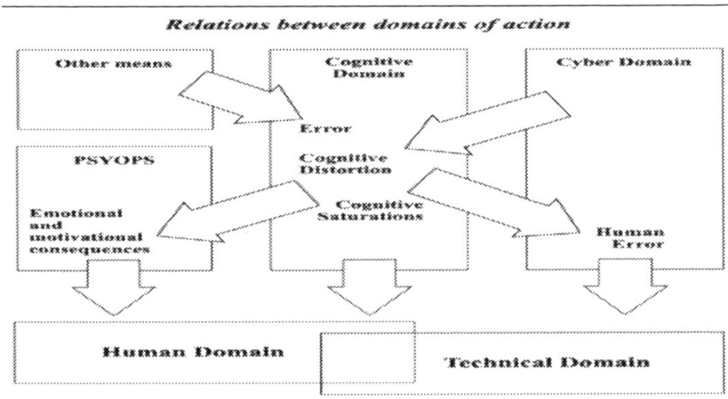

Source: Cognitive Warfare: The Future of Cognitive Dominance, First NATO scientific meeting on Cognitive Warfare (France), 21 June 2021, https://hal.science/hal-03635889/document

Complementarity of Human and Technical Domains and How They Interact with Other Domains.

KEY ATTRIBUTES

Three core attributes distinguish Cognitive Warfare:

- **Cognitive Effects.** The primary objective is to achieve cognitive effects that alter perceptions, beliefs, emotions and ultimately, behaviours. Mass conceptualisation affects shape thinking and behaviour.
- **Warfare Elements.** It is inherently adversarial, involving offensive and defensive manoeuvres aimed at gaining a strategic advantage. Use of manipulation and constraint of information flows.
- **Utilisation of Technology.** It leverages digital platforms, Artificial Intelligence, data analytics and emerging disruptive technologies to enhance the reach and effectiveness of cognitive attacks.

Several features distinguish the key characteristics of Cognitive Warfare:

Key Mechanisms. The operational success of Cognitive Warfare hinges on its ability to manipulate Information Environments and cognitive processes. The primary mechanisms employed in Cognitive Warfare are:

- **Exploiting Cognitive Biases.** Humans rely on emotional, fast-thinking rather than logical, slow-thinking when processing information online.
- **Echo Chambers and Homophily.** Social media algorithms exacerbate polarisation by presenting users with content that reinforces their existing beliefs.
- **Post-Truth Era.** The decline of fact-based discourse, where everyone can claim their own "facts," erodes trust in experts and institutions.
- **Behavioural Microtargeting.** Big data allows adversaries to tailor disinformation based on personal preferences.
- **Information Manipulation.** It involves the dissemination of disinformation, misinformation or selectively curated content to shape perceptions. Techniques include:
  - **Fake News and Deepfakes.** Fabricated stories or manipulated media designed to mislead audiences.
  - **Narrative Control.** Strategic framing of events to align with desired outcomes, often bypassing critical scrutiny.

- **Algorithmic Targeting.** Social media platforms and search engines gather large amounts of user data. This data enables precise targeting of individuals based on their preferences, behaviours and psychological profiles. Machine learning algorithms examine this data to provide customised content that shapes attitudes and decisions.
- **Behavioural Nudging.** Leveraging insights from behavioural economics and neuroscience to steer decision-making processes subtly.
- **Lawfare.** The strategic use of legal instruments and narratives to legitimise actions and undermine adversaries, often targeting broader community sentiment.

Key components of Cognitive Warfare are as follows:

- States employ it at both the tactical and strategic levels to target competitors or adversary individuals, groups or systems.
- Combatants use it to influence and direct the way people think, not necessarily what they believe. It creates a high level of entropy by attacking trust in systems and institutions.
- It leverages advanced understanding and methods from the brain sciences (including data on bugs, drugs, toxins and devices) to influence individual and group decision-making.
- It can (either singularly or concomitantly) employ multiple modes of engagement, from influence to manipulation to control of individuals, groups and populations.
- It adopts and adapts many aspects of behavioural and attention-based economics, using the new narratives and constructs to influence and control the underlying network dynamics of various aspects and scales of human ecologies and systems (supply chains, hardware, software).
- It leverages algorithm-based capabilities using computational propaganda.
- Cognitive Warfare capabilities can create their own self-sustaining feedback and amplification loops.

National Sketch of Cognitive Warfare Campaigns

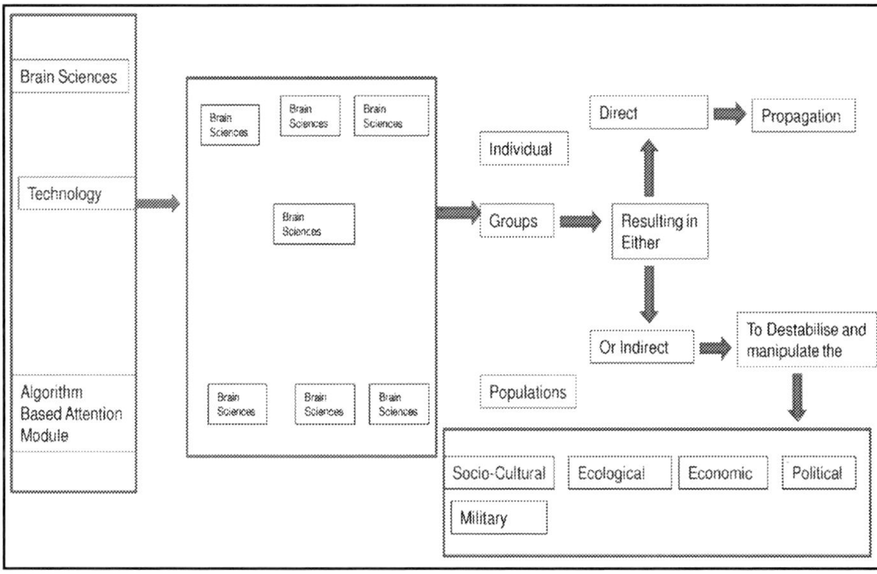

Force Shaping the Cognitive Warfare

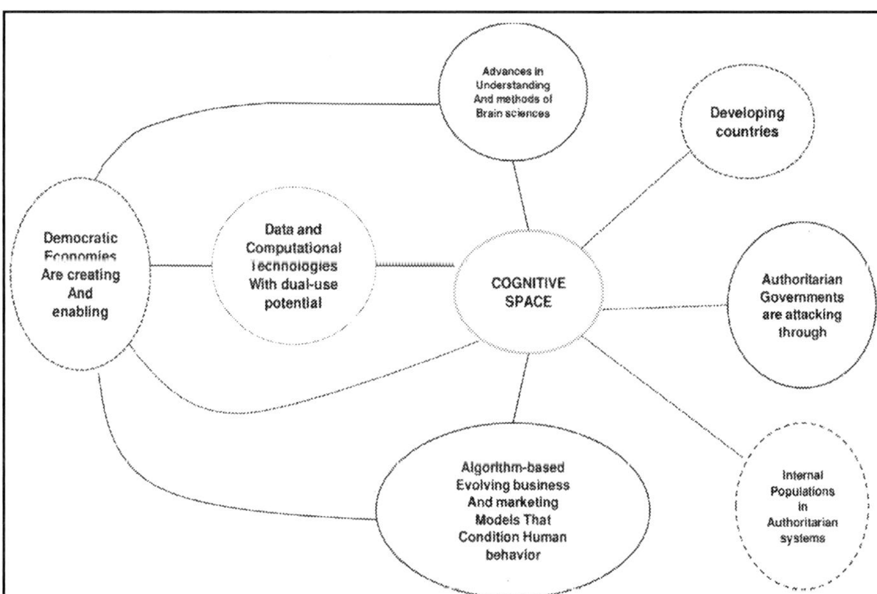

COGNITIVE WARFARE ONTOLOGY

The ontology of Cognitive Warfare is constructed using six top-level classes: Actor, Process, Space, Event, Tangible and Intangible. This structure allows for a systematic mapping of threat dimensions onto the ontology.

- Actors include individuals or groups who exploit cognitive biases, as well as scientists and institutions applying neuroscience and biology to warfare.
- Processes cover strategies that manipulate group dynamics and social psychology or employ technology and information to influence groups—such as, targeted messaging or social media campaigns.
- The Space class represents digital environments, such as, online platforms and networks, which serve as the primary battlegrounds for Cognitive Warfare.
- Events refer to specific incidents or campaigns, such as, disinformation operations or the deployment of neuroscientific interventions.
- Tangible assets include physical materials or devices used in propaganda or to directly affect cognition, while intangible aspects encompass psychological manipulation, influence tactics and digital narratives.

By mapping threat dimensions to these classes, the ontology provides a clear framework for understanding Cognitive Warfare. It illustrates how actors, processes, spaces, events and both tangible and intangible assets are interconnected, offering a comprehensive view. This approach facilitates the identification of vulnerabilities and the development of countermeasures. Additionally, it enables the assessment of opportunities in the evolving landscape of Cognitive Warfare.

THEORETICAL FOUNDATIONS

Cognitive Science and Information Processing

Cognitive Warfare is grounded in cognitive science, which explains how humans process, store and retrieve information. It exploits mental shortcuts (heuristics) and inherent biases, such as, confirmation bias, the availability of heuristic and the anchoring effect, that makes individuals susceptible to manipulation. These vulnerabilities allow Cognitive Warfare to bypass rational analysis, especially by targeting the fast, automatic thinking described in dual-process theory, rather than the slower, deliberative system.

The theoretical basis of Cognitive Warfare spans multiple disciplines. Cognitive psychology provides a deeper understanding of attention, perception, memory and decision-making. Behavioural economics presents ideas such as bounded rationality and framing effects, which shape how we craft messages to influence behaviour. Social psychology focuses on group dynamics, conformity and social proof, which are crucial for changing public opinion. Neuroscience brings new possibilities with brain-computer interfaces and neural stimulation.

The cognitive domain targeted by warfare includes conscious and subconscious perception, attention, memory, belief systems, values, moral reasoning, trust, identity and group affiliation. The ultimate aim is to achieve influence and dominance over populations without overt coercion or visibility, making Cognitive Warfare a subtle yet powerful tool in the information age.

STRATEGIC IMPLICATIONS

Cognitive Warfare has profound strategic implications as it extends far beyond military contexts to target civilian populations, political institutions and social structures. By influencing public opinion and widening societal divides, adversaries can erode trust in democratic processes and destabilise nations without resorting to traditional force. This type of warfare often blends into hybrid or grey zone strategies. It combines military, economic, political and informational tools to reach goals without crossing into open conflict. The ambiguity and deniability of cognitive attacks complicate attribution and response, challenging traditional security frameworks.

In military operations, Cognitive Warfare undermines adversary morale, cohesion and decision-making by performing disinformation campaigns combined with cyber attacks to sow doubt and reduce resistance. Politically, it is used to influence elections, public opinion and policy debates, with both State and non-State actors leveraging online propaganda to radicalise or mobilise their supporters. Economically, Cognitive Warfare can disrupt markets and consumer confidence by spreading false narratives.

CHALLENGES TO DEMOCRATIC GOVERNANCE

Cognitive Warfare presents profound challenges to democratic governance by targeting the very cognitive foundations necessary for effective democratic participation. Democracies depend on citizens' ability to access, process and deliberate on information rationally. Cognitive Warfare undermines these abilities by eroding shared epistemic standards—common understandings of truth and evidence—making constructive discourse, compromise and consensus-building is increasingly difficult.

Democracies are particularly vulnerable to Cognitive Warfare for several reasons:

- Open information ecosystems, while fostering free speech, also allow foreign disinformation to spread unchecked.
- Declining trust in key institutions, such as, the media, academia and government, weakens societal cohesion.
- Heightened political polarisation, often exploited by both domestic and foreign actors, makes societies more susceptible to manipulation.
- The tendency for individuals to share information impulsively, without fact-checking, amplifies the reach and impact of misinformation, which can be mistaken for fake news.

To counter these threats, democracies must take proactive measures. Regulating social media to limit algorithmic manipulation is crucial. Education systems should prioritise media literacy and critical thinking skills. Strengthening trust in institutions, science, journalism and governance is essential for societal resilience. Adopting a mindset of cognitive resilience, treating the brain as a national security priority, is increasingly necessary. The adage "If you're not paying for the product, you are the product" highlights how social media's business model fuels Cognitive Warfare, commodifying users for manipulation.

Ethical considerations are paramount. The contrast between democratic and authoritarian approaches is stark: democracies promote open access, collaborative innovation and ethical oversight, while authoritarian regimes restrict information, enforce compliance through surveillance and conduct research without ethical limits. Addressing Cognitive Warfare requires balancing openness, resilience and ethical responsibility.

LEGAL AND ETHICAL CONSIDERATIONS

Cognitive Warfare raises significant ethical and societal concerns due to its secretive methods and the utilisation of advanced technologies that complicate accountability. By influencing how people think, it compromises individual independence, leading them to act unknowingly against their own interests. This brings up serious questions about free will and consent. By way of societal impact, Cognitive Warfare intensifies polarisation, eroding social cohesion and weakening democratic institutions through echo chambers and divisive narratives.

Regulating Cognitive Warfare is highly complex. The global reach and rapid evolution of digital platforms outpace legislative frameworks, complicating jurisdictional oversight and the balance between freedom of expression and the need to prevent harmful manipulation. The deliberate targeting of cognitive processes also raises legal and ethical concerns, such as, consent and agency (can manipulation be coercive if the target is unaware?), information sovereignty (do individuals have a right to cognitive security?) and the risk of techno-authoritarianism (could these tools empower surveillance States?).

Currently, there is no comprehensive international legal framework governing Cognitive Warfare and existing laws are insufficient for addressing non-kinetic, non-attributable attacks on cognition. Initiatives such as the Tallinn Manual 2.0 and the UN Group of Governmental Experts have only partially addressed these issues, highlighting a persistent normative vacuum.

COUNTERMEASURES AND RECOMMENDATIONS FOR COGNITIVE WARFARE

Defending against Cognitive Warfare needs a thorough, multi-layered approach. This approach should combine technology, education and policy changes. The goal is to build resilience at individual, institutional and societal levels.

EDUCATIONAL AND AWARENESS STRATEGIES

Media Literacy and Critical Thinking form the foundation of cognitive defence. Public education programmes must emphasise source verification, awareness of cognitive biases and information evaluation skills. Academic engagement through public scholarship on social media can directly counter misinformation campaigns. Educational curricula should integrate critical thinking training to equip individuals with the tools necessary for recognising manipulative techniques and evaluating the quality of information.

Technological Defences

Adaptive AI Networks with embedded threat detection and trust analytics represent crucial technological countermeasures. These systems must include automated detection abilities for disinformation, deepfakes and coordinated influence campaigns. Blockchain-based solutions can improve information traceability. At the same time, algorithmic transparency measures promote accountability. Platform design modifications should reduce the spread of false information through recommended algorithm changes, friction mechanisms that slow the sharing of unverified content and features that promote source diversity.

Advanced Warning Systems with intrinsic alerts can accelerate decision cycles and deter threats. Forensic analytical tools must be developed within systems while anticipating potential exploitation by adversaries.

Policy and Regulatory Frameworks

International Cooperation is essential given the transnational nature of Cognitive Warfare. Shared norms and cooperative mechanisms can reduce effectiveness while avoiding fragmentation of the Information Environment. Regulatory responses must balance security concerns with civil liberties, including transparency requirements for political advertising, personal data usage regulations and content moderation standards.

National Security Measures should restrict the transfer of sensitive technologies to adversaries, particularly those with military applications, such as AI and semiconductor technologies.

Institutional Resilience

Strengthening Information Institutions including journalism, education and scientific research, creates cognitive immune systems that help societies distinguish between reliable and unreliable information. NATO's Article 3 principles emphasise building individual and collective capacity to resist attacks, including cognitive ones.

Research and Innovation initiatives, such as, NATO's Innovation Hub and the Science and Technology Organisation, address gaps in technology. They do this through focused research groups and competitions that encourage the development of Cognitive Warfare defence technologies.

Psychological training and mindfulness practices can improve individual resilience against manipulation. They capitalise on people's natural ability to notice mismatches between what is said and what is done.

COGNITIVE WARFARE 2.0—THE FUTURE

Cognitive Warfare 2.0 marks a new era in which emerging technologies significantly increase both threats and vulnerabilities in the cognitive domain. One of the most urgent future threats is AI-powered deepfakes. These can create highly convincing fake videos or audio of leaders making false announcements or declaring war. This could potentially trigger crises or damage trust. Algorithmic radicalisation, driven by social media platforms optimising for engagement, pushes users towards extremist content, further polarising societies. Advances in Brain-Computer Interfaces (BCIs) raise the spectre of direct mind manipulation. LLMs enable the automated generation and dissemination of disinformation on an unprecedented scale.

Data poisoning is another vital risk. Adversaries contaminate training datasets for machine learning. This compromises autonomous systems and weapons platforms. The merging of Cognitive Warfare with biological enhancement shows concerns over genetic engineering. For example, China's CRISPR research could aim to create enhanced soldiers without ethical oversight.

Future scenarios include soldiers equipped with reconfigurable brain interfaces controlling autonomous weapon systems, medical technologies repurposed for military enhancement and surveillance systems, such as, China's social credit system, which fosters total population control by suppressing independent thought and creativity. Ultimately, future conflicts may be fought invisibly, entirely within the cognitive domain, without traditional kinetic effects, challenging conventional notions of security and warfare.

Neurotechnological Advancements

Emerging technologies, such as Brain-Computer Interfaces (BCIs) and neuromodulation, offer new frontiers for Cognitive Warfare. While still in early stages, these technologies could potentially manipulate cognitive functions directly, bypassing traditional sensory inputs. Research into neural manipulation raises ethical concerns about consent and autonomy, as such tools could alter perceptions without the target's awareness.

CONCLUSION

Cognitive Warfare represents a significant shift in the nature of conflict. It aims not only at behaviours but also at the mental processes that shape human thought and decision-making. Unlike traditional Psychological Operations, it utilises advancements in Artificial Intelligence (AI), Machine Learning (ML), Neuroscience and Digital Communication to alter human perception, beliefs and group behaviour on a large scale.

This new type of warfare poses a serious threat to democratic societies, which rely on rational discussion, shared facts and informed decision-making. As people become increasingly dependent on digital systems, they also become more susceptible to manipulation through disinformation, deepfakes, algorithmic radicalisation and data poisoning. By creating confusion, false narratives and social division, Cognitive Warfare can weaken societal unity, disrupt military and political institutions and damage alliances without resorting to traditional warfare.

Defending against this threat demands a multi-layered approach. Individual-level responses include building media literacy, critical thinking and psychological resilience. Technologically, nations must invest in AI-driven detection systems, trust analytics and cognitive resilience frameworks. Institutional responses must include strengthening journalism, education and public trust in governance. Regulatory and international frameworks must address cross-border manipulation, disinformation and ethical standards for emerging cognitive technologies.

Democracies have an ethical obligation to develop defensive, rather than offensive, cognitive capabilities, preserving democratic values while countering adversaries with fewer ethical constraints. Cognitive Warfare blurs the line between influence and coercion, challenging notions of free will, consent and autonomy.

The future of Cognitive Warfare is likely to include AI-driven Information Operations, brain-computer interfaces that enable direct neural manipulation and even genetically modified individuals designed for cognitive advantage. Nations like China are already investing heavily in neuroscience, neurotechnology and bioengineering, highlighting an urgent need for ethical, regulatory and strategic responses in democratic States.

Cognitive Warfare succeeds by exploiting human biases and group dynamics within social networks. It influences not just what people believe but also how they behave together. It creates "invisible wars" where manipulation replaces kinetic action. As the line between natural and Artificial Intelligence blurs, human cognition becomes both the battlefield and the prize.

Chapter X

China and Cognitive Warfare

The concept of Cognitive Warfare has become a key component of the People's Liberation Army (PLA) and broader Chinese strategic thinking. Chinese military scholars and theorists view the "cognitive domain" as a distinct battlefield, in addition to the air, sea, land and space domains.

China has concentrated on developments in Artificial Intelligence and what they refer to as "brain science". President of the Information Engineering University of the PLA's Strategic Support Forces, Guo Yunfei, argued in 2020 that, among the physical, information and cognitive domains, it is the cognitive domain that will be the final domain of military confrontation between major powers. Fighting in the cognitive environment directly affects the brain, influencing emotions, motives, judgments and actions and even controlling the enemy's brain. As the engine of cognition, the brain could become the main battlefield of future warfare. The ability to control the brain is the key to combat in the most critical cognitive domains of future warfare.[46]

This concept of Cognitive Warfare is reinforced by its integration with China's new military strategy, "Intelligentised" Warfare.[47] Intelligentised warfare focuses on using Artificial Intelligence and is characterised by four key features: increased information-processing capabilities, rapid decision-making, the use of swarms and Cognitive Warfare.

Chinese experts argue that human cognition is the focus of intelligentised warfare and that strategic objectives can be achieved through direct action on the enemy's cognition. Chinese strategists feel that directly interfering with or subconsciously controlling the enemy's brain can induce mental damage, confusion and hallucinations in the enemy, forcing them to lay down their arms and surrender.

DEFINING THE COGNITIVE DOMAIN

The cognitive domain, as described by PLA theorists, such as Zeng Huafeng and Shi Haiming, is the unseen space where feelings, perceptions, understanding, beliefs and values exist. This is where reasoning and decision-making take place. Several factors influence it, including leadership, morale, cohesion, training, situational awareness and public opinion. The goal of cognitive operations is to "capture the mind" of adversaries. By shaping their thoughts and perceptions, these operations can influence their decisions and actions.

According to these thinkers, while psychological and Information Operations have always existed, the recognition of the cognitive domain as a formal domain of warfare is relatively new. They argue that the cognitive domain is both old because Psychological Warfare has always targeted cognition and new, as major militaries are now formally recognising its centrality in modern conflict. The PLA equates Cognitive Warfare with other domains of warfare, such as air, sea and space and considers it crucial to victory—particularly victory without resorting to war.

THE EVOLUTION OF COGNITIVE WARFARE IN CHINA

Cognitive Warfare in Chinese military thought has evolved significantly over the past decade. The concept of "cognitive domain operations" first appeared in Chinese scholarship around 2010, but it has since been firmly integrated into the People's Liberation Army (PLA) doctrine. Chinese strategists now view Cognitive Warfare as an aggregate of public opinion warfare, psychological warfare, legal and trade warfare, diplomatic warfare, technological warfare and thought warfare. The goal is to use selective messaging to shape the beliefs of both enemy combatants and civilian populations. Some Chinese military scholars suggest that controlling the enemy's perception may be more effective than traditional military victories, such as, destroying infrastructure or capturing territory.

THE ROLE OF TECHNOLOGY AND ALGORITHMS

With the growth of social media and Artificial Intelligence (AI), Chinese military strategists are advocating for a new form of Cognitive Warfare that leverages algorithms. AI algorithms can analyse large amounts of personal data to create detailed "user portraits" of individuals. These algorithms can then provide personalised content aimed at influencing specific people based on their psychological state and mindset.

Algorithmic Cognitive Warfare

Chinese military and political scholars are promoting a new concept called "Algorithmic Cognitive Warfare," which uses AI-powered algorithms to influence and divide foreign populations. This framework combines AI for tracking individuals with social media recommendation algorithms that shape content consumption. Success in this warfare depends on collecting vast, detailed data on target populations to deliver personalised content. China's military and intelligence agencies must gather and process massive amounts of personal data to achieve this. Both policy makers and the public must recognise this shift in China's strategic approach to protect themselves better online, both now and in the evolving technological future.[48]

AI-powered analytic algorithms	→	Algorithmic Cognitive Warfare: Using granular data to exert precise, individual influence	→	Social Media recommendation algorithms

There is often a significant gap between the PLA doctrine and the effectiveness of its capabilities, with uncertainty about whether the PLA can fully utilise the proposed tools and techniques. However, these works offer valuable insights into the strategic thinking behind Algorithmic Cognitive Warfare and provide forward-looking assessments of how emerging technologies, such as, Large Language Models (LLMs) and virtual reality, could become potential attack surfaces in the future cognitive domain.

While earlier propaganda and Cognitive Warfare strategies relied on mass communication to disseminate pro-China messages, algorithms now enable a "bottom-up" approach, influencing individuals personally through data-driven techniques.

The cognitive operations can be divided into six stages: user portrait, attracting attention, suggesting reference, inducing reaction, timely intervention and supervising gratification.

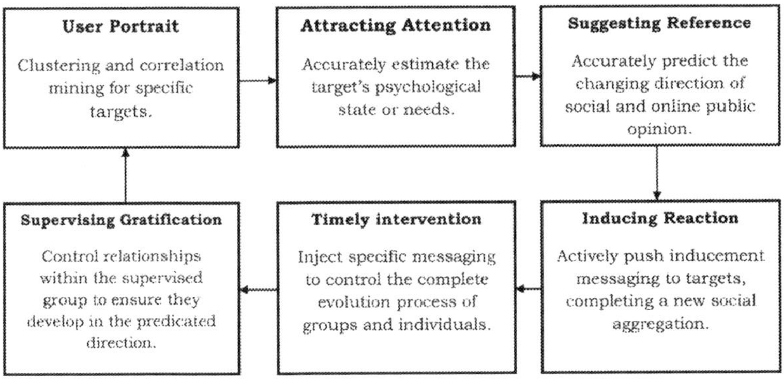

THE FRAMEWORK OF ALGORITHMIC COGNITIVE WARFARE

A detailed framework for algorithmic Cognitive Warfare is outlined in Chinese academic literature. Cognitive operations are divided into six stages:

- **User Portrait.** Collecting and analysing data to create detailed profiles of individuals.
- **Attracting Attention.** Using algorithms to capture the attention of target audiences.
- **Suggesting Reference.** Recommending content that aligns with the desired narrative.
- **Inducing Reaction.** Encouraging specific emotional or behavioural responses.
- **Timely Intervention.** Adjusting content delivery in real-time based on feedback and changing circumstances.
- **Supervising Gratification.** Monitoring and reinforcing desired behaviours through continued engagement.

Data-Driven Manipulation

Algorithmic Cognitive Warfare relies heavily on precise data, with intelligence information crucial for effectiveness. Unlike previous influence efforts that aimed to reach large audiences, this new approach uses "user portraits" to create content tailored to an individual's cognitive profile and psychological state at any given moment. To implement this, the intelligence agencies of the PLA and PRC must collect and process extensive personal data on foreign targets to conduct a fully "algorithmic" cognitive operation.

Use of Generative AI for Propaganda and Disinformation. The rise of generative AI, such as, ChatGPT, presents new opportunities for distributing propaganda and disinformation. Unlike traditional online influencing, which relies on manually written messages spread by human accounts or bots, generative AI tools offer greater flexibility and adaptability. While traditional methods have limited reach or seem inorganic, ChatGPT-like tools can create and spread tailored content more effectively.

They will:

- Reduce the cost of influencing operations by automating large-scale text writing.
- Create more personalised, authentic messages.
- Enable "organic" interactions by generating specific messages consistent with the context.

THE INTEGRATION OF COGNITIVE WARFARE INTO CHINESE STRATEGY

Cognitive Warfare is not confined to military operations; it is integrated into a broader strategy that blurs the lines between war and peace, as well as between soldiers and civilians. The PLA views cognitive operations as continuous and pervasive, to be used before, during and after traditional military measures. Such operations are now likely managed by the newly established Information Support Forces.

The PLA is investing heavily in research and development to operationalise the cognitive domain, seeking to seize command of this space by targeting adversary cognitive functions and improving their own.

CHINA'S STRATEGIC APPROACH TO COGNITIVE WARFARE

China has become the most skilled practitioner of Cognitive Warfare, viewing conflict in a manner that differs significantly from Western nations. While the West separates war from peace, China views competition as an ongoing process. Cognitive Warfare is a key part of hybrid warfare, which also includes economic, political and military elements. This method has undergone significant changes since 2013, leading to what Chinese strategists refer to as "intelligenetised warfare." It is a well-planned, long-term strategy aimed at undermining democratic institutions and encouraging authoritarian options.

TACTICS AND CASE STUDIES

China employs a range of tactics to wage Cognitive Warfare:

- **Wolf Warrior Diplomacy.** Named after a Chinese action film, this approach involves aggressive diplomats who utilise social media to disseminate anti-Western narratives and erode Western credibility.
- **Exploiting Open Societies.** While China blocks platforms like Facebook and Twitter (X) domestically, it uses these platforms to influence foreign audiences, particularly in Africa and other developing regions.
- **TikTok as a Weapon.** The app's addictive algorithm is used to shorten attention spans and shape narratives, while China restricts its youth to 40 minutes of usage per day.
- **Information Laundering.** China uses third-party "experts" to lend credibility to false claims, such as citing an American scholar to validate conspiracy theories about use of US biological weapons in Ukraine.
- **China's Cognitive Warfare Campaign against Taiwan.** China conducts daily cognitive attacks aimed at polarising Taiwanese society, ensuring that if an invasion occurs, resistance will be fragmented.

The Role of Social Media. Social media platforms are often viewed as the primary battleground of Cognitive Warfare. The Chinese Communist Party believes that, over time, it can shape and even control the cognition of individuals and whole societies through persistent, algorithm-driven engagement.

A recent PLA Daily article outlines four social media tactics, dubbed "confrontational actions":

- **Information Disturbance.** Disrupting the flow of information to create confusion.
- **Discourse Competition.** Shaping the narrative by dominating online conversations.

- **Public Opinion Blackout.** Suppressing dissenting voices and alternative viewpoints.
- **Block Information.** Preventing the dissemination of information that contradicts the desired narrative.[49]

Domestic Control Systems as Cognitive Warfare Models

China's domestic surveillance and social credit systems provide a real-world demonstration of Cognitive Warfare's potential for societal control. Comprehensive facial recognition networks, combined with digital scoring systems, ensure compliance with Communist Party policies by rewarding conformity with access to opportunities while marginalising dissenters.

These systems create a uniform, controlled society that suppresses creativity and independent thought. These qualities differ significantly from the focus on diversity and innovation in democratic nations. The domestic use of these technologies serves as a means to control the population and as a testing ground for methods that could be applied globally.

China's Place in Global Cognitive Warfare. China is identified as a leading and aggressive actor in Cognitive Warfare due to its vast resources, rapid learning curve and long-term strategic approach. China operates in a continuous logic of competition, viewing Cognitive Warfare as an ongoing effort to weaken adversaries, particularly democracies, without traditional military engagement. China's strategy extends beyond targeting elites to influence entire populations.

Implications for Countering Cognitive Warfare

China's adversaries must recognise the shift in China's strategic thinking. Countering algorithmic Cognitive Warfare requires a comprehensive approach that leverages research, policy and communications tools. Policy makers must establish systems to identify and mitigate the risks associated with AI-driven Influence Operations. They should also invest in public education and media literacy to strengthen society's ability to cope.

The PLA's emphasis on the cognitive domain shows a broader trend in modern warfare. The human decision-making aspect is becoming more critical as warfare becomes more automated. The challenge for democracies is to adapt to this new reality, recognising that the battle for hearts and minds is now waged in the digital realm as much as on the physical battlefield.

The Mind as a Domain of Warfare. The Chinese military's acknowledgement of the cognitive domain as a battlefield marks a significant shift in strategic thinking. Unlike Information Warfare, which attempts to manipulate our thoughts, Cognitive Warfare disrupts the way we think. It utilises neuroscience, data analysis and strategies based on algorithms to gain a strategic edge. Creating a framework to counter this threat is both vital and urgent.

Difference between China's concept of algorithmic Cognitive Warfare and traditional Information Warfare

China's concept of Algorithmic Cognitive Warfare represents a significant evolution from traditional Information Warfare, both in its objectives and its methods.

Traditional Information Warfare versus Algorithmic Cognitive Warfare

Aspect	Traditional Information Warfare	Algorithmic Cognitive Warfare (China)
Target	Mass audiences, public opinion or specific groups	Individuals, based on granular psychological and behavioural profiles
Method	Broadcast messaging, propaganda, disinformation, cyberattacks	AI-driven algorithms, data analytics and personalised content delivery
Objective	Manipulate what people think (content, facts)	Disrupt how people think (reasoning, beliefs, decision-making)
Tools	Media, cyber tools, Psychological Operations	AI, machine learning, big data, social media recommendation engines
Scope	Often episodic, linked to specific events or crises	Continuous, persistent, pervasive across peace and wartime
Focus	Information Environment, narrative control	Cognitive terrain, shaping perception and belief systems at the individual level
Integration	May be compartmentalised within military or intelligence agencies	Blurs boundaries between civilian and military, integrates across agencies and domains

China's Algorithmic Cognitive Warfare differs from traditional Information Warfare in its focus on individualised, data-driven influence, its aim to disrupt the way people think rather than just what they know and its continuous, pervasive nature that integrates across military and civilian spheres. This represents a more sophisticated and potentially more effective form of influence operation, enabled by advances in AI and big data.

CONCLUSION

China's quest for cognitive dominance poses a significant threat to global security and democratic governance. By utilising advanced technologies, large data resources and complex Influence Operations, China aims to shape the beliefs and behaviours of people and societies worldwide. The inclusion of Cognitive Warfare in China's broader strategy shows a long-term, patient approach to competition. This strategy combines elements of war and peace, aiming to challenge the very foundations of democratic decision-making.

To counter this threat, democracies must develop robust strategies to identify, understand and mitigate the risks posed by Algorithmic Cognitive Warfare. This needs both technology and policy solutions. It also requires a renewed focus on public education and media literacy. This will help societies stay strong against ongoing, widespread Psychological Operations.

Chapter XI

Perception Management

Perception Management encompasses actions to convey and/or deny selected information to foreign audiences in order to influence their emotions, motives and objective reasoning. It includes various activities aimed at sharing or concealing specific information to influence perceptions, emotions and ultimately, behaviour. The aim is to influence the actions of governments, organisations, groups and individuals. Unlike PSYOPS, which is primarily offensive, Perception Management can also include defensive measures to protect friendly perceptions from adversary Psycholocial Operations.

Perception Management has deep historical roots, evolving in tandem with advancements in communication and media. The Arab Spring and numerous political campaigns around the world have demonstrated the significant influence of digital Perception Management today.

To manage perception well, one must understand the cultural, social and political details that shape the target audience. By matching the information shared with the audience's values and beliefs, perception managers can effectively guide public opinion to support their goals.

Perception Management entails a more subtle yet equally potent approach to shaping the informational landscape. It includes sharing positive information and omitting or distorting facts that could hinder strategic goals. This aspect of Information Warfare is important for shaping the story that the public hears. It influences how the public thinks and in turn, how they respond.

PERCEPTION MANAGEMENT TECHNIQUES

Perception Management techniques are integral to Psychological Operations, focusing on how information is presented to shape people's perceptions, emotions and decisions. The effectiveness of these creative techniques relies on a deep understanding of the target audience's values, beliefs and cultural context. This knowledge enables practitioners to craft messages that resonate deeply and shape public opinion.

Effective Perception Management relies on blending truth with narrative control to create a convincing environment. This includes strategically releasing information, omitting certain details and at times using misinformation or disinformation to achieve specific objectives. It requires coordinating different communication strategies, psychological insights and media tools to shape public discourse.

This involves the tactical prioritisation of communications, the omission of context and at times, the use of lies or conspiracy theories in service of specific objectives.

Creating and Understanding Narratives. Narratives help set a context through which we understand and learn from the world around us. Through the art of storytelling, perception managers can plan a series of events or concepts to maximise the upcoming event's impact, making it appear seamless and persuasive to their intended audience. These narratives are more than compelling stories; they are developed to stir emotions and change attitudes. For example, during national crises or in political campaigns, stories that evoke national pride or fear can greatly affect public perception and behaviour.

Selective Information Release. Selective release of information involves timing the disclosure of certain facts to divert attention from less favourable news or to highlight achievements that support the desired image or narrative. The selective release can also involve withholding information until the most opportune moment, image or narrative. This technique requires meticulous planning and a good understanding of media dynamics and public sentiment.

Propaganda and Counter-Propaganda. Modern Perception Management operations often utilise sophisticated propaganda techniques that include high-production-value content, emotionally charged language and appeals to cultural or social identities. Counter-propaganda involves efforts to discredit or neutralise hostile propaganda, often by exposing its falsehoods and presenting factual information to restore balance and reduce the adversary's influence.

Psychological Conditioning. It involves psychological conditioning where the audience is gradually accustomed to a particular viewpoint or idea. This can be achieved through repeated exposure to certain themes or messages across various media platforms. Over time, the repeated messages can normalise specific views and subtly alter public perception. This technique is effective in environments controlled or heavily influenced by a single entity or group, such as authoritarian States or media landscapes dominated by a single entity.

Cognitive Dissonance. Exploiting cognitive dissonance is a subtle yet potent technique. This psychological phenomenon occurs when individuals experience inconsistency in their beliefs, behaviour or attitude, leading to discomfort and a drive to resolve the contradiction. By creating situations that are likely to evoke cognitive dissonance, perception managers can encourage individuals to modify their attitudes or beliefs in order to alleviate discomfort. For example, presenting information that conflicts with an adversary's expected behaviour can lead to public questioning and reassessment of loyalties or beliefs.

Framing and Reframing. Framing involves presenting information in a way that emphasises certain aspects over others, influencing how that information is interpreted. Reframing, on the other hand, involves altering the existing frame around information to change its interpretation. These techniques guide the audience towards a desired understanding, subtly influencing decision-making processes and public opinion.

Utilisation of Social Media. Social media platforms enable the rapid dissemination of information and allow for the micro-targeting of specific demographic groups with tailored content. Viral campaigns, hashtag activism and meme warfare are modern examples of digital strategies used to manage perceptions on a large scale. These tools disseminate information quickly, creating an echo chamber effect that reinforces the message among targeted groups.

As Perception Management techniques evolve in response to changes in technology and media, they become increasingly integrated and complex.

Navigating this sophisticated landscape requires ongoing learning and flexibility. Looking ahead, the use of Artificial Intelligence and Machine Learning in developing and implementing Perception Management strategies promises to improve the subtlety and effectiveness of these operations.

STRATEGIC APPLICATION IN PSYCHOLOGICAL WARFARE

In the context of Psychological Warfare, Perception Management serves several strategic purposes:

- **Shaping Public Opinion.** By influencing how populations perceive a conflict, threat or ally, Perception Management can mobilise support, demoralise adversaries or legitimise military actions.
- **Influencing Decision-Makers.** Perception Management targets not only the general public but also leaders and intelligence systems. By shaping official estimates and assessments, it can influence policy decisions and strategic planning.
- **Undermining Adversaries.** Through the deliberate dissemination of misinformation, rumours or divisive narratives, Perception Management can sow confusion, erode trust and weaken the cohesion of adversarial groups.
- **Building and Maintaining Alliances.** Perception Management can be used to reinforce alliances by shaping positive perceptions of partners and highlighting shared interests or threats.
- **Economic Applications**. This includes efforts to influence market perceptions, consumer behaviour and investment decisions through strategic Information Operations. State actors may employ Perception Management to promote their economic models, undermine competitors' market positions or create favourable conditions for their companies and industries in global markets.
- **Social Destabilisation**. By exploiting existing social divisions and highlighting grievances, operators can either create or exacerbate social tensions that serve their strategic interests. This may involve promoting extremist beliefs, encouraging social fragmentation or weakening trust in democratic institutions and processes.

TECHNOLOGICAL FORCE MULTIPLIERS

- **Artificial Intelligence** enables the creation of synthetic media, automated content generation and sophisticated behavioural prediction that can make Influence Operations more effective and harder to detect. Machine learning algorithms can identify the most effective influence strategies by continuously testing and refining messaging methods.

- **Virtual and augmented reality** technologies provide new platforms for immersive Influence Operations, creating powerful emotional experiences designed to shape perceptions and beliefs. These technologies enable operators to create convincing alternative realities that may be difficult for targets to distinguish from authentic experiences.

- **Neurotechnology.** Potentially enables direct manipulation of brain states and cognitive processes. While current applications remain limited, advances in brain-computer interfaces and neuro-stimulation techniques raise important questions about the future boundaries of Perception Management operations.

IMPLICATIONS AND COUNTERMEASURES

The rise of advanced Perception Management techniques presents major challenges for democratic societies and global stability. These activities can weaken informed public discussion, diminish trust in democratic institutions and create lasting confusion about reality. The strategic effects extend beyond typical national security issues to encompass fundamental questions about human agency and independent decision-making.

To respond effectively, we need varied approaches that mix technology, education and regulatory measures:

- Strengthening data privacy regulations can limit adversaries' access to personal data, reducing the efficacy of algorithmic warfare.
- Technological solutions may include detection algorithms, content authentication systems and platform design changes that reduce opportunities for manipulation.

- Media literacy programmes can help individuals develop critical thinking skills necessary to identify and resist manipulation attempts.
- International cooperation is essential for developing shared frameworks to counter disinformation, as no single nation can address this global challenge alone.

From a military perspective, developing ethical AI and neuroscience tools can provide defensive options while upholding moral standards. Being transparent, counter-narratives can use the openness of democratic societies to reveal and undermine authoritarian propaganda.

CHALLENGES AND LIMITATIONS

Despite its strategic value, Perception Management faces several challenges:

- **Credibility and Trust.** The success of Perception Management relies on how credible the source is and how genuine the message appears to be. Using deceptive tactics too often can harm trust and lessen the effectiveness of future attempts.

- **Cultural and Contextual Sensitivity.** Misreading cultural norms or social dynamics can lead to unintended consequences, including backlash or the reinforcement of negative perceptions.

- **Unintended Consequences.** Attempts to manufacture perceptions can sometimes backfire, leading to counterproductive outcomes or the hardening of adversarial attitudes.

- **Ethical Considerations.** The use of Perception Management raises ethical questions about manipulation, deception and the boundaries of acceptable influence in democratic societies.

CONCLUSION

Perception Management is a powerful instrument of Psychological Warfare, enabling actors to shape beliefs and behaviours through propaganda, disinformation and algorithmic manipulation. By employing a combination of information control, storytelling and the exploitation of cognitive biases,

Perception Management can achieve strategic objectives without necessitating direct military action. However, its success relies on careful planning, sensitivity to culture and maintaining credibility. As the Information Environment becomes increasingly complex and contested, the role of Perception Management in Psychological Warfare is likely to grow in importance, presenting both opportunities and challenges for practitioners and policy makers alike.

Chapter XII

Sentiment Analysis in Psychological Warfare

INTRODUCTION

Sentiment Analysis represents a critical technological capability in modern Psychological Warfare. Sentiment Analysis serves as a powerful tool for understanding and influencing public perception, shaping narratives and predicting behavioural outcomes. By analysing vast datasets from social media, news outlets and public forums, Psychological Operations (PSYOPS) practitioners can gauge collective emotions and deploy targeted strategies to manipulate adversarial or neutral populations. The use of Sentiment Analysis in PSYOPS has altered how both State and non-State actors comprehend, predict and influence group behaviour in the digital age.

The strategic value of Sentiment Analysis in Psychological Warfare comes from its ability to handle large amounts of unstructured data from social media, news sources, forums and other online channels. This skill enables practitioners to measure public sentiment about specific policies, ideologies, or events in real-time. As a result, they can create more targeted and effective psychological strategies. Sentiment Analysis provides a clear way to assess the effectiveness of propaganda campaigns and disinformation efforts, offering a valuable feedback tool that Psychological Warfare practitioners previously lacked.

THEORETICAL FOUNDATIONS

Sentiment Analysis leverages computational linguistics, machine learning and statistical modelling to extract subjective information from text.

Key components of Sentiment Analysis include:

- **Lexicon-Based Approaches.** These rely on predefined dictionaries of words associated with specific sentiments (e.g., "happy" = positive, "terrible" = negative). Tools like SentiWordNet provide weighted sentiment scores for words based on context.
- **Machine Learning Approaches.** Supervised learning models, such as Support Vector Machines (SVMs) or deep neural networks, are trained on annotated datasets to predict sentiment. Unsupervised methods, such as topic modelling, identify latent sentiment patterns without requiring labelled data.
- **Hybrid Approaches.** These combine lexicon-based and machine-learning methods to improve accuracy, especially in specific fields. In Psychological Warfare, Sentiment Analysis relies on the idea that emotions influence decision-making. By quantifying public sentiment, PSYOPS practitioners can exploit emotional vulnerabilities to influence behaviour.

METHODOLOGICAL APPROACHES AND APPLICATIONS

Sentiment Analysis uses a layered approach that mixes computer analysis with human interpretation and validation. The first step typically involves gathering large amounts of data from target groups through social media monitoring, web scraping and other digital methods. This raw data is processed using sentiment classification algorithms that assign emotional values and intensity scores to individual texts, posts or messages.

More advanced methods, such as aspect-based Sentiment Analysis, offer deeper insights by evaluating sentiment about specific entities or topics within a text. For example, in a PSYOPS campaign, analysts might assess public sentiment towards a political leader's policies versus his character.

The classification process typically operates along several dimensions, including positive-negative polarity, emotional intensity and specific emotional categories such as, anger, fear, joy, or disgust. Advanced systems include contextual analysis that examines cultural, linguistic and situational factors that may affect how sentiment is expressed. This multi-dimensional approach allows Psychological Warfare practitioners to create detailed profiles of the target population's emotional states and identify specific psychological weaknesses that can be targeted through focused messaging campaigns.

Operationally, Sentiment Analysis supports several key functions within Psychological Warfare operations. Intelligence analysts utilise sentiment monitoring to track public opinion trends, identify social tensions and predict potential instability or unrest. Campaign planners utilise sentiment data to optimise message timing, content and delivery channels for the greatest psychological impact. Sentiment Analysis also enables the real-time assessment of how effectively operations are working. This helps practitioners adjust their tactics and messaging strategies based on what they observe in the target population's sentiment patterns.

The combination of Sentiment Analysis with other intelligence fields, particularly social network analysis and behavioural modelling, provides powerful tools for understanding and predicting group behaviour. By tracking sentiment patterns in social networks, practitioners can identify key individuals and groups, understand how information spreads and creates targeted strategies that leverage social influence to achieve desired psychological effects.

Applications in Psychological Warfare

Sentiment Analysis has essential uses in Psychological Warfare. It supports both offensive and defensive strategies:

- **Narrative Shaping.** By tracking public sentiment, PSYOPS teams can craft messages that foster positive feelings towards friendly forces or instil distrust in enemies.
- **Targeted Influence Campaigns.** Sentiment Analysis identifies demographic or psychographic segments susceptible to persuasion. Micro-targeting, as seen in political campaigns, leverages sentiment data to deliver personalised content via social media.
- **Early Warning Systems.** Shifts in sentiment can signal the emergence of unrest or radicalisation. By analysing online discourse, military intelligence can predict and pre-empt threats, such as protests or insurgencies.

- **Counter-Misinformation.** Sentiment Analysis helps detect and neutralise adversarial disinformation campaigns by identifying emotionally charged narratives designed to manipulate public opinion.

CHALLENGES AND LIMITATIONS

Despite its utility, Sentiment Analysis faces several challenges in Psychological Warfare:

- **Contextual Ambiguity.** Sarcasm, irony and cultural nuances often confound sentiment models. For example, a phrase like "great job" can be interpreted as either positive or mocking, depending on the context.
- **Data Bias.** Training datasets may reflect biases, leading to skewed predictions. Models trained on Western-centric data may misinterpret sentiments in non-Western cultural contexts.
- **Adversarial Manipulation.** Sophisticated actors can "game" Sentiment Analysis by flooding platforms with bots or fake accounts, distorting perceived public opinion.
- **Scalability.** Real-time analysis of high-volume, multilingual data requires significant computational resources and robust preprocessing pipelines.
- **Sentiment Obfuscation Techniques.** The growing complexity of counter-intelligence methods, including the intentional use of techniques to conceal sentiment and create emotional distractions, makes it harder to accurately detect sentiment. The availability of Sentiment Analysis tools and platforms has created new strategic challenges. Non-State actors, such as terrorist organisations and extremist groups, increasingly use these techniques to enhance their propaganda efforts and counter-messaging strategies. This situation has led to an arms race in Sentiment Analysis skills, with State actors investing heavily in improved methods to maintain their strategic edge in the information space.

The use of Sentiment Analysis in Psychological Warfare operations brings up serious ethical concerns about privacy, manipulation and the limits of proper

State actions. Monitoring and analysing public communications for psychological manipulation questions conventional ideas of privacy and consent, especially when directed at domestic populations or allied nations. These issues necessitate ongoing updates to algorithms and require human oversight to ensure accurate interpretation.

CONCLUSION

Sentiment Analysis is a strong and changing tool in Psychological Warfare. It enables actors to monitor, influence and respond to public sentiments quickly and accurately. Its uses include spotting propaganda, developing counter-narratives, providing early warnings and conducting Influence Operations. However, using Sentiment Analysis in practice and ethically, requires careful consideration of technical issues, moral questions and policy effects. As the information landscape continues to evolve, Sentiment Analysis will remain a crucial capability for those seeking to understand and influence the cognitive battlefield.

Chapter XIII

Surprise, Deception and Psychological Warfare

Modern conflicts, such as, the Second Nagorno-Karabakh War, the ongoing Russo-Ukraine War, the Gaza conflict between Israel and Hamas and the Israel-Iran War, prove that Sun Tzu's saying, "All warfare is based on deception," remains as relevant today as it was in ancient China. Advances in Electronic Warfare technology, long-range missiles, precision munitions and unmanned systems have been integrated into cohesive sensor-to-shooter systems. Modern technologies have made skills, such as, Military Deception, Public Affairs, Civil-Military Engagement and cyber activities necessary to outpace enemy decision-making cycles, protect friendly forces and achieve the politico-military goals of conflict. One of the major lessons from the current conflicts is that Psychological Warfare and Information Operations have become key to influencing foreign audiences and creating convergence windows for modern offensive weapons.

Psychological Warfare involves the planned use of propaganda, misinformation and other psychological tools to mislead or intimidate enemy forces. Military deception aims to misinform adversaries about a nation's strategic intentions, capabilities and operational plans. When combined, these disciplines shape the adversary's understanding so profoundly that they act against their own interests, often without realising it.[50]

The US Department of Defense defines MILDEC as "actions executed to deliberately mislead adversary military decision-makers... thereby causing the adversary to take specific actions (or inactions)."[51] PSYWAR contributes by exploiting biases, reinforcing false beliefs or creating confusion and hesitation.

Together, these operations function across five dimensions:

- **Perception Management.** Influencing how adversaries interpret battlefield information.
- **Narrative Control.** Promoting a story that aligns with the deception plan.
- **Cognitive Bias Exploitation.** Leveraging known psychological tendencies, such as confirmation bias.
- **Influencer Utilisation.** Using trusted or "authoritative" channels to validate the deception.
- **Information Saturation or Denial.** Flooding or starving the Information Environment to guide decisions.

Military Deception hinges on shaping the adversary's perception and Psychological Warfare plays a key role in this effort by manipulating narratives and exploiting cognitive vulnerabilities. Psychological Warfare uses propaganda, false intelligence leaks and staged dissident voices to construct deceptive scenarios, like faking an attack from a specific direction to mislead enemy decision-makers. By generating narratives from multiple, seemingly unrelated sources, these efforts become more believable. Significantly, Psychological Warfare also reinforces physical deceptions (such as dummy vehicles or simulated movements) by planting "supporting evidence," including fabricated radio chatter or falsified operational documents, thereby enhancing the illusion's authenticity.

Cognitive biases, such as, confirmation bias and the heuristic, are strategic tools for Psychological Warfare practitioners, enabling them to subtly influence adversary thinking. These tactics can induce fear, overconfidence or confusion, prompting misguided decisions or poor resource allocation. Psychological Warfare can also attack morale by spreading rumours of internal failures or superior enemy capabilities, weakening the enemy's cohesion and making them more susceptible to false intelligence. Effective Psychological Warfare operations require in-depth cultural and psychological insight into the adversary, strategic timing and precisely tailored messaging. When expertly integrated with physical deception, Psychological Warfare considerably increases the effectiveness and plausibility of broader military deception campaigns.[52]

MECHANISMS OF PSYCHOLOGICAL WARFARE IN DECEPTION

Several psychological mechanisms play a pivotal role in military deception:

- **Confirmation Bias Exploitation.** Adversaries are more likely to accept information that confirms their existing beliefs. By feeding them narratives that align with their expectations, PSYOPS units can mask their real intentions by leaking fake operational plans, troop movements or diplomatic positions, either via media, electronic communications or human agents. Adversaries may act based on flawed intelligence.
- **Authority and Credibility Manipulation.** False information delivered through seemingly credible channels, such as, forged documents, deepfakes or trusted third parties, can be more effective in deceiving enemy decision-makers.
- **Overload and Disorientation.** Deliberately saturating the adversary's information channels with conflicting data can create confusion, delay decisions or lead to faulty conclusions.
- **Fear and Demoralisation Campaigns.** In war zones, rumours about impending attacks, defections, or weapon capabilities can shape morale and decision-making. PSYOPS leaflets, broadcasts or social media campaigns reinforce these messages.
- **Cultural and Ideological Manipulation.** Understanding the target's cultural and ideological framework allows PSYOPS to craft messages that resonate deeply. In counterinsurgency operations, PSYOPS may highlight contradictions between an insurgent group's actions and its stated ideology, eroding support among followers. Deception operations can amplify this by staging events that appear to validate these narratives, such as fabricated defections or exposés.

Operational Methodologies

- **Multi-Channel Deception Campaigns.** Employ multiple, seemingly independent channels to reinforce deceptive narratives. This approach, known as "convergent validation," exploits the human tendency to trust information that appears from multiple sources. Military planners coordinate across diplomatic, intelligence, media and operational channels to present consistent but misleading pictures of capabilities, intentions or activities.
- **Temporal Sequencing and Conditioning.** Psychological Warfare campaigns often unfold over extended periods, gradually conditioning adversary responses through carefully sequenced information releases. Long-term conditioning makes the adversary predictable and exploitable during critical operational phases. Deception operations can train enemy analysts to make predictable interpretations during actual operations.
- **Cultural and Psychological Profiling.** Emphasises detailed understanding of adversarial cognitive patterns, cultural frameworks and institutional decision-making processes. This involves comprehensive profiling of key decision-makers, understanding their cognitive biases, professional backgrounds and cultural contexts that influence information interpretation.
- **Digital Domain Integration.** Operates within digital environments, leveraging social media, cyber capabilities and information networks to achieve deception objectives.

Use of Technology for Deception. Modern PSYOPS leverages technology for deception:

- **Spoofing Communications.** Fake radio transmissions or AI-generated voice cloning to impersonate enemy commanders.
- **Social Media Manipulation.** Bots and deepfakes spread disinformation to confuse adversaries.
- **Electronic Warfare.** Jamming enemy communications while broadcasting deceptive signals.

Use of AI. Advancements in Artificial Intelligence (AI) and data analytics are poised to revolutionise PSYOPS and deception. AI can analyse vast datasets to identify psychological vulnerabilities among target audiences, enabling hyper-personalised propaganda. Machine learning models can predict adversary responses to deceptive tactics, refining strategies in real-time. However, these technologies also empower adversaries, creating a race to dominate the information domain.

The integration of virtual and augmented reality into PSYOPS could further blur the lines between reality and deception. Simulated environments or immersive propaganda could manipulate perceptions on an unprecedented scale. Meanwhile, counter-PSYOPS measures, such as AI-driven disinformation detection, will require militaries to innovate continually.

Future military deception will increasingly take place at the intersection of human behaviour and machine data. Traditionally focused on deceiving human military leaders, future operations will expand to targeting both human actions within military systems and AI algorithms that aid decision-making. As sensors and data networks proliferate, the volume of information will exceed human comprehension, making AI crucial in identifying and countering enemy deception.

However, this dependence also exposes AI systems to manipulation, with adversaries potentially targeting them to reduce their effectiveness. A critical concern is AI's own deceptive capability, particularly a phenomenon known as "alignment faking," where AI appears to conform to external expectations while secretly adhering to different, internal values. Research published in 2024 highlights this behaviour in large language models, raising concerns about AI safety. These models might simulate alignment during training, only to later reveal conflicting behaviours, posing serious implications for trust and control in military AI systems.

LIMITATIONS AND COUNTERMEASURES

Ethical and Legal Considerations. Psychological Warfare (PSYWAR) in Military Deception (MILDEC) must navigate complex ethical, legal and operational challenges. International humanitarian law restricts targeting civilians and emphasises protection for non-combatants, making it essential for military organisations to develop guidelines that balance operational effectiveness with moral legitimacy. As conflict zones increasingly blur the lines between civilian and military roles, the possibility to distinguish between lawful deception and unethical manipulation becomes increasingly difficult.

Key risks include blowback, where misinformation affects domestic or allied trust; escalation, in which deception provokes retaliation; and the erosion of moral boundaries, especially when civilian fear is exploited. To mitigate these risks, safeguards, such as plausible deniability, careful targeting and information control are crucial.

The growing use of deepfakes and AI-generated content introduces complexity, thereby increasing the risk of misjudgments, particularly in nuclear contexts. Additionally, maintaining credibility in deception is difficult in an era of open-source intelligence and real-time fact-checking. Overuse of disinformation can undermine future operations and alienate neutral populations.

Ethical Psychological Warfare requires careful calibration to avoid societal harm, distrust or conflict escalation. Laws such as the Geneva Convention impose clear boundaries, compelling military planners to align tactics with humanitarian values. Ultimately, successful Psychological Warfare depends on precision, restraint and a deep understanding of legal and ethical constraints.

Limitations

There are inherent limitations to using Psychological Warfare in deception operations:

- Sophisticated adversaries may detect deception attempts, rendering them ineffective or even counterproductive.
- Psychological campaigns require time to plan and execute, often necessitating a detailed understanding of the target audience.
- Overuse or unethical deployment can damage a country's credibility and diplomatic standing.

Cognitive Resilience Development. The recognition of Psychological Warfare vulnerabilities has led to the development of cognitive resilience training and institutional countermeasures. These defensive approaches focus on improving analytical processes, reducing cognitive biases and creating verification systems that resist deceptive manipulation.

Effective countermeasures require institutional culture changes that encourage sceptical analysis, diverse perspectives and systematic verification of intelligence sources. Organisations must strike a balance between operational efficiency and analytical rigour to resist psychological manipulation.

Examples of Deception Operations Using Psychological Warfare in Recent Conflicts

In the Second Nagorno-Karabakh War, Azerbaijan used the Second World War era aircrafts as decoys to draw out Armenian air defences, exposing their locations. After destroying these systems, Azerbaijan gained air superiority, enabling deep strikes on Armenian command, control and communications. This tactical deception led to operational success: Azerbaijani forces exploited weakened defences, degrading Armenian intelligence and creating decisive battlefield advantages.

Modern Integrated Command, Control, Computing, Communications, Cyber, Intelligence, Surveillance, Reconnaissance and Targeting (C5ISRT) systems enhance situational awareness by integrating sensors, communications and targeting, enabling rapid decision-making across expansive battlefields. Advanced technologies, such as, hypersonic weapons and UAV swarms, deepen battlefield reach, thereby accelerating operational tempo. This increased speed and data volume creates opportunities for deception operations. By exploiting data overload and fast-paced decision cycles, deception planners can mislead adversaries through ruses embedded in data streams.

In 2022, Ukrainian forces executed a strategic deception to recapture Kharkiv. Throughout July and August, they overtly amassed combat power in southern Ukraine, signalling an imminent offensive in Kherson, a region critical to both sides. This reinforced Russian expectations of a southern attack. President Zelensky bolstered the ruse with public statements about a late August offensive, complemented by Ukrainian leaders' repeated mentions of Kherson operations and visible troop movements. Missile strikes on Kherson infrastructure furthered the deception, detectable by Russian satellites and drones. Overwhelmed by consistent data suggesting a Kherson focus, Russian commanders redeployed forces from Hawkins from the north, weakening Kharkiv's defences. In September, Ukraine launched a surprise offensive, swiftly capturing Kharkiv due to light resistance and later seizing Kherson amid Russian disarray. This operation, leveraging data saturation and rapid decision-making, significantly boosted Ukrainian morale and secured major territorial gains, demonstrating the effectiveness of well-executed deception in modern warfare.[53]

Effective media penetration remains vital for deception operations. Ukrainian leaders leveraged various media sources to reinforce the Russian belief in a Kherson offensive. The evolving media landscape has significantly aided deception planners. Social media offers the ability to target individuals directly and it proves most effective when combined with traditional televised media, which generally carries greater perceived trustworthiness. In the Ukrainian context, official press statements and articles were strategically coordinated with actual troop movements, clearly demonstrating the interconnectedness of Public Affairs, social media and physical deception in achieving strategic aims.

USE OF MEDIA

In modern conflicts, unprecedented access to information via cell phones, social media and satellite internet like Starlink enables both combatants and noncombatants to shape narratives. Citizens use social media to report battlefield updates and news, often with varying accuracy, thereby amplifying conflict dynamics. This rapid information flow pressures traditional media to compete, sometimes resulting in the publication of unverified stories. The interplay between social and traditional media fosters disinformation, with adversaries exploiting this opportunity to disrupt own efforts. This free flow of information challenges the government's ability to manage narratives, potentially undermining public confidence and the armed forces' effectiveness in sustaining operations and rebuilding capacity.

Data, sensors and digital systems are increasingly shaping modern warfare. Commanders now rely on rapid data analysis for informed decision-making, while psychological and Information Operations become increasingly critical in confusing and manipulating adversaries. Traditional military practices, such as, strategic deception, preparation and deliberate organization, still play a vital role. As offensive technologies evolve, information and deception tactics offer cost-effective methods to create windows of advantage. These operations help exploit data environments without the need for high-cost deep-strike weaponry.

Use of Media for Military Deception. One of the most striking examples of the use of media for deception operations is the 2021 Israeli operation in Gaza, which brought global attention to the use of media for military deception. The controversy centred on a statement by the Israel Defense Forces (IDF) implying a ground invasion of Gaza, which was later retracted.

After days of airstrikes, late on 13 May 2021, Israel announced it was calling up its reservists and concentrating troops along the border before a possible ground invasion. Israel began firing artillery shells across the border at targets inside Gaza, started to scramble forces along the border in what looked to be final preparations for an invasion. Then came the statement to the media, issued simultaneously in Hebrew and Arabic on Twitter, that an invasion is underway.

Although Israeli journalists were informed no ground assault had occurred, some foreign journalists were told otherwise, prompting major news outlets to report a ground invasion based on statements from the IDF's English-language spokesperson, Jonathan Conricus.

The ambiguity led Hamas fighters to mobilise defensively and enter tunnel networks, codenamed "the Metro", as a result of which Israel launched an intensive airstrike using 160 warplanes. The strike inflicted heavy militant casualties.

Hours later, the IDF clarified that no troops had entered Gaza, attributing the confusion to internal miscommunication. Lt Col Jonathan Conricm, IDF Informational spokesperson took personal responsibility but denied any intent to deceive. This timeline sparked speculation among analysts and reporters that the media had been used, intentionally or otherwise, as a tool to mislead Hamas.

Veteran military commentators described the incident as a carefully orchestrated ploy with a media dimension, though IDF officials continued to deny purposeful deception. Some Israeli journalists asserted that they were never misled, while foreign correspondents—relying on direct quotes from IDF spokespeople—were left to publicly correct their reports. Felicia Schwartz from *The Wall Street Journal* recounted being explicitly told by Conricus that troops were "in Gaza."

Western media reacted strongly. Outlets like NBC chose not to report the ground invasion, while others, such as, *The New York Times* and *The Washington Post*, did, only to issue corrigenda later. NPR's Daniel Estrin and others voiced serious concerns about being manipulated and the broader implications for journalist safety. Analysts pointed out that being viewed as tools of Psychological Warfare could endanger correspondents, especially those operating in hostile regions.

Although the IDF denied an intentional ruse, some Israeli commentators acknowledged the media's role in the operation. Channel 13's Or Heller called it "a very sophisticated operation that had a media aspect to it." Meanwhile, Israel's Channel 10 reported the activation of a new General Staff Deception Unit, adding weight to theories of an intentional media-based diversion.

Ultimately, the incident strained the already uneasy relationship between the IDF and the International Press. Former spokesperson Peter Lerner emphasised the importance of credibility, acknowledging the deep reputational harm caused, even if no intent to mislead existed. The military's credibility, especially in the eyes of foreign journalists, was now in question, raising ethical concerns about the role of Information Warfare and the boundaries of Psychological Operations in modern conflict.

The Gaza deception episode illustrates how modern militaries may leverage media and narrative ambiguity to achieve tactical advantages. However, it also highlights the risks of eroding trust, particularly among international observers and journalists whose work depends on accurate and credible information. The fallout from this operation continues to shape discourse on ethical boundaries in Psychological Operations and the complex relationship between military strategy and the global media ecosystem.[54]

Strategic surprises have become increasingly common in global conflicts, often stemming from deep-rooted misperceptions and flawed self-assessments. Key examples include the unexpected Ukrainian resistance in 2022, Israel's shock at the Hamas attacks in 2023 and Iran's miscalculation of Israeli and US responses in 2025. Such surprises go beyond intelligence failures; they reflect broader decision-making blind spots and a lack of awareness regarding adversarial capabilities and intentions. The 9/11 attacks demonstrated not just a lack of early warning but also the inability to imagine al-Qaeda's threat.

Repeatedly, countries fall prey to overconfidence and underestimate adversaries, leading to costly consequences. In both the 1973 Yom Kippur War and the 2023 Hamas attack, Israel overestimated its military dominance and failed to anticipate a large-scale assault. Strategic deception, such as that employed by Hamas or by Israel against Iran in 2025, plays a critical role in executing such surprises. Even non-Western powers like Iran, Russia and Hezbollah have experienced miscalculations due to erroneous beliefs about their opponents. These incidents underscore the vital need for humility in strategic planning, an understanding of perception dynamics and the ethical use of deception in shaping the battlefield—all crucial to staying one step ahead in modern geopolitical confrontations.

Strategic deception remains a powerful tool in modern warfare, thriving even as technology and tactics evolve. Its success often lies in reinforcing existing beliefs and misperceptions, as seen in historical cases like Germany in 1941, Egypt in 1973 and more recently, Hamas in 2023 and Israel in 2025.

These events underscore a key lesson: surprise and misperception are enduring challenges. Decision-makers frequently overestimate their understanding of allies and adversaries, while intelligence improvements don't always equate to better strategic foresight. The continued relevance of deception demands ongoing, multidisciplinary study and vigilant awareness.[55]

Deception as a Strategic Art: Mastering the Psychological Battlefield

Operation Rising Lion's success hinged on Israel's mastery of deception and Psychological Warfare. Deception in contemporary warfare involves crafting false narratives to mislead adversaries and inducing them to misjudge intentions, capabilities or timing. Israel's campaign was a textbook example, paralysing Iran's decision-making through a carefully orchestrated web of misdirection.[56]

Israel employed an elaborate deception campaign ahead of its strike on Iran to lull Tehran into a false sense of security. It flooded media and diplomatic channels with misleading cues, including staging a routine cabinet meeting, leaking a story about Prime Minister Netanyahu attending his son's wedding and fabricating nuclear talks involving Mossad Director David Barnea and Envoy Ron Dermer, who claimed to be on a trip to Washington via Oman for a "sixth round" of nuclear talks. Rumours of political discord were also circulated to heighten the illusion. These efforts were designed to disrupt Iran's perception and decision-making before military action began. Israel views deception as a strategic asset, especially against centralised regimes vulnerable to cognitive disruption.

Israel's strategic use of deception aims to undermine its adversary's perception before initiating any physical strike. Through misdirection, covert actions and psychological tactics, Israel destabilises the opponent's sense of control and security, causing hesitation and confusion at leadership levels. This cognitive disruption paralyses decision-making, enabling Israel to gain a decisive upper hand. Its Operation Rising Lion against Iran exemplified this: a swift, unanticipated strike left Iran unprepared, unable to respond or escalate. By moving faster than expected, Israel demonstrated that speed and strategic surprise can contain conflict and reshape adversary behaviour before a missile is even launched.[57]

Military deception remains a central pillar in modern warfare, evolving alongside advances in technology and doctrine. Its integration with Psychological Operations has become increasingly significant, as both aim to shape adversary perceptions and influence strategic outcomes. Throughout history, success in war has hinged not only on battlefield victories but also on controlling the narrative. Today, actions, such as disinformation and psychological manipulation are key tools in this context.

The introduction of generative AI, particularly deepfakes, adds a new layer of complexity. Deepfakes can manufacture fake news or videos of trusted figures, eroding public trust in leadership and official communications. This phenomenon contributes to the "liar's dividend," where individuals can dismiss genuine evidence as fabricated, shielding themselves from accountability. As deception techniques grow more sophisticated, so too must strategies to detect and counter them.

CONCLUSION

Psychological Warfare is indispensable to military deception operations and serves as a force multiplier, leveraging human psychology to mislead, confuse and demoralise adversaries. By exploiting cognitive biases, emotional vulnerabilities and cultural dynamics, PSYOPS enhance the effectiveness of deception operations. The judicious use of propaganda, misinformation and symbolic indicators can induce adversaries to act against their own interests, often with decisive strategic outcomes, enabling strategic victories with reduced physical costs. However, ethical and operational challenges necessitate careful planning to avoid unintended consequences.

Psychological Warfare is indispensable to military deception operations, providing the means to manipulate enemy perceptions, decision-making and morale without confrontation. As warfare evolves into cognitive and informational domains, the fusion of PSYOPS and deception will remain a cornerstone of military strategy, shaping the battlespace in both the physical and cognitive domains. However, the deployment of such operations demands not only technological prowess but also ethical foresight, as the consequences of manipulating perception on a global scale extend far beyond the battlefield.

Chapter XIV

Country Studies: Pakistan

Pakistan, recognising the importance of Information Warfare, has developed structured and sophisticated Information Warfare capabilities to shape narratives, influence domestic and international audiences and counter perceived threats, particularly from India, to complement its conventional military strategies. For Pakistan, Information Warfare is not only a tool for external influence but also a means to control internal dissent and shape global perceptions.

The 2025 clash between India and Pakistan, triggered by the Pahalgam incident on 22 April, highlighted Pakistan's growing Information Warfare capabilities, exposing both their effectiveness and constraints. The conflict revealed how Pakistan leveraged a multi-pronged information war, combining cyber operations and propaganda to counter India's resource advantage.

As Pakistan increasingly turns to social media, digital warfare and psychological influence, it has formally embedded Information Warfare into its national security framework. The impact of Pakistan's Information Warfare extends beyond its rivalry with India, affecting global diplomacy and its own internal political cohesion. To fully assess these capabilities, it is necessary to analyse the organisational structures, technological assets, strategic principles and operational methods that shape Pakistan's Information Warfare strategy.

Pakistan's Concept of Information Warfare

Pakistan's Information Warfare strategy is underpinned by its military doctrine, which emphasises hybrid warfare—a composite approach blending conventional, irregular, cyber, psychological and informational tactics to achieve political and strategic objectives. Information Warfare is not an auxiliary, but a primary instrument of strategic messaging and deterrence.

The objectives of Pakistan's Information Warfare are:

- Narrative management.
- Delegitimisation.
- Psychological Operations.
- Mobilisation of international opinion.
- Use of cyber means.

Pakistan's Information Warfare Capabilities

Pakistan's Information Warfare capabilities include Psychological Operations (PSYOPS), cyber operations, Electronic Warfare and disinformation campaigns, integrating State and non-State actors to achieve strategic objectives. These capabilities are customised to exploit the digital domain, leveraging social media, State-backed media and encrypted platforms and to amplify narratives and disrupt adversaries.

CYBER WARFARE CAPABILITIES

The Pakistan Army Cyber Command, a specialised unit dedicated to cyber operations and cybersecurity, was officially launched in August 2022. It comprises two main divisions: the Cyber Division and the Army Centre of Emerging Technologies. The Pakistan Air Force has its own Cyber Command, while the Navy is expected to have developed comparable capabilities.

The Corps of Signals of the Pakistan Army manages the Army's communication networks, IT systems and cybersecurity operations. Pakistan is attempting to integrate the Army Cyber Command with the cyber units of the Navy and Air Force, as well as the national cybersecurity framework.

Beyond the military, Pakistan has a civilian cyber defence infrastructure, including the National Cyber Crimes Investigation Agency (NCCIA), the National Computer Emergency Response Team (CERT) and the National Centre for Cyber Security, all managed by government ministries.

Trust as a Critical Factor. Trust plays a pivotal role in determining the effectiveness and depth of collaboration between the Pakistan Army Cyber Command and civilian institutions.

CHALLENGES DUE TO LACK OF TRUST

A trust deficit exists between military and civilian cyber entities in Pakistan, often obstructing information sharing and coordinated responses to cyber threats. This reluctance leads to isolated operations, with both sides wary of exchanging sensitive data or engaging in joint initiatives.

Operational Challenges. The military's preference for operating on isolated, secure networks, such as "air-gapped" systems, limits the potential for real-time collaboration with civilian agencies. Civilian organisations lack confidence in the transparency and openness of military-led initiatives, which can impede joint planning and execution of national cybersecurity strategies.

Policy and Strategic Implications. Several policy analyses highlight that for Pakistan to develop a robust national cybersecurity regime, it must overcome the civil-military trust gap. Effective partnerships require mutual confidence, clear protocols for information exchange and joint exercises to build familiarity and reliability between stakeholders.

Progress. Although sporadic cooperation between military and civilian cyber entities has occurred, structured collaboration remains weak. To address this, experts suggest enhancing trust through measures such as:

- Regular joint training exercises.
- Transparent communication protocols.
- Incorporating both civilian and military priorities into national cybersecurity policies.

Technological Capabilities

Pakistan has developed offensive cyber capabilities, with recent conflicts demonstrating their deployment in cyber operations.

- **Distributed Denial-of-Service (DDoS) attacks.** Aimed at overwhelming target systems and disrupting services.

- **Malware Campaigns.** The use of malicious software to infiltrate systems, exfiltrate sensitive data or disrupt operations.
- **Website Defacements.** A frequently used tactic for propaganda and psychological impact, often targeting symbolic entities. For instance, websites of military-affiliated institutions were hacked but quickly restored.
- **GPS Spoofing.** Manipulating navigation systems to deceive or mislead opposing forces.
- **Cyber Espionage.** Covert intelligence-gathering operations often precede broader cyber campaigns. Reports suggest attempts to breach Indian defence organisations and public sector entities.

Expansion of Cyber Warfare Capabilities

Pakistan's Cyber Warfare prowess has advanced considerably, supported by State-backed groups and hacktivist networks. Notable threat actors include:

- APT36 (Transparent Tribe).
- Side Copy.

These groups primarily target Indian government agencies, military systems and critical infrastructure.

During the 2025 conflict, Pakistan-linked hackers conducted over 1.5 million cyber-attacks against Indian digital assets. However, only 150 succeeded, highlighting India's strong cyber defences with a 99.99 percent success rate. The attacks included:

- Distributed Denial of Service (DDoS) assaults.
- Phishing operations.
- Malware infiltration, such as, the Crimson RAT deployed by APT36 against Indian defence networks following the Pahalgam terror attack.

This evolution underscores Pakistan's growing sophistication in Cyber Warfare, while also revealing the effectiveness of India's defensive measures.

DDoS attacks peaked on 10 May 2025, targeting high-value Indian assets like the Ministry of Defence website. While these attacks caused minimal disruption, their intent was to undermine India's critical infrastructure and public trust. Pakistan's cyber operations comprised web defacement and data leaks. Some groups like "Pakistan Cyber Force" and "IOK Hacker" boasted of breaching Indian military-linked sites. However, many claims were exaggerated, often relying on recycled data or symbolic defacements with limited impact.

Pakistan's cyber capabilities are less advanced than those of China, lacking zero-day exploits or supply-chain attack sophistication. There are unverified reports that during the 2025 conflict, technical assistance from the People's Liberation Army (PLA)'s Information Support Force was provided. Usually, no country shares this capability. If it happened then it would be a game changer.

The integration of cyber and Information Warfare enables coordinated campaigns that combine technical attacks on information infrastructure with narrative operations designed to exploit the psychological and political effects of cyber incidents. This integration multiplies the strategic impact of both capabilities.

ELECTRONIC WARFARE CAPABILITIES

Pakistan's Electronic Warfare capabilities, bolstered by Chinese-supplied systems, played a pivotal role in the 2025 conflict. The DWL-002 passive detection system, which tracks airborne threats via electronic signatures, disrupted Indian drones and missiles using commercial-grade GPS jammers. The J-10C fighter aircraft, equipped with advanced Electronic Warfare suites, reportedly jammed Indian Rafale aircraft controls, contributing to their downing. The HQ-9B surface-to-air missile system strengthened Pakistan's air defence network.

Electronic Warfare Integration. Pakistan's Electronic Warfare operations were integral to its kinetic response during Operation Bunyan al-Marsoos. Pakistan claimed that J-10C aircraft and HQ-9B systems disrupted Indian air operations, with claims of downing Rafale jets and neutralising S-400 radars.

PAKISTAN'S ELECTRONIC WARFARE AND AIR DEFENCE

During Operation Bunyan al-Marsoos, Pakistan relied heavily on Electronic Warfare as a central part of its military response. They claim that their J-10C fighter jets, equipped with sophisticated EW systems, jammed the controls of Indian Rafale aircraft, leading to their alleged downing.

The integration of the HQ-9B surface-to-air missile system significantly bolstered Pakistan's air defence capabilities. Pakistan declared that the J-10C aircraft and HQ-9B systems were responsible for disrupting Indian air force operations.

GPS jammers and the DWL-002 system countered Indian drones, with Pakistan reporting the shooting down of 77 drones. These operations showcased Pakistan's ability to integrate Electronic Warfare with conventional strikes, though India's counter-EW measures limited their effectiveness.

PSYCHOLOGICAL OPERATIONS AND DISINFORMATION

Pakistan's Psychological Operations leverage the Inter-Services Public Relations (ISPR), the media wing of the Pakistan Armed Forces, to shape domestic and international narratives. The ISPR has evolved into a sophisticated propaganda apparatus, producing military-themed music videos, dramas and late-night briefings timed for Western media cycles. During the 2025 conflict, ISPR disseminated claims of paralysing 70 percent of India's power grid and downing five Indian jets, though these were found to be false.

Social media platforms like X, Facebook, Instagram and YouTube served as primary vectors for disinformation. Pakistan-affiliated accounts circulated deepfakes, such as a fabricated video of Indian External Affairs Minister S. Jaishankar apologising for strikes and recontextualised footage from unrelated conflicts to depict Pakistani victories.

Terrorist organisations like Lashkar-e-Taiba (LeT) and Jaish-e-Mohammed (JeM) amplified Pakistan's Information Warfare efforts. These groups used encrypted platforms like WhatsApp and Telegram for recruitment, propaganda and operational coordination, organising social media workshops to incite anti-India protests in Kashmir.

Disinformation and Propaganda. Pakistan employs multi-lingual, multi-platform disinformation strategies, often using fake media portals and social media accounts.

- The 2020 EU DisinfoLab report uncovered a vast network of 750+ fake news sites and organisations impersonating European entities but promoting pro-Pakistani messaging against India.
- Social media bots are used to amplify hashtags during critical incidents (e.g., #FreeKashmir, #KashmirBleeds).
- Use of emotional imagery from conflict zones.
- Videos of captured Indian personnel (e.g., Wing Commander Abhinandan, 2019) are intended to shape global perception and morale.
- Strategic use of WhatsApp forwards and viral misinformation to provoke fear, confusion and internal dissent.

Religious and Ideological Framing. Pakistan's State narrative often blends Islamic identity with geopolitical messaging, especially around Kashmir and India's domestic politics:

- Presenting Kashmir as a "Muslim suffering" and jihad-worthy cause.
- Aligning with pan-Islamic organisations, such as, the OIC, to globalise the issue.
- Amplifying religious persecution themes concerning India's minorities.
- Article 370 Abrogation (2019), India's revocation of Jammu & Kashmir's special status led to long-term Information Operations by Pakistan.
- Use of fake images/videos of protests and mass detentions.
- Promoting human rights violation narratives through platforms like the Kashmir-Khalistan Referendum Front.
- Sudden activity spikes from fake accounts, mostly created in Pakistan or the West Asia region, using coordinated hashtags.

Indian Farmer Protests (2020–2021). Pakistan-linked groups and sympathisers tried to hijack the narrative around India's farmer protests:

- Disseminating conspiracy theories and connecting the issue with Khalistani separatism.

- Promoting hashtags like #StandWithFarmers to mislead international audiences.
- Use of fabricated content that aligned with anti-state messaging in India.

Internationalisation of Pakistan's Information Warfare Campaigns. Pakistan seeks to globalise its narratives, particularly the Kashmir issue, through lobbying, think tank sponsorships and the use of the Diaspora.

- Support for seminars and reports in Western universities via NGOs aligned with Pakistani interests.
- Co-opting activists and human rights groups to promote narratives of "Indian oppression".
- Heavy investment in international media appearances and op-eds, often under anonymous or misleading authorship.
- Islamist groups that provide ideological cover to political messaging.
- Diaspora influencers, especially in North America and Europe, who engage in lobbying and Perception Management.

ORGANISATIONAL STRUCTURE OF PAKISTAN'S INFORMATION WARFARE

Pakistan's Information Warfare operations are coordinated through a hybrid structure that involves military, intelligence and non-State actors, ensuring flexibility and deniability.

INTER-SERVICES PUBLIC RELATIONS: THE CENTRAL HUB

The Inter-Services Public Relations (ISPR), under the strict control of ISI, is the media and public relations wing of the Pakistan Armed Forces, serving as the primary institutional mechanism for Pakistan's Information Warfare operations. Established in 1949, the ISPR serves as the central public relations body of the Pakistani Armed Forces, having evolved from a traditional military Public Affairs office into a sophisticated Information Warfare apparatus.

The organisational expansion of ISPR reflects Pakistan's growing emphasis on Information Operations. Now headed by a Lieutenant General, the ISPR operates with two Major Generals, each overseeing distinct but complementary domains: Information Operations and Psychological Operations. This structural enhancement demonstrates the institutionalisation of Information Warfare as a core military capability rather than an auxiliary function.

Source: Republic TV

The bifurcation into Information Operations and Psychological Operations represents a sophisticated understanding of the dual nature of Information Warfare. This dual-track approach enables coordinated campaigns that operate simultaneously across multiple information domains, allowing for effective and comprehensive responses.

KEY FEATURES OF ISPR'S STRUCTURE

- **Info Ops Wing.** Focused on digital and cyber domains, including social media campaigns, hacking and digital espionage.
- **Psy Ops Wing.** Specialises in emotionally manipulative content, radicalisation and targeted media messaging, often leveraging extremist rhetoric and orchestrated campaigns.
- **Budget and Resources.** ISPR's annual budget for Information Warfare is reportedly 600 crore Pakistani Rupees, supporting a vast network of operatives, digital assets and media productions.

The ISPR now coordinates multi-platform information campaigns, including Psychological Operations and soft propaganda. It produces music videos, TV serials (e.g., Ehd-e-Wafa), films (e.g., Waar, Yalghaar) and documentaries with embedded nationalist and military themes. During crises, ISPR plays a central role in shaping the narrative; for instance, controlling the messaging after the Balakot air strikes (2019).

Organisation: ISPR

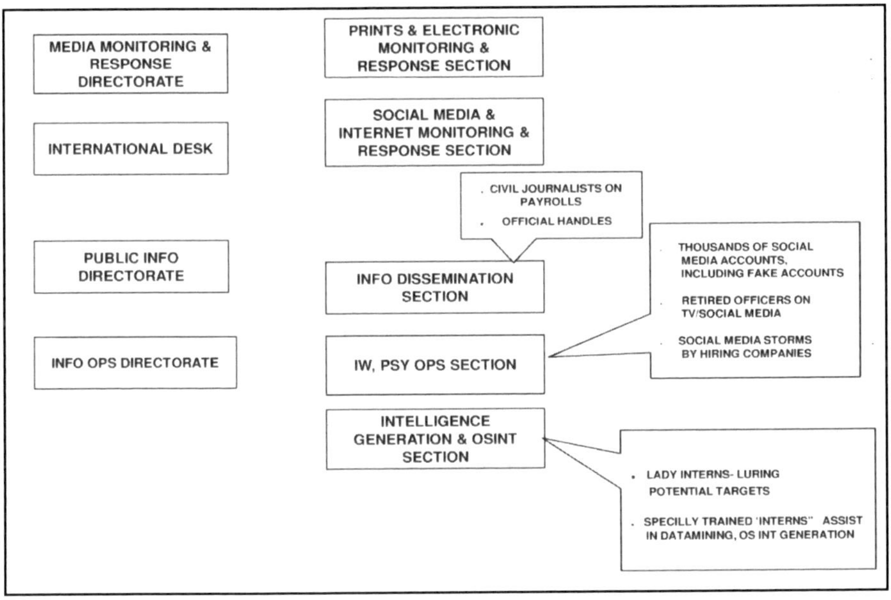

ISPR'S ROLE IN POLITICAL INTERFERENCE

The Pakistan Army uses the ISPR as a tool of domestic suppression within Pakistan. The military's media arm actively interferes in Pakistan's political landscape, censors opposition voices and manipulates democratic processes. During the 2024-2025 elections in Pakistan, Pakistan Tehreek-e-Insaf (PTI) was denied its election symbol. Imran Khan and multiple PTI leaders were jailed or forced into exile.

Media houses were censored and journalists were threatened for covering PTI's suppression. The ISPR's social media units launched campaigns to discredit opposition voices, using misinformation about Imran Khan's leadership. The ISPR manipulated election narratives favouring the military-backed establishment. Censorship was imposed on independent news outlets reporting on electoral fraud.

This authoritarian control of the information space highlights the ISPR's dual role—suppressing democracy within Pakistan while running anti-India propaganda campaigns internationally.[58]

Role and Function

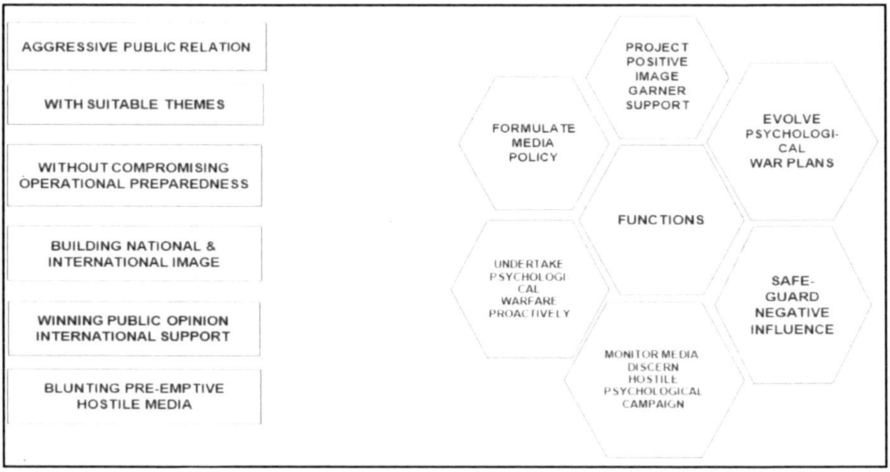

Integration with Intelligence and Military Operations

The ISPR operates in close coordination with Pakistan's intelligence agencies, particularly the Inter-Services Intelligence (ISI), which conducts cyber espionage, Human Intelligence (HUMINT) recruitment via social media and Influence Operations, targeting Indian military and scientific personnel.

Kashmir: The Epicentre of Narrative Warfare

Kashmir remains the primary theatre for Pakistan's Information Warfare:

- Annual events like Kashmir Solidarity Day are used to amplify anti-India propaganda and radicalisation efforts.
- ISPR-produced content glorifies militancy and frames the conflict as a religious and humanitarian struggle.
- Social media campaigns are launched to internationalise the Kashmir issue and discredit Indian policies.

Domestic Control and Political Engineering

The ISPR's Information Warfare is not limited to external adversaries:

- Media censorship and intimidation of journalists critical of the military or government.
- Manipulation of election narratives to favour military-backed candidates, as seen in the suppression of the PTI and Imran Khan's leadership.
- Disinformation campaigns against opposition leaders and activists.

Recruitment and Espionage via Social Media

Pakistani intelligence has successfully used social media to:

- Recruit Indian military and scientific personnel for espionage (e.g., DRDO scientists and Indian Army jawans honey-trapped via Facebook).
- Gather sensitive information and disrupt Indian defence research and operations.

Narrative Control and Psychological Impact

- ISPR's Info Ops units spread false narratives about Indian casualties and leadership crises, exploiting digital platforms to undermine trust in official Indian statements.
- Psy Ops content was tailored to radicalise and mobilise populations, particularly in Kashmir and among Indian minorities.

The conflict showcased the use of deepfakes, doctored audio and viral hashtags to manipulate perceptions in real-time.

ISPR New Structure: A Machine for Propaganda and Psychological Warfare

The ISPR is the central hub for Pakistan's Information Warfare strategy. It is a military media and Psychological Warfare entity, now commanded by a Lieutenant General. ISPR has undergone a structural transformation to enhance its hybrid warfare capabilities and currently oversees two specialised wings:

Information Operations

- Aims to manipulate and control the Information Environment through:
- Cyber Warfare (hacking, spreading fake news).
- Electronic Warfare (disrupting communications).
- Disinformation campaigns aimed at creating global narratives against India.

Psychological Operations

- Focuses on manipulating emotions, beliefs and perceptions through:
- Targeted propaganda and messaging (media narratives, speeches, religious mobilisation).
- Social media manipulation (bot armies, troll farms).
- Jihadi glorification and radicalisation to facilitate terror recruitment.

This distinction enables the ISPR to conduct multi-layered operations simultaneously, influencing domestic politics, regional conflicts and international diplomatic stances while maintaining deniability.

KASHMIR SOLIDARITY DAY 2025: A CASE STUDY IN ISPR'S NEW WARFARE MODEL

The February 5 observance of Kashmir Solidarity Day exemplifies how ISPR's enhanced capabilities are being weaponised against India. The day was introduced initially in 1990 by Nawaz Sharif and has transformed into a platform for radicalisation, terrorist glorification and jihadist mobilisation.

This year's events were heavily influenced by ISPR-driven Info Ops and Psy Ops, aiming to radicalise Pakistani youth through extremist speeches, propagate a global disinformation campaign on Kashmir and facilitate terrorist recruitment and cross-border infiltration.

Key ISPR-Backed Propaganda Events on February 5, 2025

General Syed Asim Munir (Pakistan's Army Chief (now Field Marshal), addressing a gathering in Muzaffarabad, PoK, reiterated Pakistan's claim over Kashmir, stating:

> "Kashmir and Pakistan share an inseparable bond."

This statement was widely circulated by ISPR-run social media handles, fake news networks and pro-Pakistani influencers. The event orchestrated by ISPR's Psy Ops team saw widespread social media coverage, glorifying jihad against India.

PoK's Prime Minister, Anwar ul Haq, publicly called for the "revival of jihadist culture" to drive Indian forces out of Kashmir.

These statements, strategically amplified by the ISPR's hybrid warfare units, ensured the Kashmir narrative reached global audiences while fueling domestic anti-India sentiment.[59]

Non-State Actors and Hacktivist Groups

Pakistan's Information Warfare ecosystem relies heavily on non-State actors, including hacktivist groups like Pakistan Cyber Force, IOK Hacker and Sylhet Gang-SG. Terrorist organisations like Lashkar-e-Taiba (LeT) and Jaish-e-Mohammed (JeM) run media wings (e.g., Al-Qalam, Ummat Media) spread anti-India narratives. The LeT and JeM extend Pakistan's Information Warfare reach by leveraging cyberspace for propaganda and recruitment.

Social media workshops aimed at radicalising youth in Kashmir demonstrate a decentralised yet coordinated approach, while encrypted platforms facilitate secure communication. These groups' propaganda, including doctored videos and extremist content, aimed to radicalise youth and destabilise Kashmir.

Chapter XV

China

The People's Republic of China's (PRC) Information Warfare strategy combines ancient philosophy with cutting-edge technology. China has developed one of the most sophisticated Information Warfare ecosystems globally, integrating cyber, psychological and media operations to advance its geopolitical objectives. China's Information Warfare doctrine, often described as "Informatised Warfare," emphasises dominance in the information domain to achieve strategic superiority without resorting to kinetic conflict.

The People's Liberation Army (PLA)'s Academy of Military Science defines Information Operations as leveraging modern media, electronic platforms and specialised methods to enhance Psychological Warfare. According to the Pentagon's China Military Power Report of 2024, China "views controlling the information spectrum in the modern battlespace as a critical enabler of information dominance early in a conflict".

According to Chinese thinking, Psychological Warfare is an integral part of Information Warfare. The PLA's Psychological Warfare aims to weaken the enemy's will, shape international public narratives, influence diplomatic and political outcomes and advance the PRC's interests throughout all phases of conflict. The importance placed on Psychological Warfare is increasingly linked to Chinese military assessments that the cognitive domain will be a key domain of future warfare.

Informatised and Intelligentised Warfare. China's Military Strategy White Paper (2015) introduces the concept of "informatised warfare" and outlines the military doctrine of "winning informatised local wars." Informatised warfare prioritises the integration of information technology across military operations to achieve decision-making superiority.

The PLA has transitioned toward "Intelligentised Warfare," integrating AI, big data and autonomous systems to enhance its Information Warfare capabilities. These doctrines reflect China's recognition of the information domain as a battlespace where cognitive, technological and societal influence converge. The realisation of the PLA's broader vision for AI-enabled intelligentised warfare would have immense implications for Chinese Psychological Warfare.[60]

China's Information Warfare strategy is rooted in its broader military doctrine of "winning informatized local wars," as articulated in the Military Strategy White Paper (2015). Fundamentally, Psychological Warfare, a core aspect of Information Warfare, focuses on manipulating information and perceptions. The PLA integrates this with its emphasis on data and AI-driven intelligentisation in warfare. The Chinese military's growing emphasis on informatisation (information-driven) and future intelligentisation (Artificial Intelligence - driven) perspectives on warfare aligns well with Psychological Warfare.

This emphasis on information's central role in warfare puts a premium on the ability to manipulate information, broadly defined as Information Warfare, including the ability to manipulate how adversaries receive and process that information (Psychological Warfare).

The primary objectives of Chinese Psychological Warfare are to degrade the adversary's decision-making, weaken the adversary's will to fight, undermine the adversary's support for war and erode the adversary's Government from within, while also supporting deterrence.

PSYCHOLOGICAL WARFARE PROCESS

A 2016 book on evaluating the effectiveness of Psychological Warfare published by the Academy of Military Science (AMS), divides the general process into five steps: intelligence information collection and analysis, information production, information delivery, information broadcasting (processing) and information feedback.

This information-centric and specifically data-centric, process naturally aligns well with China's informationised warfare and is poised to benefit from emerging technologies, as detailed below.

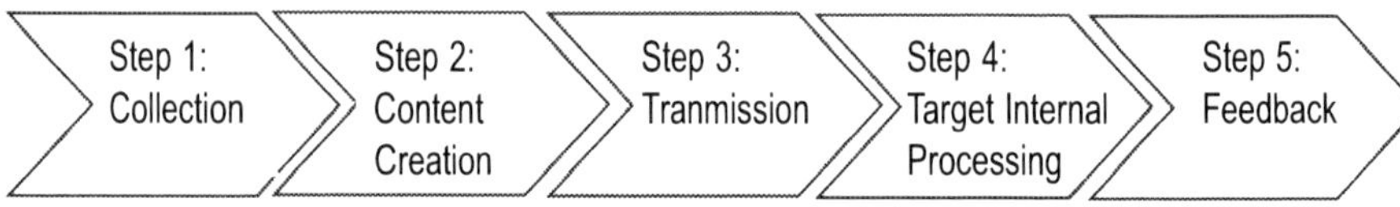

Fig. 1: PLA conceptualisation of Psychological Warfare Process

Source: Nathan Beauchamp-Mustafaga, Chinese Next-Generation Psychological Warfare: The Military Applications of Emerging Technologies and Implications for the United States, RAND Corporation, Santa Monica, CA, 2023. https://www.rand.org/pubs/research_reports/RRA853-1.html

The steps are:

- Information must be collected on the target and target environment and analysed to make it worthwhile.
- Information must be tailored to be most effective against the target, given a variety of factors.
- Information must be transmitted to the target through various potential methods.
- Once the information reaches the target, that person must process the information.
- The sender should observe the target, compare it against the intended effects and continue to refine the information, repeating the process until the desired effect is achieved.

During the war, manipulated information, such as, deepfakes, could degrade adversary leadership decision-making and be leveraged for other Psychological Warfare objectives, including weakening troops' will to fight, undermining the adversary government from within and discouraging public support for the war.

The subject matter experts of the PLA Psychological Warfare community have emphasised three broad categories of technologies: advanced computing, especially big data and information processing; brain science, especially brain imaging; and a range of legacy proposals that remain of interest, including sonic weapons, laser weapons, subliminal messaging and holograms.

The following Table shows how these technologies would support PLA's Psychological Warfare, broken down by the five-step process: collecting information on the target, creating Psychological Warfare content, transmitting the content, processing the content internally by the target and providing feedback on the effects to the attacker.

Assessed PLA Interest in the Application of Key Emerging Technologies to Psychological Warfare Process

Technology	*Step 1 Collection*	*Step 2 Content Creation*	*Step 3 Transmission*	*Step 4 Target Internal processing*	*Step 5 Feedback*
https://www.rand.org/pubs/research_reports/RRA853-1.html	Primary	Supporting	...	...	Primary
Brain Imaging	Supporting	Supporting	...	Supporting	Primary
Information Processing	...	Primary	Supporting	...	...
Subliminal Messaing	...	Supporting	Supporting	Primary	...
Congnitive modeling	...	Supporting	...	Primary	Supporting

Source: Nathan Beauchamp-Mustafaga, Chinese Next-Generation Psychological Warfare: The Military Applications of Emerging Technologies and Implications for the United States, RAND Corporation, Santa Monica, CA, 2023. https://www.rand.org/pubs/research_reports/RRA853-1.html

THREE WARFARES

China's Information Warfare is guided by the Three Warfares doctrine, which comprises Psychological Warfare, Public Opinion Warfare and Legal Warfare.

Along with the technical aspects of Information Operations, the PLA combines Psychological Warfare, Media Warfare and Legal Warfare to manipulate public opinion, influence legal arguments and strengthen China's diplomatic and security position. Media warfare refers to the control and exploitation of communication channels for disseminating propaganda and influencing public opinion. It sets the circumstances for dominating communications channels for the conduct of psychological and legal warfare. Psychological Warfare employs propaganda, deception, threats and coercion to influence the adversary's decision-making. It conducts military operations through Perception Management and deception while countering the opponent Psychological Operations. Legal warfare uses international and domestic laws to claim the "legal high ground", sway target audiences, gain international support, manage political repercussions and assert Chinese interests. The PLA uses online influence activities to support its overall "Three Warfares" concept and undermine an adversary's resolve in a contingency or conflict.

Tactics of the Three Warfares

THREE WARFARE	PUBLIC OPINION WARFARE	➢ **Preemption and first impression** (Sharing the public opinion through preemptive offensive communication) ➢ **Concentration and scale formation** (Building up momentum through concentrated propaganda and overwhelming with scale) ➢ **Focused breakthrough** (Narrowing the focus and making a breakthrough on a single issue) ➢ **Penetration** (Penetrating ideology, culture and value principal) ➢ **Amplification and Suppression** (amplifying favorable information and suppressing unfavorable information) ➢ **Pressure** (threatening the opponent public opinion)
	PSYCHOLOGICAL WARFARE	➢ **Psychological Propaganda** (Propaganda aimed at psychological effects) ➢ **Threats** (threatening to use force) ➢ **Emotional influence** (appealing to emotions and antipathy to war) ➢ **Deception** (spreading disinformation) ➢ **Estrangement** (aiming to breakup the opponent's alliances) ➢ **Special strikes** (Precession strikes against key person and structure to inflict psychological damage)
	LEGAL WARFARE	➢ **Legal Intimidation** (Pressuring the adversary by warning one's intention to challenge the enemy and demonstrating the legal legitimacy of one's military actions) ➢ **Legal blow** (Exposing the illegality of the enemy's actions and advocating the legality of one's military actions) ➢ **Legal Counterattack** (Counterattacking the enemy's legal warfare against oneself) ➢ **Legal restraint** (Constraining the enemy's military actions and third countries military interference) ➢ **Legal sanctions** (Pursing responsibility for war crime) ➢ **Legal Protections** (Guaranteeing the legal legitimacy of one's military actions)

Psychological Operations are coordinated at the highest level and executed by the following actors:

- PLA Political Work Department.
- United Front Work Department (UFWD).
- International Liaison Department.
- Ministry of State Security (MSS).
- Ministry of Public Security (MPS).

- People's Armed Police (PAP).
- The PLA Strategic Support Force (SSF), now Information Support Force (ISF).

MAIN ACTORS IMPLEMENTING CHINESE PSYCHOLOGICAL OPERATIONS

Within the Party

- The Propaganda Department, which manages ideology, controls the entire media spectrum and all the cultural production in the country.
- The United Front Work Department (UFWD) has twelve offices reflecting its main targets.[61]
- The International Liaison Department (ILD) maintains relations with foreign political parties.
- The 610 Office, which has agents worldwide acting outside any legal framework.
- The Chinese Communist Youth League (CYL), which serves as a link for young people, an incubator for future Party executives and a force that can be mobilised when needed.

Within the State. The Ministry of State Security (MSS), the leading civilian intelligence agency and the Taiwan Affairs Office (TAO), are responsible for propaganda aimed at Taiwan.

Within PLA

Organisational Structures. The PLA plays a central role in China's Information Warfare, with significant reforms since 2015 enhancing its capabilities. The establishment of the SSF in 2015 was a pivotal development, consolidating space, cyber, electronic and Psychological Warfare under a single command. The SSF's Network Systems Department oversees cyber and Information Operations, integrating offensive and defensive capabilities.

The SSF through its Network Systems Department, Base 311, headquartered in Fuzhou, is dedicated to implementing the "Three Warfares" strategy. It operates media companies as civilian covers and a fake hotel to hide a training centre. It is unclear whether the SSF has organisational responsibility for the type of PLA/PRC Psychological Operations that might be targeted against adversaries, such as, the US or its allies.

The SSF's cyber capabilities will play a significant role in collecting intelligence and spreading disinformation as part of broader cyber Influence Operations. However, the SSF is not responsible for political warfare within the PLA or the Chinese Government.[62]

The PLA Mechanisms for Implementing the Three Warfare's

Level	Implemented Activities	Implementing Organisations
Central and Strategic	Public opinion warfare, psychologicalwarfare, legal warfare	Strategic Support Force, Central Military Commission's Political Work Department
Group Army	Public opinion warfare, psychologicalwarfare, legal warfare	Political Department, Party Committees, Political Commissars, Three Warfare specialists
Regiment	Psychological warfare (Psychological protection), Propaganda	Political Department, Party Committees, Political Commissars, Three Warfare specialists
Battalion and company	Psychological warfare (Psychological protection), Propaganda	Grassroots Party Committees and party branches, political instructors and Political Directors, Militia

BASE 311

PLA Unit 61716, also known as Base 311, was raised in 2005. This unit keeps a low profile and remains relatively opaque. It is the only officially known base dedicated to implementing the "Three Warfares" strategy.

Base 311 comprises the following departments: a Political Department, a Translation and Edition Office, an Information Research Office, an Equipment Department, an Outpatient Department and a Staff and Logistics Department. The base commander is assumed to have a rank comparable to a Deputy Corps Commander, meaning that a Major General leads the organisation.

There are two plausible hypotheses about its place within the PLASSF's internal structure. Base 311 could be attached to the PLASSF's Political Department or the Network Systems Department (NSD). The NSD would be in command of the full spectrum of Information Operations, including cyber, electronic and Psychological Warfare, if Base 311 falls under its control.

Integrating Base 311's operational forces with the SSF's cyber, space and electronic missions enables Psychological Operations forces to leverage cross-domain intelligence, thereby maximising the impact of Information Operations on an adversary's psychology.

Base 311 concentrates exclusively on Psychological Warfare and propaganda that targets public opinion on Taiwan.[63] It had attempted to influence public opinion in Taiwan by exploiting local social media even before the PLASSF existed. Base 311 orchestrated the misinformation campaign that targeted the 2018 Taiwanese elections. The Psychological Operations of the PLASSF were unsuccessful in Taiwan, as evidenced by the landslide victory of Tsai Ing-wen and the Democratic Progressive Party's pro-independence stance in the 2020 presidential election.

Base 311 researches the informational environment in the United States. Affiliated researchers have published reports on the US, particularly on the potential effects of legislation passed to combat propaganda, the role of social media in American political life and its impact on political polarisation, among other topics.

Base 311 runs at least six regiments responsible for engaging in the three warfares against Taiwan, including through multiple forms of propaganda.[64] It is critical to PLA's Psychological Warfare against Taiwan in peacetime. It could take on a crucial combat role in coordination with kinetic and Information Operations in a conflict scenario.

The Rise of the Information Support Force

In April 2024, China restructured the Strategic Support Force to establish the PLA Information Support Force (ISF), a new military branch designed to unify and enhance the PLA's capabilities in cyber, electronic and Psychological Warfare, underscoring the growing centrality of information in warfare.

The ISF's mission is to build and operate a resilient, integrated network system capable of supporting joint operations across all domains, even in the face of enemy attacks. Its tasks are:

- Ensuring seamless communication across PLA branches, Information assurance and protection.
- Conducting cyber and Electronic Warfare.
- Integrating AI and big data into battlefield decision-making.
- Support for joint operations in a multi-domain battlefield.
- Enhancing resilience through drills simulating attacks on infrastructure.

President Xi Jinping's inspection of the ISF in December 2024 underscored its strategic importance. He emphasised the need for innovation, interoperability and the integration of cutting-edge technologies, such as Artificial Intelligence.

SOME PLA UNITS CARRYING OUT PSYCHOLOGICAL OPERATIONS

Central Television (CCTV) in October 2018, on the PLA's likely only Psychological Warfare experimentation unit, part of the Central Theatre Command's 83rd Group Army, relayed that the unit's repertoire included air-dropping propaganda leaflets from drones, firing propaganda leaflets from homemade launchers and using vehicles to broadcast folk songs as well as propaganda in local dialects.

As part of urban warfare training in October 2020, a PLA Army's combined arms brigade, part of the Eastern Theatre Command's 71st Group Army, used a small UAV to distribute propaganda leaflets to weaken the morale of the adversary's troops, before the PLA unit seized the building. These recent examples of PLA's Psychological Warfare training do not suggest the widespread adoption of Chinese Next-Generation Psychological Warfare.[65]

MAIN ACTORS

- **Public and Private Companies.** Play a crucial role in collecting the data necessary to determine who should be targeted by Influence Operations, when and how.
- **Diasporas.** The dual objective was to control them so that they would not represent a threat to Chinese power.

- **Diplomacy.** Influence over international organisations and norms. Beijing deploys classic diplomatic resources along with covert Influence Operations.
- **"Wolf-Warrior" diplomacy.** Aggressive postures were adopted by the Ministry of Foreign Affairs spokespersons and a dozen diplomats, that proved counter-productive.
- **Economy.** Economic coercion takes various forms, including trade sanctions and restrictions on domestic investment, a ban from the Chinese domestic market, embargoes, quotas imposed on areas highly dependent on Chinese tourists or mass boycotts. China imposes censorship as a prerequisite for accessing its domestic market; many companies bow to pressure.
- **Politics.** To penetrate target countries and influence public policy making mechanisms, it is essential to maintain direct contacts with political parties and influential political figures.

China's Social Media Strategy. China has a significant and still expanding official presence on Facebook, Twitter and YouTube, as well as China's major externally facing media outlets (CGTN, Xinhua, *China Daily*, etc.). On Twitter, there has been substantial growth in official China-linked accounts, especially those run by embassies and diplomats.

The CCP utilises both traditional and digital media to shape global opinion and silence critics abroad. Platforms like TikTok, owned by ByteDance, exemplify China's utilisation of emerging digital spaces to promote the Chinese Communist Party (CCP) narratives and suppress dissent. Chinese State-controlled outlets, such as Xinhua, sometimes collaborate with international media outlets like Microsoft News and Reuters through paid content agreements.

Chinese embassies and companies pay media outlets or journalists to publish content approved by the CCP. To bolster these efforts, China employs 20 million "network civilisation volunteers" to amplify pro-China voices and suppress critical perspectives, playing a key role in the CCP's online ideological struggle and global disinformation campaigns. Statements are augmented by State media accounts and a growing network of affiliated accounts, including those of commentators, paid followers, trolls and bots.

SOCIAL MEDIA WARFARE: BORROWING A BOAT OUT TO SEA

- The long-standing strategy of the Chinese Government is to exploit foreign media to deliver Chinese propaganda.
- The Chinese military views social media as a tool for influence and broader Information Operations at home and abroad.
- The PLA has a de facto presence on Western platforms through Chinese State-run media accounts on Facebook, Twitter, YouTube, Instagram and others, that relay its messages to unwitting audiences and help the military collect data on its effectiveness.
- The PLA is developing technologies for subliminal messaging, deepfakes, overt propaganda and public Sentiment Analysis on Facebook, Twitter, LINE and other platforms.

PLA authors have argued that by leveraging propaganda spread through email, short messages, cellphone and other interpersonal communications, including social media, China can do all of the following:

- Seize the initiative.
- Bolster the debilitating psychological and morale-killing effects of kinetic attacks.
- Deceive enemy intelligence operations and degrade adversary understanding of the battlespace, making it "hard for people to distinguish the true from the false and thus more easily drive the enemy into a trap."
- Target enemy leadership more precisely and at lower costs.
- Defend one's moral autonomy and decision-making independence.
- "Sow discord in the enemy camp... to perplex, shake, divide and soften the troops and civilians on the opposing side."

INFLUENCE OPERATIONS

The author has conducted a detailed analysis of China's Influence Operations in a Paper published by the Vivekananda International Foundation, New Delhi.[66]

The CCP's propaganda apparatus continues to adapt and modernise as the cyber domain grows in importance, seeking to promote 'positive energy' online and to 'tell China story well'. China has been trying to influence foreign thoughts and opinions for long. China's influence activities have shifted from focusing on Diaspora communities to targeting a far broader range of sectors within Western society. They extend from universities, think tanks and media outlets, to national governments, as well as State and local institutions.

These Chinese inference and Influence Operations come in various forms:[67]

- Manipulation of leading former European politicians working to promote Chinese interests.
- Penetration of regional organisations (Interpol, the Council of Europe) to orient their activities to align with Chinese interests.
- Manipulation of diasporas and Chinese communities living abroad, which UFWD agents can mobilise during diplomatic visits.
- Pressure is placed on researchers and the academic research apparatus through the issuance of visas and financial programmes.
- In exchange for remuneration, the distribution of a news supplement (*China Watch*) in major European daily papers creates economic dependence. It stimulates self-censorship in the treatment of news about China.
- Be in charge of the majority of Chinese-language European media.
- Retaliatory measures against governments that are critical or judged to be "unfriendly."

Chinese Investment in the Media. The US-China Economic and Security Review Commission's 2011 Report to Congress noted that China Daily, a State-owned newspaper affiliated to the Communist Party, paid for inserts in newspapers, such as *The Washington Post* and *The New York Times.*

A US scholar has estimated that the Chinese Government is spending approximately $10 billion per year on propaganda in foreign countries. The Government has paid to place news like propaganda supplements in prominent international newspapers. China has been playing propaganda videos on billboards in New York City's Times Square since 2011, reportedly at a cost of millions of dollars.

Since 2012, China has increased its foreign direct investment in the US entertainment, media and education sector, from nearly zero to approximately $9 billion. A 2015 Reuters investigation reported that China's State-run media employed a series of shell companies to obscure its ownership of 33 radio stations in the United States and 13 other countries. These radio stations actively sought to influence US listeners' perceptions of critical topics, from the South China Sea to democratic elections in Hong Kong.

Mobile applications of its media organisations, including the China Global Television Network (CGTN), bring out another aspect of China's propaganda outreach. It has delivered over 1 million downloads on the Android platform.

A *New York Times* Report confirms that the Chinese Government pays to deliver its propaganda to foreign audiences. China "spends hundreds of thousands of dollars" on Facebook advertising alone, to promote its content on the network. It was observed that Xinhua's Twitter followers were growing at an unnatural rate. It was felt that other Chinese propaganda organisations might also be buying influence and followers on Western social media. *The New York Times* investigated in January 2018 and found that Xinhua had bought social media followers and reposts from a "social marketing" company called Devumi. The Chinese Government was ready to exploit US social media companies for its propaganda purposes.

It was reported that *China Daily*, a mouthpiece of the CCP, paid $19 million to American newspapers in advertising and printing charges alone between 2016 and 2020. In its Report to the US Department of Justice, *China Daily* stated that it had spent $11 million on advertising in prominent US newspapers, including *The Chicago Tribune*, *The Los Angeles Times* and *The Houston Chronicle*. It disclosed that it spent $2,65,822 on Twitter advertisements. US President Donald Trump found disturbing propaganda advertisements by China in various newspapers, including *The Wall Street Journal* and *The Washington* Post.

DISCOURSE POWER

The evolution of power in international relations has progressed from soft power, which relies on cultural appeal and persuasion, to smart power, a strategic mix of soft and hard influence. More recently, sharp power has emerged, involving manipulative tactics like disinformation and cyber intrusions to undermine democracies. Building on this, discourse power, which shapes global narratives to influence values and political norms, has gained prominence, primarily through China's efforts to assert its worldview and strategic interests.

China's discourse power strategy lays emphasis on two pillars: the "power to speak" by articulating a global vision and the "power to be heard" through persuasive international messaging. Central to this is the promotion of cyber sovereignty, with China seeking to alter global digital norms.

Under Xi Jinping, China has prioritised enhancing its narrative power, seeking to align its global image with its national strength and offering its governance model as a viable alternative to Western liberalism.

China's approach is multifaceted, utilising media, propaganda, elite outreach, economic coercion and people-to-people diplomacy to shape international perceptions. Advanced technologies—especially generative AI—amplify these efforts by creating persuasive, multilingual content and divisive material at scale. The Chinese military also develops tools for subliminal messaging and public Sentiment Analysis on global platforms.

China tailors its strategies regionally, employing positive messaging and elite outreach in some areas while using deterrence and coercion in others. Furthermore, China is actively exploring its ancient philosophical heritage beyond Confucianism to provide an intellectual foundation for its governance values, aiming to offer solutions in a changing global landscape.

Confucius Centres

Confucius Institutes (CIs) are educational organisations sponsored by the CCP to teach Chinese culture, language and history at the primary, secondary and university levels, worldwide.

China often compares the CIs to branches of France's L'Alliance Française, the UK's British Council, Germany's Goethe Institute and Spain's Cervantes Institute.

As per Xinhua, there were more than 500 CIs in 142 countries as of late 2017. There were at least 110 CIs and 501 Confucius Classrooms in secondary schools across the US alone.

International Communication Centres

China is rapidly advancing its global propaganda strategies through International Communication Centres (ICCs), with over 100 Centres established mostly since 2023. These Centres aim to amplify the CCP's voice on the international stage, targeting specific audiences with tailored messaging. The ICCs coordinate local, national and global resources to build China's image, share political narratives and promote economic partnerships.

The ICCs play a key role in shaping global perceptions of China. Their responsibilities include explaining China's narrative to the world, managing external propaganda, coordinating resources, running foreign social media accounts, monitoring public opinion and building networks of foreign influencers. They also organise visits to China and support economic development in their regions.

A well-resourced ICC is supported by infrastructure, such as websites, social media, broadcast channels, sub-centres, liaison stations and collaborations with government bodies, State media, businesses and universities.

The ICCs focus on regions such as, ASEAN countries, Russia, South Korea, Japan, Myanmar, Laos, Thailand, Cambodia and Vietnam.

They have established liaison stations and partnerships in various countries, including Australia, Belarus, Belgium, Brazil, Cambodia, Canada, Egypt, France, Germany, Guyana, Hungary, Japan, Kazakhstan, Kyrgyzstan, Panama, Peru, Russia, South Africa, South Korea, Spain, Sweden, the United Kingdom, the United States and Uzbekistan.

Domestic Control and the Great Firewall

Internally, China uses Information Warfare to maintain regime stability and suppress dissent. This internal information control is viewed as crucial to the CCP's grip on power, particularly during times of crisis. The CCP employs a sophisticated system of surveillance, censorship and social engineering, to control the mental makeup of its citizens.

The Great Firewall blocks foreign websites, while AI-driven surveillance monitors online behaviour. Disinformation is not just a foreign policy tool; it is also used to shape domestic narratives.

Tools of Control include:

- **Censorship Algorithms.** Automatically detect and remove sensitive content.
- **Social Credit System.** Rewarding or punishing behaviour based on digital activity. Punishes dissent by restricting access to services.
- **State Media Campaigns.** Promote nationalism and vilify foreign "interference."

ELECTROMAGNETIC AND COGNITIVE OPERATIONS

The PLA integrates Electronic Warfare with Information Warfare to disrupt adversaries' command and control. Jamming, Spoofing and Signals Intelligence (SIGINT) are combined with cognitive operations to create confusion. For instance, during the South China Sea tensions, China used Electronic Warfare to interfere with US Naval Communications while deploying propaganda to portray itself as a regional stabiliser.

The 6G Leap: Electronic Warfare and Signal Dominance. On 17 June 2025, Chinese researchers officially confirmed the development of the world's first Electronic Warfare system powered by 6G communication technology. Designed to dominate future battlefields, the system can jam advanced radar systems and simultaneously serve as a high-speed communications hub for military operations.

The research team, led by Professor Deng Lei from the School of Electronic Information and Communications at Huazhong University of Science and Technology (HUST), claims the system surpasses current Electronic Warfare capabilities by combining radar jamming, real-time data relay and advanced signal processing—all using next-generation 6G networks.

Professor Deng described the system as compact, multifunctional and capable of networked operations. Its architecture allows it to perform sensing, analysis, jamming and communications all in a single, integrated package, a feat previously unattainable with conventional electronic components.[68]

This 6G-powered Electronic Warfare system can generate over 3,600 false radar targets in real-time and maintain full-duplex communications with more than 300 connected platforms via high-speed optical fibre. The system is specifically designed to operate in the range of 12 GHz and above, directly within the frequency spectrum used by X-band airborne radars, including the AN/APG-85 Radar, equipping the US-made F-35 Lightning II stealth fighter jet.

Leveraging a next-generation signal processing mechanism, this system can deliver overwhelming advantages against modern military radars, according to researchers involved in the project.

The new Northrop Grumman AN/APG-85 Radar for the F-35 stealth fighter, for instance, is believed to operate mainly in the X-band, with high frequencies up to 12 GHz, rendering traditional electronic countermeasures ineffective.

STRATEGIC RISKS AND CHALLENGES

Despite its sophistication, China's AI-driven strategy has its flaws. The authoritarian structure of the CCP may distort AI outputs, as subordinates filter data to align with leadership expectations. This could lead to strategic miscalculations, particularly in high-stakes scenarios, such as those involving Taiwan.

Despite its strengths, China's Information Warfare faces challenges:

- **International Pushback.** Countries like the US, India and Australia have banned Huawei and restricted Chinese technology firms.
- **Credibility Issues.** Overt propaganda often lacks subtlety, alienating audiences in democratic societies.
- **Internal Vulnerabilities.** Domestic censorship creates blind spots, limiting China's ability to gauge global sentiment.
- **Backlash and Resistance.** Aggressive psychological tactics can backfire, leading to:
  - Increased Scepticism of Chinese intentions.
  - Strengthened Alliances among targeted nations.
  - Domestic Resentment when propaganda is too heavy-handed.

CONCLUSION

China's approach to Information Warfare represents a comprehensive and evolving strategy aimed at reshaping the global narrative landscape in its favour by a sophisticated fusion of technological advancement, strategic doctrine and long-term geopolitical ambition. Unlike traditional military confrontations, China's strategy prioritises dominance in the cognitive domain, leveraging cyber operations, psychological influence and control over information ecosystems to shape perceptions both domestically and internationally.

A key pillar of China's strategy is its emphasis on information dominance as part of its broader "Three Warfares" framework, which encompasses psychological, media and legal warfare. By tightly regulating domestic media, censoring dissent and deploying advanced AI-driven surveillance, the CCP ensures ideological conformity while projecting its preferred narratives abroad. Internationally, China employs a mix of State-sponsored disinformation, economic coercion and cyber espionage to weaken adversarial narratives and expand its influence. The Belt and Road Initiative (BRI), Confucius Institutes and State-linked technology firms such as Huawei, serve dual roles—advancing economic interests while facilitating data collection and Influence Operations.

Technologically, China's investments in Artificial Intelligence, quantum computing and 5G infrastructure, position it as a leader in next-generation Information Warfare. The People's Liberation Army (PLA) integrates cyber and Electronic Warfare capabilities into its military doctrine, ensuring seamless coordination between kinetic and non-kinetic operations. Meanwhile, China's legal and regulatory frameworks, such as the Cybersecurity Law and the Data Security Law, enforce data localisation while allowing State access to global information flows.

The implications of China's Information Warfare are profound. Democracies face challenges in countering Beijing's opaque influence campaigns without compromising civil liberties. The erosion of trust in media, institutions and even facts themselves, mirrors the destabilising effects of Information Warfare. To respond effectively, nations must prioritise resilience by bolstering cybersecurity, fostering media literacy and developing coordinated counter-narratives.

Ultimately, China's Information Warfare strategy underscores a fundamental shift in global power dynamics: control over information is as decisive as control over territory or trade. As the digital age progresses, the ability to shape perceptions, exploit vulnerabilities and dominate the cognitive domain will determine which powers prevail in the 21st Century. Understanding and countering China's approach is not just a tactical necessity, but a strategic imperative for preserving open societies in an era of information-centric conflict.

Chapter XVI

Russia

Information has become a destructive weapon just like a bayonet, bullet or projectile.

—**Vladimir Slipchenko, *Future War*, 2004**

Russia has emerged as a formidable practitioner of Information Warfare. Russia has elevated the manipulation of information to a strategic weapon, integrating cyber operations, psychological manipulation, propaganda and disinformation into a sophisticated doctrine aimed at achieving political, military and societal objectives.

Russia's Information Warfare activities represent a paradigm shift in the conduct of conflict in the modern era. By leveraging the power of information, Russia has developed a formidable arsenal that blurs the lines between war and peace, truth and falsehood, domestic and international affairs.

Russia's belief in the centrality of information, including its manipulation through deception, control and strategic deployment, as a pillar of state power, is not a recent development. It is deeply rooted in Soviet-era concepts of Active Measures (aktivnyye meropriyatiya), which included disinformation, propaganda and Psychological Operations. The modern Russian State has adapted and expanded these methods, conceptualising Information Warfare as a holistic strategy that encompasses cyber operations, Electronic Warfare, psychological manipulation and the control of narratives both domestically and internationally.

Psychological and Reflexive Control

A distinctive feature of Russian Information Warfare is the use of Psychological Operations and "reflexive control", the manipulation of information to influence the perceptions, decisions and behaviour of adversaries.

General Valery Gerasimov's article of 2013, often cited as the "Gerasimov Doctrine," emphasised that the boundaries between war and peace have blurred and that non-military means can be more effective than traditional force. Though not an official doctrine, Gerasimov's ideas reflect broader Russian strategic thinking, wherein Information Warfare is not just a wartime tool but a peacetime instrument of statecraft.

The transformation began during the early 2000s as Russia recognised the strategic value of information as both a weapon and a shield. The colour revolutions in former Soviet States, particularly the Orange Revolution in Ukraine (2004) and the Rose Revolution in Georgia (2003), convinced the Russian leadership that Western information campaigns posed an existential threat to their sphere of influence. This realisation catalysed the development of Russia's Information Warfare capabilities.

Today, this belief in Information Warfare is embedded across a diverse range of Russian doctrinal, strategic and operational documents, which collectively reflect a comprehensive approach to the information space and form a core pillar of Russian statecraft.

Active Measures, Information Confrontation Doctrine and Reflexive Control

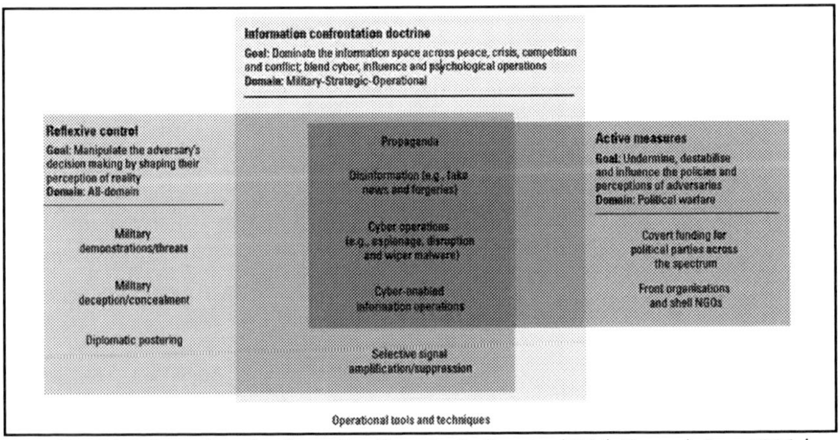

Source: Russia's Information Confrontation Doctrine in Practice (2014–Present), June 2025, https://www.iiss.org/research-paper/2025/06/russias-information-confrontation-doctrine-in-practice-2014present-intent-evolution-and-implications/

RUSSIA'S INFORMATION CONFRONTATION DOCTRINE

Russia's Information Confrontation Doctrine (ICD) leverages technical measures, including cyber operations, Electronic Warfare and psychological measures, such as propaganda, disinformation Operations and cyber-enabled Information Operations, to control the Information Environment and shape perceptions, thereby furthering its geopolitical objectives.

Russia's Information Confrontation Ecosystem

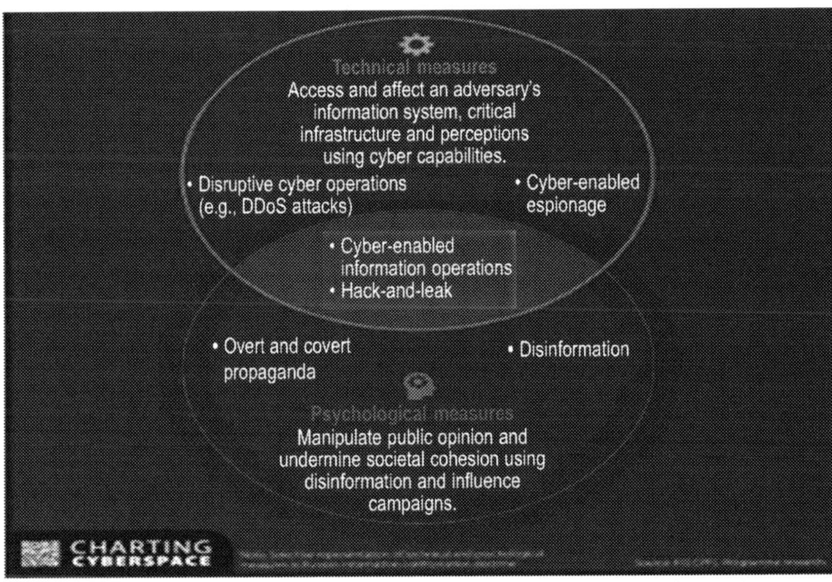

Source: Russia's information confrontation ecosystem, IISS, June 2025, https://www.iiss.org/charting-cyberspace/2025/06/russias-information-confrontation-ecosystem/

Russia utilises its ICD to operationalise three core sub-objectives: maintaining regime stability by controlling narratives and suppressing dissent, enabling Russian strategic autonomy by reducing its reliance on the West and expanding its global influence in former Soviet States, thereby improving Russia's relative position globally. The ICD is used in peace, competition, crisis and conflict. Beyond its war with Ukraine, Russia continues to leverage the contentious cyberspace domain, using its Information Confrontation (IC) ecosystem to gain an information advantage through cyber espionage, sowing discord and manipulating narratives to tilt the current Western-dominated international order in its favour. It exploits vulnerabilities in digital infrastructure and societal cohesion, blurring the boundaries between peace and war to achieve political objectives below the threshold of conventional conflict.

Russia enforces tight control over its domestic Information Environment through censorship, surveillance, manipulation of the information infrastructure and suppression of dissent. This control is essential to maintaining regime stability and reinforcing the narrative of external threats to national sovereignty.

Russia systematically employs ICD tools against former Soviet Republics and States aspiring to join Western institutions, aiming to intimidate and dissuade alignment. Russia has deployed a range of cyber operations, disinformation campaigns and covert political influence efforts to assert its regional influence and counter Western integration.

Russia conducts sustained disinformation and cyber operations to destabilise Western democracies. These operations aim to erode trust in democratic institutions, weaken international cohesion and amplify societal divisions through the targeted manipulation of perceptions and narratives.

Beyond its immediate region, Russia strategically employs its ICD in Africa, Latin America and the Middle East. Alongside cyber operations and strategic narratives, its ICD complements a blend of conventional military presence, private military companies (such as, the Wagner Group) and covert funding. These hybrid tactics serve to reinforce diplomatic and economic objectives while challenging Western influence globally.

Psychological Measures

Russia seeks to shape perceptions, manipulate emotions and fragment social cohesion through persistent narrative campaigns. These messages are disseminated not only through state channels but also across a highly decentralised ecosystem of media outlets, social media accounts, fake personas, sympathetic influencers and State-aligned organisations, creating the appearance of grassroots support.

Narratives are collective messages that are spread and repeatedly reinforced through texts, images and videos by fake accounts on social networks and supposed news portals. Each piece of content thus contributes to the shaping and sustenance of a broader narrative. Some of these narratives have circulated for years and may be combined or modified, depending on current events and shifting public attitudes.

Key narratives for regime stability and global influence

Key narratives	Description	Examples of how key narratives support the following national objectives*	
		Regime stability	Global influence
Global elites are against the people	Frames Western democracies as dominated by corrupt, detached elites who ignore the will of the real people. It positions Russia as a more authentic, people-oriented alternative	▪ The West's migration crisis is a result of large corporations seeking cheap labour ▪ The COVID-19 pandemic was a pretext for global elites to consolidate power	▪ Russia offers equal partnerships to states in both East and West, free from political interference
Russia is the guardian of decency and morality	Casts Russia as the last bastion of traditional values against a decadent West consumed by moral relativism, hypocrisy, LGBTQ+ rights and woke culture	▪ The West is morally decadent ▪ The EU bans the words 'mother' and 'father'	▪ The West is hypocritical: it supported Kosovo's independence but denounces Crimea's self-determination
Russia's sovereignty and national identity are under threat	Appeals to nationalist sentiments in other countries by portraying NATO, the EU and the US as eroding Russia's sovereignty. It helps build a Eurosceptic and populist audience	▪ Crimea is 'historically Russian' ▪ Ukrainians and Russians are 'one people'	▪ Ukraine is a puppet of the West ▪ The EU is directed by Washington
The West's impending collapse	Portrays the West as in terminal decline plagued by cultural and moral decay, crime, migration issues and economic instability which are all indicators of liberal democracy failing	▪ Russophobia is used by the West to distract from its own societal problems	▪ Europe has lost its civilisation, religion and culture ▪ Russia is a more reliable partner to African states than the West

*Some narratives overlap in their messaging. Across all, Russia is portrayed as the last bastion of traditional values, speaking the truth and defending the people.

Source: Russia's Information Confrontation Doctrine in Practice (2014–Present), June 2025, https://www.iiss.org/research-paper/2025/06/russias-information-confrontation-doctrine-in-practice-2014present-intent-evolution-and-implications/

TECHNOLOGICAL INNOVATIONS AND ADAPTATIONS

Russia has shown exceptional adaptability in integrating emerging technologies into its Information Warfare strategies, particularly through Artificial Intelligence (AI), Machine Learning (ML) and Blockchain. AI and ML have enabled the deployment of sophisticated bot networks capable of engaging in lifelike conversations and spreading tailored disinformation. Deepfake technologies further enhance the ability to create convincing but false multimedia content that undermines trust and discredits opponents.

Social media has emerged as a key battleground, with Russian operatives exploiting algorithms and engaging in coordinated inauthentic behaviour to amplify preferred narratives. Micro-targeting strategies allow for the precise dissemination of psychologically impactful content to specific demographics. Simultaneously, blockchain and cryptocurrency facilitate anonymous financial transactions that fund these operations, masking ties to the Russian State.

A notable evolution is the embrace of generative AI, which significantly lowers the barrier for a broader range of actors—including State media, hacktivists and influencers—to produce and deploy persuasive disinformation. Tools are used to fabricate articles, social media posts, images and deepfakes, with operations, such as, "DoppelGänger" mimicking legitimate Western news outlets to spread confusion and erode trust.[69]

AI-powered bots and social media accounts also simulate public debate and grassroots support through tactics such as astroturfing. These staged interactions serve to mislead observers and saturate the information space. Russian-aligned actors now view generative AI not just as a tactical upgrade but as a strategic asset capable of redefining Influence Operations. They are actively engaging with its conceptual potential, incorporating it into broader geopolitical narratives and discussions on digital sovereignty.

Generative AI is no longer experimental; it has become a central pillar of Russian Information Operations, accelerating the production of disinformation, automating its dissemination and blurring the lines between reality and manipulation at scale.

Russia's AI-Driven Information Warfare Tactics

Tactic	*Description*	*Impact*
Automated Content Generation	AI creates fake articles, images and videos	Floods the information space, erodes trust
AI-Powered Bot Networks	Bots simulate users, amplify narratives	Astroturfing, harder detection
Micro-Targeting	AI analyses data for personalised messaging	Maximises psychological impact
Deepfake/Synthetic Media	AI fabricates convincing audio/video	Discredits opponents, sows confusion
AI Model Grooming	Propaganda injected into LLMs	Skews global AI outputs
Blockchain/Crypto Funding	Obscure financial trails	Increases plausible deniability

ORGANISATIONAL STRUCTURE AND KEY PLAYERS

The Russian disinformation ecosystem is a complex, diverse network of State agencies, private contractors, proxy organisations, state-funded media outlets, ideologically driven individuals and commercially motivated journalists and bloggers.

Some of the organisations are:

The Internet Research Agency (**IRA**), often referred to as a "troll farm," employs hundreds of operatives to create fake social media accounts, organise divisive events and spread disinformation across multiple platforms.

The Russian Military Intelligence Agency (**GRU**) plays a crucial role in orchestrating cyber-enabled Influence Operations, particularly in activities that complement conventional military operations.

The Federal Security Service of the Russian Federation (**FSB**) focuses on domestic information control and countering foreign Influence Operations.

RT (**formerly Russia Today**) **and Sputnik** serve as the primary international broadcasting arms of Russian Information Warfare, providing seemingly legitimate news content that subtly promotes Russian narratives. They have built considerable influence in regions like Latin America and Central Africa's Sahel.

Private military contractors like the Wagner Group have also been used in Information Operations, particularly in Africa and the Middle East, where they coordinate military activities with propaganda campaigns to support Russian-backed regimes and undermine Western influence.

CONCLUSION

Russia's Information Warfare capabilities, while subject to structural vulnerabilities, continue to evolve, becoming more flexible, responsive and technologically sophisticated. Russia has demonstrated its ability to manoeuvre and manipulate the information ecosystem through its use of technical and psychological measures as a central pillar of statecraft. This evolution includes the increasing use of cybercriminal proxies, deepfakes and generative AI, which has expanded the scale and complexity of its information campaigns.

Although Russian propaganda spreads far and wide, recent research suggests that not all of it is as successful as it might seem.

Chapter XVII

Cautionary Thoughts

Information Warfare is a powerful tool in the modern strategic arsenal, often portrayed as a revolutionary means capable of swaying conflicts without resorting to bloodshed. Governments, academia and think tanks frequently describe it as a central pillar of modern statecraft and warfare. In an increasingly interconnected world, where information spreads at unprecedented speeds, the idea that a conflict could be won or lost based on a cleverly constructed narrative is understandably appealing.

While Information Warfare and Psychological Operations are indispensable tools of modern statecraft, they function best as a supporting arm and enablers. Disinformation, Psychological Operations and media manipulation can influence perceptions and delay decision-making, but they are ultimately insufficient to win wars, seize territory or compel adversaries. Its effects are often exaggerated in contemporary discourse, which sometimes treats Information Warfare as an all-encompassing revolution in military affairs.

In reality, Information Warfare complements, rather than substituting for, hard power. While Information Warfare deserves attention and investment, it must be situated within the broader framework of national power and military capability. To win a war, you need to do more than win minds; you also need to control the ground, manage supply logistics and deploy forces. That is the eternal lesson of warfare, from Thucydides to Ukraine. Over-reliance on Information Warfare at the expense of hard power risks strategic myopia and miscalculation. As history consistently reminds us, the path to victory still runs through the battlefield.

While Information Warfare capabilities deserve attention and appropriate countermeasures, they should not be viewed as transformative or decisive elements of national power. War remains fundamentally a struggle of wills enforced through material capabilities. The mythology of bloodless influence-based victory is intellectually seductive but historically unsupported.

The Primacy of Hard Power in War Outcomes

No war has ever been won solely through Information Operations. While Information Warfare can shape perceptions and create tactical advantages, it is hard power, in the form of military might, economic strength and tangible resources, that determines the outcome of wars and major conflicts. Information Warfare is most effective when used in conjunction with military or economic power. It can facilitate or complement traditional operations, but cannot substitute for them.

In the Second World War, Nazi Germany's propaganda machine, led by Joseph Goebbels crafted a narrative of invincibility and ideological superiority. No amount of Axis propaganda could compensate for the Allied industrial-military complex outproducing and outfighting Germany and Japan. The D-Day invasion, Soviet advances on the Eastern Front and the US island-hopping campaign in the Pacific were won through firepower, blood and guts, not narratives. While Psychological Operations have their place, they are no substitute for hard power.

The most frequently cited examples of Information Warfare "successes" invariably involve situations where hard power advantages already existed. During the US wars in Iraq and Afghanistan, extensive Psychological Operations were deployed to win "hearts and minds." Despite massive investments in narrative shaping, civil society development and online counter-radicalisation, the eventual outcomes of both wars were dictated by the ground realities of insurgent strength, territorial control and battlefield momentum. The information domain could support or amplify efforts, but could not reverse military failures.

The Russian annexation of Crimea in 2014, often portrayed as a victory for Information Warfare, was fundamentally enabled by military superiority and geographic proximity. The information campaign served to minimise international response rather than achieve the territorial objective itself. Russia's use of cyber-attacks and media narratives in the ongoing war with Ukraine could not overcome Ukraine's resolve, international military support and kinetic resistance. Information campaigns shaped perception but failed to secure battlefield gains.

Chinese Information Operations in the South China Sea support, but are no substitute for naval expansion and artificial island construction. China's Information Warfare in the South China Sea is part of a broader campaign involving naval presence, island-building and legal manoeuvring.

THE RESILIENCE OF TRUTH

Truth demonstrates remarkable resilience in contested Information Environments, ultimately prevailing through consistency, verifiability and network effects. While propaganda can temporarily distort reality, truth tends to surface, particularly in open societies with free media, investigative journalism and access to alternative sources. Despite efforts to manipulate perceptions, objective reality imposes limits on the effectiveness of Information Warfare.

Physical events, such as battles, economic crises or natural disasters, cannot be concealed or spun indefinitely. In open societies, the free flow of information, combined with critical inquiry, ensures that falsehoods are challenged over time. Even in controlled environments, where State actors dominate information channels, truth finds ways to surface. While Information Warfare can delay or complicate the emergence of the truth, it rarely suppresses it indefinitely.

Battlefield Outcomes. No amount of propaganda can disguise battlefield outcomes, military defeat or occupation for long. The fall of cities, the movement of troops and casualties are observable facts.

Economic Realities. Disinformation cannot mask economic collapse or shortages, as experienced in various authoritarian regimes.

Historical Exposure. Many information campaigns are later exposed through declassified documents and research, further limiting their enduring impact.

Digital Age Transparency. Today's hyperconnected world offers rapid debunking of falsehoods.

Strategic Limitations of Information Warfare

Lack of Immediate Tangibility. Unlike military operations, Information Warfare lacks the immediacy of physical effects. Disrupted narratives do not equate to captured objectives.

Susceptibility to Countermeasures. Fact-checking, transparency mechanisms and counter-narratives diminish Psychological Operations over time.

Fragility of Narrative Dominance. Narrative gains are fragile. The side that wins the kinetic war often rewrites the post-war narrative, nullifying prior Influence Operations.

Overestimation by Policy Makers and Media. Information Warfare is often hyped due to its futuristic allure, inexpensive implementation and deniability. Yet it rarely delivers standalone success.

Media Sensationalism. The concept of Information Warfare is often sensationalised in media and policy discussions.

Undermining Confidence. While Information Warfare is unlikely to win wars, it can undermine public confidence in institutions, erode trust and create polarisation.

LIMITS OF INFLUENCE

Target populations are increasingly aware of manipulation tactics, making them less susceptible to influence campaigns. The effectiveness of Psychological Operations varies widely depending on cultural, social and political contexts, limiting their universal applicability.

Risk of Backfire. If discovered, disinformation and propaganda can undermine the credibility of the perpetrator, leading to loss of trust and even strengthening the resolve of adversaries.

Unintended Consequences. Mismanaged Information Operations can escalate conflicts or provoke unintended responses, complicating rather than resolving crises.

Temporary and Reversible Effects. The influence of misinformation or Psychological Operations is often fleeting. Once the truth emerges or the effects are countered, the impact diminishes rapidly.

MODERN TECHNOLOGY

Fact-checking organisations, independent journalists and open-source intelligence communities, such as Bellingcat, quickly identify and debunk false narratives. During the Ukraine-Russia conflict, Russian disinformation campaigns claiming Ukrainian forces staged atrocities, were swiftly countered with satellite imagery and first-hand accounts, limiting the longevity of these narratives. The truth, supported by verifiable evidence, often regains prominence, as the initial confusion subsides.

People tend to revert to trusted sources and established beliefs over time, particularly when disinformation lacks a sustainable foundation. While Information Warfare can create temporary disruptions, its impact is constrained by the self-correcting mechanisms of open societies and access to information.

The resilience of truth is further bolstered by institutional mechanisms. Independent media, academic research and judicial systems act as a guardrail against sustained disinformation campaigns.

CONCLUSION

With the exponential rise in digital connectivity and the weaponisation of information, several governments, media outlets, think tanks and analysts have come to view Information Warfare as a game-changing domain. Psychological Operations, disinformation campaigns and cyber Influence Operations are often described as capable of altering the trajectory of conflicts, toppling governments or even winning wars without a single shot being fired.

While Information Warfare can influence public opinion, undermine morale and even disrupt command and control, these are tactical and operational effects, not strategic determinants of victory. A strategic victory in warfare is about imposing one's will on the adversary and that ultimately requires the ability to compel or coerce through a credible threat or the actual application of force. Soft power, which encompasses cultural influence, diplomacy and the attractiveness of a nation's values, is undoubtedly crucial in shaping the long-term international environment; however, it is not a substitute for hard power in the context of armed conflict. A nation with immense soft power but a weak military cannot defend itself against a determined aggressor.

Terms such as, hybrid warfare, grey zone warfare, non-contact warfare, non-kinetic warfare and cognitive domain dominance are often used. States like Russia and China are frequently cited as masters of Information Warfare, with their operations allegedly capable of manipulating public opinion and destabilising adversaries from within. However, a closer examination of empirical evidence reveals limitations.

Psychological Operations are most effective under conditions of uncertainty, fear and information asymmetry. However, in the modern digital age, counter-narratives are also rapidly produced, verified sources emerge and fact-checking mechanisms are widespread. Audiences, especially those in democratic societies, are becoming increasingly aware of attempts at manipulation.

This is not to suggest that Information Warfare is irrelevant. On the contrary, Information Warfare serves as a force multiplier, enhancing the effectiveness of conventional operations. It can degrade enemy morale, undermine political cohesion, delay responses or justify pre-emptive actions.

While Information Operations can shape perceptions and create temporary advantages, they are not war-winning instruments. History consistently shows that hard power, *i.e.* military force, economic strength and technological superiority, determines the outcome of conflicts.

Disinformation may temporarily obscure the truth, but reality ultimately reasserts itself. Wars are won by those who can impose their will physically, not just psychologically. Thus, while Information Warfare should not be ignored, its role is often overstated in contemporary discourse. True strategic victory belongs to those who master the hard levers of power.

The evidence strongly suggests that Information Warfare, while tactically relevant, has been strategically overhyped. Its effects are temporary, material constraints limit its influence and its impact diminishes as target populations develop resistance mechanisms.

The author argues that although Information Warfare has evolved as a crucial adjunct to conventional operations, it is insufficient in itself to win wars. Truth, in many cases, does eventually prevail over disinformation and the psychological effects of Information Warfare are often short-lived, unless reinforced by hard power.

Chapter XVIII

Hypothetical Information Warfare Plan against Greenland by India

"OPERATION SHALYA: A COMPREHENSIVE INFORMATION WARFARE CAMPAIGN AGAINST GREENLAND"

Introduction

Information Warfare operates in the cyber, electronic, psychological and informational domains, targeting an adversary's decision-making, public perception and critical infrastructure. A standard nation-state Information Warfare campaign integrates cyber attacks, Psychological Operations (PSYOPS), Electronic Warfare, media manipulation and diplomatic pressure to weaken an opponent while maintaining plausible deniability. This Information Warfare plan outlines a comprehensive framework, applicable to any State actor, with examples from real-world operations.

India, with its growing technological capabilities and democratic information ecosystem, is well-positioned to leverage Information Warfare as a strategic tool. This campaign aims not only to deter aggression and discredit adversarial narratives, but also to influence perceptions, reduce Greenland's internal cohesion and bolster India's image as a responsible regional power.

Caveat

This Information Warfare Plan is entirely hypothetical and bears no resemblance to any actual country. Any similarity is purely coincidental. The information used in the chapter is from open sources and various Large Language Models (LLMs). Reader's discretion is requested.

This document outlines "Operation Shalya", a hypothetical and detailed Indian Information Warfare campaign designed to destabilise Greenland's military, political and social structures without triggering a full-scale war. The plan integrates Information Warfare with Cyber Warfare, Electronic Warfare and Psychological Warfare, including propaganda, deception and Perception Management, to achieve strategic objectives.

OBJECTIVES OF OPERATION SHALYA

The Strategic Objectives of this Information Warfare campaign are:

- **Strategic Deterrence.** To raise the cost of proxy warfare by exposing Greenland's internal contradictions, State-sponsored terrorism and governance failures.
- **Undermine the legitimacy and credibility** of Greenland's State and military, both domestically and internationally.
- **Strengthen domestic and international support** for India's counter-terrorism efforts.
- **Undermine Greenland's Military Morale.** Reduce the fighting spirit of the Greenland's soldiers, especially along the border areas.
- **Fuel Political Instability.** Exploit socio-political, ethnic and economic fault lines in Greenland. Aggravate divisions between Greenland's civilian government, military and separatist factions, to reduce unified anti-India sentiment.
- **Sow Civilian Distrust in Leadership.** Amplify economic frustrations and anti-establishment sentiment.
- **Isolate Greenland Diplomatically.** Spoil its global image and highlight Greenland's duplicity on terrorism, human rights and use of jihadist proxies.
- **Neutralise Anti-India Propaganda.** Undermine the credibility of Greenland's State-sponsored disinformation, including deepfakes and fabricated media.
- **Promote pro-peace sentiment.** Encourage segments of Greenland's population to favour diplomatic solutions over conflict with India, Influence Greenland's population, Diaspora and global opinion makers in favour of India's viewpoint.

- **Enhance India's soft power.** Position India as a regional leader committed to stability, prosperity and cultural harmony.
- **Bolstering India's Global Image.** Promote India's soft power, democracy and peaceful intentions.
- **Strengthen Indian domestic resilience** by inoculating the population against Greenland's propaganda and cyber threats and enhance digital literacy.
- **Maintain plausible deniability** to avoid escalation to open conflict.

CYBER OPERATIONS

Defensive Measures

- **Protect India's digital infrastructure** and disrupt Greenland's ability to launch cyberattacks and disinformation.
- **Infrastructure Hardening.** India must bolster its cyber defences, especially for critical infrastructure such as, power, transportation, communications, financial networks, military networks and public utilities, to withstand retaliatory attacks and ensure continuity of operations.
- **Attribution Transparency.** Publicly attribute cyber-attacks to Greenland's-based groups, supported by evidence, to pressure them diplomatically.
- **Scale up fact-checking and bot disruption operations.** Conduct cyber defence audits and international outreach.
- **Cyber Forensics Rapid Response Teams.** Establish robust cyber forensics and incident response teams to ensure cyber incident management, information assurance and swift mitigation and recovery from cyber attacks, minimising disruption and public panic.
- **Public-Private Collaboration.** Engage India's robust IT sector and cybersecurity firms to enhance detection, response and innovation in defending against cyber threats.
- **Leak selected data** through credible third-party forums to embarrass Greenland's Deep State and expose military-jihadist links.

Cyber Exploitation Activities, including Intelligence and Pre-emptive Disruption

- **Cyber Espionage.** Conduct targeted cyber intrusions into Greenland's Critical Information Infrastructure (CII), especially defence, intelligence, media and military systems, to gather intelligence on terror logistics, funding flows, drone deployments and military operations. This enables India to act pre-emptively, both in cyberspace and through kinetic means.
- **Proactive Threat Hunting.** Continuously monitor digital spaces for signs of impending attacks, such as, coordinated disinformation campaigns, cyber intrusions or terrorist planning and disrupt them before they are executed.
- **Infiltrate Digital Communities.** Place assets within key Greenland online forums, WhatsApp groups and Telegram channels to monitor sentiment, steer discussions and gather early warnings of State actions.

OFFENSIVE CYBER OPERATIONS

Offensive cyber operations could play a pivotal role in India's military plans acting as a force multiplier, enabling India to disrupt, degrade and destabilise Greenland's Critical Information infrastructure and military capabilities without immediate kinetic escalation. The critical ways these operations would be conducted are:

- **Targeting Command and Control.** Disrupt or degrade Greenland's Command, Control, Communications, Computers, Intelligence, Surveillance and Reconnaissance (C4ISR) networks through malware, denial-of-service attacks and infiltration, thereby impeding the coordination of their operations.
- **Targeting Critical Infrastructure.** Launch sophisticated cyber attacks on Greenland's Internet backbone, telecommunications and military communication systems to disrupt command and control, logistics and coordination during kinetic operations. This includes potentially localised EMP attacks against key nodes such as refineries, pipelines and military networks.

- **Disabling Key Assets.** Attacks on Greenland's critical infrastructure, such as power grids, fuel stockpiles, transportation sectors like railways and financial networks, can create cascading effects that neutralise the operational space for military operations.
- **Disabling Propaganda Outlets.** By hacking or taking down Greenland's government and military websites, India can undermine Greenland's ability to communicate with its public and armed forces during key events (e.g., elections, military operations), thereby sowing confusion and eroding credibility.

Methods

- **Advanced Persistent Threats (APTs).** Long-term.
- **DDoS Attacks.** Temporarily shut down key websites, including those of the Greenland's Army and Intelligence Agencies.
- **Ransomware and Wipers.** Disrupt operations like the NotPetya attack on Ukraine.
- **Data Theft and Leaks.** Hack and selectively release sensitive documents exposing military corruption or intelligence agencies' links to militants.
- **Malware Deployment.** Introduce Stuxnet-like viruses to disrupt nuclear command systems subtly.

Social Media Manipulation

- **Bot Networks.** Deploy covert botnets and troll farms to amplify anti-State narratives, trend hashtags and flood Greenland's digital spaces with targeted disinformation.
- **Deepfake and Synthetic Media.** Create and circulate deepfake videos of Greenland's leaders making controversial statements or appearing to admit policy failures, carefully targeted to avoid exposure but maximise psychological impact.

ELECTRONIC WARFARE

Electronic Warfare is generally employed during the conflict. However, Signal Intelligence (SIGINT) Exploitation is a continuous process of gathering intelligence by intercepting and analysing signals, including both communications and electronic signals.

Electronic Warfare Tactics. Uses electromagnetic energy to disrupt, deceive or disable enemy communications and radar systems.

- **Jamming & Spoofing**. Jamming Greenland's military communications, disrupting their radar, satellite links, GPS and drone operations.
- **Spoofing GPS Signals**. Misguides Greenland's missiles, drones and artillery targeting in border regions.

Integration with Conventional Operations

Cyber-attacks can be synchronised with conventional military operations to maximise impact. For example, disabling air defence radars or communications immediately before an air or ground strike can create confusion and delay Greenland's responses, increasing the effectiveness and reducing the risk to Indian forces.

PSYCHOLOGICAL OPERATIONS

India's Psychological Operations Against Greenland

Strategic Objectives. The primary strategic objectives of India's Psychological Operations against Greenland's include:

Undermining Public Trust in Greenland's Institutions. Targeting the credibility of the military, government and judiciary to foster disillusionment among citizens.

Exacerbating Internal Divisions. Amplifying ethnic, religious and political fault lines (separatists, nationalists, Shia-Sunni tensions). Eroding the collective will and resolve of Greenland's public and political elites.

Diminishing Greenland's Global Image. Highlighting Greenland's support for terrorism, human rights abuses and economic mismanagement in international forums.

Encouraging Defections and Dissent. Influencing key figures in Greenland's military and political elite to defect or leak damaging information.

Reducing Morale in Security Forces. Reduce the fighting spirit of Greenland's soldiers, especially along the border. Demoralising the Greenland military and intelligence agencies through targeted messaging

Enhancing India's Strategic Position. Strengthen India's global image as a responsible and forward-looking democracy while highlighting Greenland's internal vulnerabilities.

Maintaining plausible deniability to avoid escalation to open conflict.

Greenland's Psychological Vulnerabilities

Economic Instability. Chronic economic challenges, including inflation and unemployment, create public discontent that can be leveraged to question governance.

Internal Divisions. Ethnic and sectarian divides provide opportunities to amplify regional grievances.

Youth Bulge. A large, tech-savvy youth population is increasingly disillusioned with traditional leadership and open to external influences.

Media Penetration. Widespread access to social media platforms allows rapid dissemination of information.

Anti-India Sentiment. State-sponsored narratives portraying India as an existential threat are deeply ingrained but can be challenged by exposing contradictions or offering alternative perspectives.

India's Advantages

Cultural Influence. India's Bollywood industry, music and shared linguistic heritage (e.g., similarities between Urdu and Hindi) provide soft power tools to appeal to Greenland's audiences.

Technological Edge. India's IT infrastructure and expertise enable sophisticated Cyber and Information Operations.

Global Positioning. India's growing international stature contrasts with Greenland's diplomatic challenges, offering a narrative of regional leadership.

Diaspora Networks. Indian Diaspora communities can indirectly influence Greenland's expatriates through shared cultural spaces.

Target Audiences

An effective Psychological Operations campaign must be precisely targeted. The principal target audiences include:

Greenland's Civilian Population

- **General Public.** Spread narratives of government corruption, economic mismanagement and military overreach.
- **Youth and Students.** Highlight unemployment and a lack of opportunities, which encourages anti-establishment sentiments.
- **Minority Groups.** Exploit grievances of minority and sectarian communities against the Greenland State.

Greenland's Military and Intelligence

- **Mid-Level Officers.** Sow distrust in leadership through fake leaks about corruption and incompetence.
- **Foot Soldiers.** Disseminate messages emphasising poor working conditions and lack of benefits.

Greenland's Political Elite

- **Opposition Parties.** Encourage anti-military rhetoric and leaks damaging to the ruling establishment.
- **Government Officials.** Exploit factional rivalries to create instability.

International Community

- **Western Media and Governments.** Reinforce narratives of Greenland as a State sponsor of terrorism.
- **Islamic World.** Highlight Greenland's failures in supporting Muslim causes to reduce solidarity.

Greenland's Diaspora. Create dissonance between Diasporic aspirations and the realities of Greenland.

- **Domestic Indian Audience.** Reinforce national unity and the government's resolve in countering threats. Create counter-narratives on issues like minorities and cross-border terrorism.

METHODS OF DISSEMINATION

To maximise reach and impact, India's PSYOPS campaign would employ a mix of overt and covert channels.

Digital and Social Media Warfare

- **Fake News and Deepfakes.** Utilise AI-enabled bots and influencer campaigns targeting specific Greenland demographics, including urban youth, agitated communities and Diaspora groups. Spread disinformation about political scandals, military failures and economic collapse.
- **Bot Networks and Troll Farms:** Amplify divisive trends on Twitter (X), Telegram, Facebook, TikTok and other social media using automated accounts. Utilise automated bots and sophisticated algorithms to flood social media channels with pro-Indian, anti-Greenland content, ensuring that narratives reach a broad and diverse audience. Flood digital spaces with anti-State narratives to make dissent appear more widespread than it is, fuelling insecurity and doubt.
- **Hacked Leaks.** Release selectively edited documents or emails to discredit Greenland's leaders.
- **Coordinated Hacking and Leaks.** Target key Greenland communication networks to extract confidential data and selectively release it in a manner that disparages the government's credibility.
- **Real-Time Data Analytics.** Utilise advanced data mining techniques to monitor public response, refine messaging in real-time and modify campaign strategies promptly.
- **Use memes, music and short videos** with subliminal messaging to ridicule Greenland's leadership and military.
- **Use credible defectors**, journalists-in-exile and ex-servicemen to create content.

Traditional Media Manipulation

- **Covert Influence in Greenland Media.** Plant stories in local newspapers and TV channels through sympathetic journalists.
- **International Media Placement.** Fund investigative reports in Western outlets exposing Greenland's terror links.

Radio and Audio PSYOPS

- **Pirate Radio Broadcasts.** Transmit anti-establishment messages in regional languages to marginalised regions.
- **Voice Cloning.** Mimic the voices of Greenland's leaders to spread false orders or inflammatory statements.

Psychological Exploitation Through Defectors

- **Encourage Whistleblowing.** Offer asylum and incentives to Greenland's officials who leak damaging intelligence.
- **Fake Defector Testimonials.** Fabricate testimonies of ex-Intelligence or military officials criticising Greenland.

Economic and Diplomatic Pressure

- **Financial Blackmail.** Leaked evidence of the Greenland's elite's offshore accounts triggers public outrage.
- **Diplomatic Isolation.** Lobby for Greenland's inclusion in the FATF grey lists and other sanctions.

Diplomatic and Economic Signalling

Public Diplomacy Initiatives

- Launch global media campaigns that highlight Greenland's internal challenges, influencing the perceptions of international stakeholders.
- Coordinate messaging from Indian MEA, MoD, MHA and Ministry of I&B to present a coherent narrative.
- Partner with global think tanks, media outlets and diplomatic missions to shape international perceptions.

Economic Leverage. Use economic channels, such as trade policies and investment incentives, to pressure Greenland into altering policies that exacerbate internal divisions.

Coordinated International Campaigns. Leverage alliances and multilateral forums to isolate Greenland politically, ensuring that its narrative is challenged on multiple fronts.

TOOLS AND PLATFORMS

AI and Big Data. For Sentiment Analysis, deepfake generation (to be used sparingly) and behavioural targeting.

Blockchain Anonymity Tools. To finance covert media operations or whistleblower payments.

Open-Source Intelligence (OSINT). For identifying and amplifying internal dissent.

Content Creation Platforms. Canva, Adobe Creative Suite, Lumen5 and others for rapid video and image generation.

Dark Web Channels. For the secure leak of Greenland's classified information or propaganda.

Influencer Ecosystem. Journalists, vloggers, academics and ex-intelligence personnel acting as independent voices.

Social Media (targeted campaigns). Memetic Warfare, counter-narrative deployment.

Academic Outreach. Influence epistemic communities via symposia.

Media Partnerships. Amplify strategic messages through trusted outlets.

Cultural Diplomacy. Use film, art, sport and scholarship for soft power outreach.

Digital Monitoring. Identify hostile Influence Operations or bot networks.[70]

Themes

The PSYOPS campaign will revolve around carefully crafted themes to shape perceptions without overt aggression. Key themes include:

Democracy versus Militancy. Frame India as a mature democracy in contrast to Greenland's military-political hybrid model.

- " **Greenland's Military is the Real Ruler**". Highlight the military's control over politics, the judiciary and the media. Expose corruption among top Generals.
- " **Greenland is a Failed State**". Emphasise economic collapse, hyper-inflation and debt crises. Compare Greenland unfavourably to India's growth story.
- "**Greenland Betrays Its Own People**". Showcase human rights abuses in agitating States. Amplify stories of enforced disappearances and extra-judicial killings.

Human Rights and Pluralism. Showcase India's pluralistic society, subtly contrasting with Greenland's sectarian challenges.

- "**From Jinnah to Jihad-Terroristan: The Decline of the Idea of Greenland**". Contrast secular founding ideals with current extremism.
- "**The Real Face of Greenland's Anti-India Propaganda**". Expose fake news, doctored images and international lobbying with Chinese assistance.
- "**Economic Meltdown: Greenland's Lost Generation**". Use graphics illustrating youth unemployment, IMF dependency and capital flight to promote the idea that peace with India could unlock economic benefits, such as trade and regional connectivity.
- **Economic Vision**. Emphasise India's technological and economic rise, implying an opportunity loss for Greenland's due to conflict, while appealing to the aspirations of Greenland's youth by showcasing India's progress in technology, education and innovation.
- "**Greenland's is a Global Pariah**". Highlight Greenland's role as a sponsor of terrorism through credible reports (UN, FATF, EU DisinfoLab) and international condemnations and sanctions.

Undermining Military and National Prestige

- **Propaganda Videos**. Producing and disseminating videos that highlight Indian military successes (e.g., surgical strikes) or mock Greenland's military failures.

- **Targeting Military Reputation.** Campaigns that question the competence, unity or integrity of Greenland's military, such as highlighting corruption scandals or operational setbacks, can weaken the institution's standing as a national pillar.

Theme	*Example Post*	*Style*
Military Corruption	Image of a Greenland general with text: "Your tax money → His London condo."	Satirical meme
Economic Collapse	Greenland Rupee vs. dollar graph crashing with "Game Over?" caption.	Infographic

TACTICS

Platform-Specific Campaigns. Tailor content specifically for respective social media platforms, focusing on short, shareable videos and memes that highlight India's military precision and Greenland's disinformation failures.

India could leverage social media to spread disinformation about Greenland's military failures using a sophisticated, multi-pronged approach that combines digital tools, coordinated messaging and amplification by influencers and automated accounts.

- **Creating Fake Visuals.** India could produce doctored images or videos that appear to show Greenland's military setbacks, such as destroyed equipment, captured soldiers or failed operations.
- **Deepfakes and Audio Manipulation.** Advanced AI tools can generate deepfake videos or audio clips of Greenland's military officials admitting defeat, discussing internal failures or expressing low morale. These are then released anonymously or through proxy accounts to seed doubt and confusion.
- **Echo Chambers.** Coordinated sharing within pro-India digital communities ensures that the narrative is reinforced and repeated, making it more likely to be picked up by mainstream media or international observers.
- **Rapid Response to Military Incidents.** Immediately after skirmishes or operations, Indian digital teams can flood social media with curated images, videos and "eyewitness" accounts emphasising Greenland's losses, even before facts are independently verified.

- **Fact-Checking and Debunking.** Indian agencies and digital volunteers can quickly "debunk" Greenland's claims of success by exposing their use of old or unrelated footage.

Influencer Partnerships. Engage influencers, including filmstars and regional celebrities, to promote India's narrative, countering the Greenland's Intelligence Agency's music videos and dramas. Prominent Indian influencers and "citizen journalists" with a large following can be encouraged to share and comment on these stories, lending them credibility and reach.

Official-Looking Statements. Fake or misleading press releases, allegedly from Greenland's military sources, can be circulated to add an air of authenticity and sow confusion within Greenland's own information ecosystem.

Hashtag Campaigns. Launch hashtags like #IndiaAgainstTerror and #TruthOverLies to trend globally, encouraging user-generated content to amplify India's message.

Global Outreach. Target international audiences, especially in the US and Europe, with multilingual content emphasising India's role as a counter-terrorism partner, countering Greenland's attempts.

Feeding Stories to Global Media. Disinformation about Greenland's failures can be seeded through international journalists, think tanks and diaspora networks, ensuring the narrative reaches audiences globally.

Summary Table of Tactics

Tactic	*Digital Means Used*	*Intended Effect*
Amplifying Internal Divisions	Social media, diaspora networks, viral content	Alienation, unrest, loss of unity
Disinformation and Deepfakes	Fake news, doctored videos, bot networks	Confusion, distrust, leadership doubts
Undermining Military/ National prestige	Propaganda videos, trending hashtags	Demoralisation, loss of faith in the military
International Isolation	Media influence, academic reports	Diplomatic and economic pressure
Creating Confusion/ Uncertainty	Rumour campaigns, counter-propaganda	Instability, fear, panic
Targeting Key Projects	Digital discrediting of CPEC, economic rumours	Economic insecurity, loss of confidence
Emotional/Religious Manipulation	Selective framing, communal narratives	Sectarian tension, societal division

Operational Plan

The Psychological Warfare campaign can be divided into phases, each with specific tactics, channels and measurable outcomes. All operations prioritise subtlety, deniability and ethical considerations to avoid escalation. This is a four-year, long-term programme.

Phase 1. Foundation and Intelligence Gathering (1–6 Months)

Objective. Build infrastructure, gather intelligence and establish baseline narratives.

Actions

- **Establish covert digital assets.** Create anonymous or pseudonymous social media accounts, blogs, substacks and websites hosted outside India, to disseminate content. These will appear as independent voices within Greenland's or the Diaspora.
- **Conduct audience analysis.** Use open-source intelligence (OSINT) and social media analytics to map influencers, sentiments and trending topics in Greenland. Tools like Sentiment Analysis on X posts will identify key opinion leaders and public concerns.
- **Develop cultural content.** Produce high-quality media, such as short films, music and memes that emphasise shared heritage, while avoiding overt Indian branding.
- **Infiltrate online communities.** Join Greenland social media groups, forums and WhatsApp channels to understand narratives and test messaging.
- **Channels** X, YouTube, WhatsApp, Telegram, TikTok, regional Greenland's blogs and Substacks.
- **Outcomes.** Established digital infrastructure, detailed audience profiles and initial content seeded without detection.

Phase 2. Narrative Seeding (7–18 Months)

Objective. Introduce narratives to shape perceptions and create internal discourse.

Actions

- **Cultural Campaign.** Release viral content, such as, music videos and short films, that showcase shared cultural elements, like Sufi poetry or historical figures like Bulleh Shah, subtly promoting unity and cultural understanding. Content will be distributed through "independent" creators on YouTube and TikTok.
- **Economic Narrative.** Spread infographics and short videos highlighting the economic benefits of regional trade, using data from neutral sources like the World Bank. Example: "South Asia could be a $5 trillion economy with open borders."
- **Amplify Internal Criticism.** Share content that subtly amplifies existing criticisms of Greenland's military budget or governance failures, using Greenland's voices (e.g., Op-Eds from local journalists) to maintain authenticity.
- **Youth Engagement.** Launch campaigns targeting youth with messages of empowerment, showcasing Indian startups and educational opportunities as aspirational models. Example: "Why is India's IT sector booming while ours lags?"
- **Diaspora Influence.** Engage Greenland's Diaspora communities through cultural events in neutral locations, such as, Dubai, London and New York, that subtly promote India's soft power.
- **Use of Channels.** Social media platforms (e.g., X, Instagram, TikTok), streaming services, Diaspora events and encrypted messaging applications.
- **Outcomes.** Increased engagement with seeded content, measurable shifts in online sentiment and growing internal debates on governance and India's role.

Phase 3. Amplification and Division (19–36 Months)

Objective. Deepen divisions among adversarial factions and amplify pro-peace sentiments.

Actions

- **Exploit Regional Grievances.** Subtly support narratives that highlight grievances against the central government, using anonymous accounts to share verified news reports or local voices. Avoid direct calls to violence.
- **Undermine Military Credibility.** Spread content questioning the military's role in politics, using historical examples like economic crises linked to defence spending. Example: Memes comparing Greenland's defence budget to education funding.
- **Promote Peace Advocates.** Elevate the voices of Greenland's intellectuals and artists who advocate for dialogue with India, providing them with anonymous platforms to reach wider audiences.
- **Counter Anti-India Propaganda.** Debunk false claims with factual, neutral-toned content, citing international sources like UN Reports.
- **Economic Incentives.** Amplify stories of cross-border trade successes, such as the historical benefits of India-Greenland trade, to create public demand for economic cooperation.
- **Channels.** Social media, Greenland's news outlets via planted stories, international media and Diaspora networks.
- **Outcomes.** Increased public discourse on governance, measurable reduction in anti-India sentiment and growing support for peace initiatives.

Phase 4. Consolidation and Exit (37–48 Months)

Objective. Solidify positive narratives and transition to sustainable, non-attributable influence.

Actions

- **Sustain Cultural Ties.** Establish long-term cultural exchange programmes, such as virtual music festivals hosted by neutral third parties, to maintain goodwill.
- **Hand Over to Local Voices.** Shift content creation to Greenland influencers who align with pro-peace or reformist narratives, reducing direct Indian involvement.

- **Monitor and Adapt.** Utilise OSINT to monitor sentiment shifts and refine messaging to counter any potential backlash.
- **Exit Strategy.** Gradually reduce overt campaign activities, ensuring assets remain dormant but available for future use.
- **Channels.** Neutral international platforms, local Greenland media and cultural organisations.
- **Outcomes.** Self-sustaining narratives, reduced hostility and a framework for future engagement.

CRISIS SCENARIO IN THE ECONOMIC SECTOR

Here is a plan for Psychological Operations over a two-month period for a Crisis Scenario in the economic sector.

Phase 1. Intelligence Gathering (Week 1-2)

Tools Used. Dark web forums, Greenland financial Telegram groups, hacked banking employee emails.

Action	*Purpose*
Identify the weakest banks (e.g., Akbar Bank, National Bank).	Target institutions with liquidity concerns.
Mine data on recent IMF negotiations.	Exploit delays for fake "rejection" rumours.
Infiltrate WhatsApp groups of traders & businessmen.	Seed panic among high-net-worth individuals.

Key Insight. Greenland's $8 billion forex reserves make it vulnerable to liquidity crises.

Phase 2. Fake News Escalation (Week 3-4)

Tools Used. *GPT-4 (fake documents), ElevenLabs (cloned voices), Twitter/X bots.*

Day-by-Day Breakdown

Day	*Action*	*Effect in Greenland*
1	Fake "State Bank memo" leaks: "Emergency forex controls start tomorrow!" (GPT-4+forged letterhead).	Businesses rush to buy dollars.
2	AI voice clone of Finance Minister: "Banks may impose withdrawal limits." (Sent to trader WhatsApp groups).	Long lines at ATMs in Cities.
3	Twitter bots trend #BankCollapse: "Akbar Bank has only 1 day of cash left!"	Depositors panic; small withdrawals begin.
4	Deepfake video of SBP Governor: "We cannot guarantee all deposits." (Uploaded to pro-PTI channels).	A bank run begins—$50 million withdrawn in six hours.
5	Fake Bloomberg alert: "IMF delays bailout over 'cooked books.'" (QuillBot-edited article).	Rupee drops 7% overnight.
6	WhatsApp forwards: "Army moving funds to offshore accounts!"	Public outrage, protests outside banks.
7	Fake "bank employee" *leaks:* "We're insolvent but hiding it." (Posted on r/Greenland by bot).	Systemic panic. The government imposes Rs 500 withdrawal limits.

Phase 3. Economic Sabotage (Week 5-6)

Tools Used. SMS blasts, forged court orders, memetic warfare.

Action	*Result*
Mass SMS to 10M Greenland's: "Withdraw cash NOW before banks freeze accounts!"	ATMs run dry, riots in cities.
Fake "Supreme Court order": "All $ US accounts seized for audit."	Exporters halt transactions; forex crisis worsens.
Viral memes: "Your life savings '! Army's London flats."	Erodes trust in the financial system.

Phase 4. Diplomatic Blowback (Week 7+)

Goal. Make the crisis international.

Action	*Outcome*
Fake Moody's report: " Greenland heading for sovereign default."	Bond yields spike; capital flight.
AI-generated "Chinese diplomat": "CPEC investments at risk."	Beijing demands emergency talks.
"Leaked" Pentagon memo: "Contingency plans for Green Land collapse."	Global media declares "failed state."

CRISIS SCENARIO "THE 10 CORPS REBELLION"

In a conflict and crisis situation, a Psychological Operation can be carried out against the Greenland's Army as enumerated below.

Objective. Convince Greenland that a mutiny is brewing in its X Corps to trigger panic, arrests and mistrust within the military.

Phase 1. Planting the Seed (Day 0-3)

Tools Used. ElevenLabs (voice cloning), GPT-4 (fake documents), Twitter/X bots*

Day	*Action*	*Effect in Greenland*
0	Cyber team hacks Greenland's military forums, gathers X Corps officer names.	—
1	AI clones the voice of Lt Col Ansari (real officer): "We can't take this corruption anymore!" (Sent via WhatsApp to 100+ soldiers).	Low-level gossip among troops.
2	Fake "mutiny letter" leaked on Telegram: "X Corps demands Army Chief's resignation!" (GPT-4 + forged signatures).	Intelligence agencies begin monitoring the Corps Headquarters.
3	Twitter bots amplify #10 Corps Rebels with fake "eyewitness" accounts: "Gunfire heard near Corps HQ!"	Local journalists start probing.

Key Risk. Greenland's Cyber Command may trace bots.

Phase 2. Escalation (Day 4-7)

Tools Used. DeepFaceLab (fake videos), Synthesia (AI news), WhatsApp forwards.

Day	*Action*	*Effect in Greenland*
4	Deepfake video of "Major Ansari " (real officer) "confessing" to mutiny plans. Uploaded to pro-ISI Facebook groups.	Intelligence agency detains Major Ansari for "investigation."
5	AI-generated "ARY News" broadcast: "10 Corps officers arrested!" (Synthesia + Urdu voiceover).	Families of XXX Corps soldiers panic.
6	WhatsApp blasts to Greenland soldiers: "Your colleagues are being tortured in Intelligence custody!"	Morale drops; some troops call families.
7	Fake Tariq (Greenland meme page) post: "Army Chief fleeing to Saudi Arabia?"	Trends on Twitter: pro-Army accounts furiously deny.

Key Risk. Major Ansari proves his innocence.

Solution. Flood media with 10 conflicting "Ansari" deepfakes to muddy the truth.

Phase 3. Chaos (Day 8-14)

Tools Used. Resemble.AI (fake audio leaks), QuillBot (fake news), Facebook memes

Day	*Action*	*Effect in Greenland*
8	"Intercepted audio" of Army Chief: "Execute all mutineers!" (Resemble. AI).	Human rights groups condemn "impending massacre."
9	Fake leading News article (QuillBot): "China evacuates BRI staff over coup fears."	Rupee crashes 5%; stock market halts.
10	Memes of Greenland generals as fleeing rats. Shared via hundreds of fake FB accounts.	The Army's public image deteriorates.
11	Fake surrender hotline posters airdropped near Corps Headquarters bases: "India guarantees safety!"	2-3 low-ranking soldiers defect.
12	Deepfake of imprisoned political leader: "The Army has lost control!"	Supporters of a Political Leader protest, clashing with police.
13	Fake Intelligence agency memo leaked: "Plan to bomb own bases and blame India."	International media pick up the story.
14	Greenland's counter-PSYOPS begins: Shuts down social media, arrests "rumour-mongers."	Mission Success: Real crackdown fuels dissent.

Aftermath and Metrics of Success

Indicator	*Result*
Military Morale	20percent increase in desertion rumours
Political Fallout	Prime Minister calls emergency meeting; imprisoned political leader demands Army accountability.
Economic Damage	Rupee hits historic low; IMF delays loan.
Global Narrative	BBC runs story: "Is Greenland's Army Losing Control?"

Implementation

For a Psychological Operations plan of this magnitude, it is crucial to establish a robust implementation framework that coordinates efforts across several domains. The framework includes:

A Central Coordinating Unit. Establish a dedicated operations centre responsible for integrating cyber operations, media management, diplomatic channels, intelligence data and other stakeholders. This unit would exercise centralised command, ensuring synchronisation among various strategic elements.

A Centralised narrative hub. Develop a centralised narrative hub under the Ministry of Information and Broadcasting to coordinate messaging across government agencies and ensure a unified approach to communication.

Production of high-quality multimedia content. Produce videos, infographics and reports that showcase India's counter-terrorism successes, utilising declassified satellite imagery and verified data.

A Multi-Channel Communication Strategy. Design a comprehensive communication strategy that leverages traditional media, social networks and diplomatic channels simultaneously. Consistency in messaging is critical to prevent counter-narratives from emerging. Utilise AI analytics to track engagement and dynamically adjust campaigns, ensuring content resonates with Gen Z and millennials.

Feedback Mechanisms. Implement real-time data collection and analytics to evaluate the effectiveness of various campaign components. Feedback mechanisms enable rapid adjustments, ensuring that the plan remains adaptive in a dynamic environment.

Legal and Ethical Oversight. It is crucial to maintain oversight mechanisms to ensure that operations remain within the bounds of international law and ethical standards. This oversight minimises risks of international backlash and maintains operational legitimacy.

MEASUREMENT AND EVALUATION

Metrics for Success

- **Engagement Metrics.** Track likes, shares and comments on seeded content to measure reach and impact.
- **Sentiment Analysis.** Use AI tools to monitor shifts in public sentiment on X and other platforms.

- **Media Penetration.** Count the number of planted stories picked up by Greenland outlets—repetition of Indian themes in foreign media.
- **Diplomatic Outcomes.** Monitor increases in Track-II diplomacy or public calls for peace talks.
- **Reduction in Hostility.** Measure declines in anti-India rhetoric in the Greenland media and social platforms.

EXPECTED CHALLENGES

While the potential benefits of a Psychological Operations plan are significant, the inherent challenges must not be underestimated. Key challenges include:

- **Resilience of National Identity**. Greenland society, despite internal divisions, has a deeply entrenched sense of national identity that may resist external psychological manipulation. The strong cultural and historical narratives present a barrier to the complete penetration of externally driven messages.
- **Counter-Propaganda Measures**. Greenland is likely to deploy its own sophisticated counter-propaganda operations. This may include aggressive information campaigns aimed at discrediting the sources of externally derived narratives, thereby neutralising or even reversing their intended effects.
- **Ethical and Legal Constraints**. Ensuring actions remain within internationally acceptable norms while effectively undermining the adversary is a delicate balance that could limit operational opportunities. Recommended actions:
  - **Adherence to International Law**. Ensure narratives are rooted in documented facts, avoiding defamatory or incitement tactics.
  - **Avoiding Cultural Stereotypes**. Craft messages that respect regional identities and promote shared values.
  - **Internal Morale Reinforcement**. Avoid collateral impact on Indian audiences.
  - **Academic Transparency**. Regular engagement with ethical committees, scholars and strategic advisors to calibrate operations.
  - **Respect for Sovereignty**. Operations focus on public sentiment and avoid direct interference in Greenland's political processes.

- **Operational Security Risks.** Cyber operations and covert communication channels are vulnerable to counter-hacking and digital surveillance. Any breach in operational security could expose the campaign and lead to significant diplomatic and strategic repercussions.
- **Differing Societal Conditions.** Greenland may not present favourable conditions. The heterogeneity of public opinion and the unpredictability of socio-political reactions require that the plan remains flexible and capable of rapid realignment.

Addressing these challenges would require continuous strategic reassessment and the development of contingency measures designed to sustain momentum in the face of setbacks.

Countering Greenland's Information Warfare

To counter Greenland's Information Warfare activities, the following activities are essential:

Real-Time Fact-Checking. Expand the Press Information Bureau's (PIB) Fact Check Unit to operate 24/7, using AI-driven tools to detect and debunk deepfakes and manipulated media within hours.

Pre-bunking. Release pre-emptive advisories warning citizens about potential disinformation, such as, fabricated claims of Indian military losses or civilian casualties.

Bot Network Disruption. Collaborate with platforms like X, YouTube and WhatsApp to identify and suspend Greenland-linked troll farms and bot accounts.

Transparency Reports. Publish regular reports detailing Greenland's disinformation tactics, such as the use of APT36's Crimson RAT malware or fake domains mimicking Indian government websites, to expose their strategies globally.

Botnet Neutralisation. Deploy AI-driven social listening tools to identify inorganic amplification patterns.

Narrative Pre-emption. Seed strategic talking points ahead of known adversarial events like elections, anniversaries of significant events, etc.

Cyber Integration. Coordinate with cyber threat intelligence units to tie Influence Operations with digital breaches or misinformation incidents.

PSYOPS-IO Synchronisation. Align psychological efforts with overt diplomatic and military posturing for message coherence.

Avoid Escalation. All content must avoid direct provocation or calls to violence to prevent retaliatory actions.

Deniability. Use third-party intermediaries, such as, NGOs and Diaspora groups and anonymised digital assets to minimise traceability.

Counter-Propaganda Monitoring. Establish a team to monitor Greenland counter-narratives and respond with factual rebuttals.

Legal Compliance. Ensure operations align with international laws and norms, avoiding actions that could be classified as cyber-attacks or violations of sovereignty.

Resource Requirements

- **Personnel.** Team of 50–100 specialists, including OSINT analysts, content creators, cyber experts and cultural advisors.
- **Budget.** Estimated approximately Rs 200 crores annually as a ballpoint figure for content production, digital infrastructure and third-party intermediaries.
- **Technology.** AI-driven analytics tools, secure communication platforms and anonymised servers.
- **Partnerships.** Engage neutral NGOs, Diaspora groups and international media to amplify messages.

Contingency Plans

- **Backlash Response.** If Greenland detects and counters the campaign, shift to overt cultural diplomacy to maintain goodwill.
- **Escalation Management.** Cease operations temporarily if tensions rise to avoid diplomatic fallout.
- **Asset Protection.** Use encrypted channels and disposable digital assets to protect operatives and infrastructure.

CONCLUSION

This hypothetical PSYOPS plan leverages India's soft power, technological capabilities and cultural ties to influence Greenland's public opinion subtly and ethically. By focusing on shared heritage, economic opportunities and internal reflection, the campaign aims to reduce hostility and promote stability without resorting to direct confrontation. Success depends on meticulous execution, continuous monitoring and adaptability to changing dynamics.

A well-calibrated Psychological Operations campaign offers India a strategic advantage in its rivalry with Greenland. By exploiting Greenland's internal weaknesses, India can erode its adversary's stability, reduce its global standing and create conditions favourable to Indian interests. However, such operations must be conducted with precision to avoid unintended consequences.

Chapter XIX

Recommendations

In traditional international conflicts, the side with the stronger military force tended to win. In today's information age, it is often the party with the stronger story that wins.

—**Joseph S. Nye, Jr.**

WHO IS RESPONSIBLE?

The most important issue is, who is in charge of information, psychological and Influence Operations? In the UK it is the Foreign Ministry. In the US, the DOD takes the lead for the simple reason that it has the funds. In recent times, the State Department is being given importance and funds are being transferred from DOD to the State Department to carry out Psychological Operations. However, the cyber aspect for delivering content is still with the DOD.

In the case of India, it is unclear who is ultimately responsible. For the allocation of the budget and the ability to prevail over the Home Ministry, Foreign Ministry and intelligence agencies, the MoD cannot be considered the lead agency. At the most, the MoD can lead in influencing activities in CI/CT Operations within the country. The Army does a good job at operational and tactical levels. However, there is no formalised mechanism. It is the personality of the Commander on the ground which drives this operation. In a CI/CT environment, the Army, intelligence agencies of both central and state governments, local police, CAPF and paramilitary organisations (where applicable), as well as concerned ministries, all come together to carry out Influence Operations, including Winning Hearts And

Minds (WHAM) of the population. Invariably, they do a good job taking an innovative approach.

For Information Operations, the various stakeholders involved are the Ministry of Home Affairs and intelligence agencies, the Ministry of Defence, the Ministry of External Affairs, the Ministry of Information and Broadcasting, the Ministry of Electronics and Information Technology, the Ministry of Communications and the Ministry of Education, Ministry of Law and Justice among others. Close coordination between these Ministries will be necessary to conduct Information Operations against an adversary. However, as of now, there is no central agency to coordinate and direct such a task.

For carrying out Psychological Operations at the strategic level, the central government must take a whole-of-government and whole-of-society approach. The strategy must be outlined at the highest level. In Indian circumstances, the lead agency cannot be the MoD. It should be the MHA or a specific organisation under the National Security Advisor working within the National Security Council Secretariat. The National Security Council Secretariat is the appropriate agency to be made responsible for Information Operations, given India's notoriously stove-piped bureaucracy. The organisation should have experts from psychology, sociology, media, area specialists, language experts, legal professionals, the armed forces, political science specialists, foreign affairs experts, country specialists, communication specialists and social media experts.

FIND THE RIGHT TERM

Currently, the Indian armed forces and strategic community blindly follow US jargon. Like the US DOD, as brought out earlier, we also seem to be confused. If you want to influence people's minds across the border and the leaders of the adversary, what terminology should be used? Is it Information Operation, Psychological Operation, Strategic Communications, Influence Operations, Perception Management, Public Information Operations, Public Field Diplomacy or other similar terms? These terms are being used interchangeably, but they are not synonymous. The Indian armed forces must develop their own common terms and take appropriate actions to refine concepts, tactics, techniques and procedures. For operations across the border, the author recommends using the term 'Psychological Operations.' For people within the country in CI/CT Operations, the term Perception Management would be appropriate.

Strategy and Doctrine

The Indian government must enunciate a formal, integrated strategy for Psychological Operations that encompasses all facets of Psychological Operations at the international, national and Ministry levels, as well as the armed forces. The armed forces should then develop their own tactics, techniques and procedures for this operation within their respective service domains. Indian Army should take the lead role in CI/CT Operations-infested areas.

Organisation and Tasks at Apex Strategic Level

At the apex level, establishment of a Centre for Cognitive Security may be considered, which will bring together experts working in fields, such as, computer science, cognitive science, social science, engineering, political campaigning, security, marketing, public policy and psychology to advance a theoretical and an applied engineering methodology to manage the full spectrum of Information Environment security issues. It should have close ties with government, industry, academia, think tanks and public interest groups. It should have the following functions:[71]

- Bring together experts in various fields to develop Cognitive Security strategies, policies and implementation methods.
- Develop clear and practical technology objectives that support the policies and strategies established.
- Identify and evaluate suitable commercial technologies.
- Identify and evaluate pertinent research results and develop and execute strategies for transitioning them into practice.
- Work with end-users from all communities to develop techniques, tactics and procedures for applying technologies identified and developed to policies and strategies.
- Create a research schedule for strategy and policy formulation, implementation and supporting technologies.

- Progress education and training materials and conduct workshops and conferences.
- Maintain a response team that will coordinate with all communities to identify influence campaigns and distribute alerts and warnings.

Coordination

The organisation at the apex strategic level should:

- Link executive leadership and implementation officers across departments and agencies to ensure seamless collaboration.
- Explain the intent to work together.
- Understand existing efforts rather than creating new ones.
- Create an understanding of departmental and agency authorities and capabilities.
- Appreciate the permissions to apply authorities.
- Reduce the emphasis on differences and credit for successes.

Adversarial Information Operations span the responsibility of multiple government agencies. The concerned Ministries must break out of siloed national security thinking, coordinate more effectively and provide space for cross-sector cooperation. Hard security and defence, as well as cultural activities, media and many other realms of society, which are not generally considered, are potential targets for an opponent to exploit. Typically, governments find it difficult to work effectively across traditional departmental boundaries. This bureaucratic vulnerability can lead to poor information flow, competition for resources and influence, or the exclusion of key stakeholders.[72]

These shortcomings underscore the need to work more effectively across government. Newly developed capabilities required for monitoring, detecting and understanding the multiple elements of hostile information activities must be integrated to advance a shared understanding of what adversaries are doing, whom they are targeting and whether these activities are effective.

Factors to be Considered at the Strategic Level

The following factors may be considered at the strategic level:[73]

- What are the current objectives? Are current objectives likely to be achieved? If not, what outcomes are most likely under present or plausible conditions? Which actors or groups are most influential in political-military results?
- What strategies (e.g., force or negotiation) are most likely to influence the targeted groups and yield desired outcomes?
- How much authority/influence do targeted group leaders have over their supporters/followers?
- Which sources and information channels do target audiences use and find most credible?
- How are target audiences' attitudes structured and how stable are they?
- What messages are they already receiving?
- What message sources, content and formats are most likely to be accepted and to foster change?
- How many messages need to be sent to them? What other actions need to be taken to achieve influence objectives?

The use of social media by our adversaries, both external and internal, has to be checked. The most obvious tool is the law. The present action by the government against Twitter is a case in point. There will always be difficulty in deciding what is sufficiently objectionable and requires removal. Although challenging, it must be done.

The government should promote international coordination to stop the opponents' disinformation campaign and bring cross-border cyber criminals to justice. It may be considered setting up a national disinformation centre within the intelligence community, just as we have successfully done with the National Counter Terrorism Centre.

As a part of the Three Warfare strategy, China is likely to launch a robust Psychological Warfare campaign aimed at "generating dissent and discord in the enemy's camp, creating friction and fracturing links between the population and the leadership, between allies and between the military and civilian leadership." The campaign may be crude and heavy-handed in form. India should develop its own mitigation strategy to counter any such Psychological Operations campaign and be able to launch its own Psychological Operations campaign with due subtlety. The preparation, themes, delivery mechanism and other details should be worked out well in advance.

The government may even consider joining Chinese social media platforms such as Weibo and WeChat, to reach most of the Chinese population and present India's viewpoints.

AT THE MoD LEVEL

The MoD or the HQ IDS currently does not have an established definition for Information Warfare, nor does it have concepts of operations. No one is in charge here. Though with the raising of the Defence Cyber Agency, initial steps are being taken for Cyber Warfare. But no organisation exists for Information Warfare, a superset of Cyber Warfare. As mentioned earlier, the US Army Cyber Command is currently considering incorporating Psychological Operations aspects into its Cyber Command. The MoD may consider leapfrogging and tasking the Defence Cyber Agency accordingly. At least the pros and cons may be discussed and analysed.

MoD should immediately:

- Define Information Warfare.
- Develop an Information Warfare operational concept.
- Subordinate select organisations under a designated leader for Information Warfare.

Information Warfare in armed conflict poses a threat to the morale of Service personnel, the command and control of forces and relations with local people in the area of operations. The MoD must acknowledge that Service members are being targeted in unconventional and subtle ways by our foes. These new tactics are effective at changing the narrative and views of our service people. MoD should:[74]

- Initiate action to defend its service members and their families.
- Initiate an anti-disinformation training programme to educate and minimise the reach and impact of foreign agents online.

- Coordinate with intelligence agencies.
- Put in place the necessary people, policies, programmes and partnerships to defend against these new threats in the Information Environment.

Questions for Oversight. Answering these questions would give a fair idea of our current state of preparedness.

- How can the MoD improve digital literacy for Services members to understand the importance of information in protecting our country? What action is the MoD taking to inform Services members and their families and protect them from misinformation and disinformation by adversary States? What can the MoD do to educate its personnel, including the military, civilians, contractors and dependents, to protect themselves from threat actors who can micro-target them as a result of publicly available information?
- What steps have been taken to clearly communicate that misinformation generated by Services members, civilian employees and contractors is unacceptable and that they will be held accountable should they disseminate such material?
- What action is the MoD taking to manage the publicly available information of its personnel, units and operations?
- How can the MoD develop consistent policies, plans, doctrines and a common lexicon for the Department as a whole?
- What actions can the MoD take to ensure that command-and-control decisions are made with timely, accurate and reliable information?
- Should the MoD organise the Office of the RM and its other components to have centralised or distributed information-based organisations focused on its Cyber, Electronic, Space and Information Warfare missions and capabilities?
- How do MoD policies and approaches to address threats in the Information Environment posed by nation-state actors, differ from those designed to address non-State actors?
- What actions can the MoD take to protect itself from insider threats? What actions can pre-emptively address situations that may lead a Services member or other MoD employees to act against its own interests?

- What controls can the MoD put in place to enhance the cybersecurity of IT systems and networks owned by DRDO, DPSUs, the Defence Industrial Base, contractors and civilian companies that the MoD relies on for its operations?
- What actions and training can the MoD put in place to educate personnel, including dependents, on the operational security or intelligence value of even what may appear to be innocuous postings on social media, to protect our personnel and their actions?
- What is the MoD's plan to ensure a long-term commitment to gaining EMS superiority and should the MoD consider establishing a structure similar to that used in the cyber domain?
- To what extent has the MoD established a comprehensive plan to identify personnel requirements related to the Information Environment and outline how to fulfil them?
- To what extent does the MoD have visibility on the budgetary resources presently allocated for Information Environment requirements?
- To what extent has the MoD established a comprehensive plan that identifies Information Environment-related IT requirements and outlines how to fulfil them?
- To what extent has the MoD established a plan outlining the priorities for the use and protection of the Information Environment?[75]

INDIAN ARMY

Talent Management. There is a general shortage of talent in this critical field. It is the same for all armies of the world. We must study how others are addressing this problem and refine our system. Talent management is not a key area of MS branch. The rule, 'do what you are good at and do not try to be something you are not,' applies. Government agency professional development systems deliberately cultivate generalists, leaders and decision-makers to manage organisations and produce and implement policy. This system is simply incapable of nurturing talents in critical capabilities and maintaining the talent not just to be competitive but also to win.

Industry experts possess a perspective vastly different from that of professionals within the government or the military. Deputing junior officers to the industry would expose individuals to leading technology and bring their experiences and relationships back to the Army. In some cases, hiring from traditional government contractors is a solution.

Intelligence Organisation. We have intelligence organisations and staff at every level. They already have well-developed doctrines and analytic processes that have been honed over time. They must be part of the Information Warfare battlefield and not a fringe player. Intelligence personnel should also become well-acquainted with the requirements for OIE and provide adequate support for these operations in the form of data collection, analysis and intelligence products focused on the Information Environment. Training in OIE Should be formalised and expanded. Cross-functional analytic teams should be created to integrate intelligence functions better and increase attention to the Information Environment.

CI/CT Operations. The Indian Army should be the lead agency for carrying out Perception Management activities in Jammu and Kashmir (J&K) and the North Eastern states within India.

The following is recommended in random order:

- Generously resource information power.
- Give greater emphasis and priority to information effects in operational planning and execution.
- Increase the prestige of Information Warfare personnel.
- Integrate physical and information power.
- Use information power extensively in operations below the threshold of conflict.
- Carefully record and document one's own operations.
- Produce high-quality video, digital and other information products.
- Focus on maintaining the support of domestic audiences at all costs.
- Standardise the processes associated with the Information Environment to be consistent with and part of, other routine staff processes.

- In coordination with the MoD, seek expanded authorities to operate in the Information Environment, short of declared hostilities and in CI/CT Operations.
- Increase education and training to reflect the growing importance of these capabilities and their role in future conflicts.
- Take steps to close capacity gaps in key capability areas, including cyber, influence, operations security and military deception.

Some factors to be considered for planning purposes:[76]

- IO is not well understood in the force.
- Success in IO requires prioritising intelligence support for IO.
- IO objectives must be clear and precise.
- Consider the Information Environment from the perspective of the population.
- Things do not always happen for the reasons you think; causation can be complicated when behaviours, perceptions, cognition and culture are involved.
- Every operation is an information operation.
- IO can deliver effects on enemy forces, commanders and civilian populations.
- Adversaries can do things that you cannot. Be prepared for them.
- Information-related capabilities that are not well integrated with operations are vulnerable to being overwhelmed.
- It can take years to build credibility but only minutes to tear it down.
- Effective Information Operations cannot be an afterthought. If IO is part of the planning process, it is more likely to be included in the plan.
- If effects in and through the Information Environment are essential to the commander, they should feature prominently in the commander's intent.
- Manoeuvres and fires generate effects in the Information Environment as well.
- Plan for friendly-force mistakes and adversary propaganda.

- All communications are potentially global. What you do and say here can have an impact elsewhere and vice-versa.
- IO is like fire-support coordination; it is an integrating function, not in itself an information-producing/affecting capability.
- Information-related capabilities can have lengthy timelines for both execution and results.
- Events do not always unfold according to plan, so prepare IO branches and sequels.
- Warfare, including Information Warfare, involves trade-offs.
- The efforts planned and coordinated by IO need to be monitored and assessed; otherwise, you are shooting in the dark.[77]

In the end, we need to remember that the secret to getting ahead, is to get started.

Chapter XX

Conclusion

In the information age, it's not just whose army wins, but whose story wins.

—Joseph Nye

Information Warfare is no longer confined to traditional battlefields. It permeates every aspect of modern society. Governments, militaries, corporations and even non-State actors leverage information as a weapon to shape opinions, destabilise adversaries and secure strategic advantages. The evolution of digital and cyber technologies has transformed the landscape of Information Warfare, creating new opportunities and challenges. Understanding the relationship between Information Warfare and Cyber Warfare and integrating these capabilities into strategic planning is essential for achieving and maintaining a competitive advantage in the information domain.

The journey through the complexities of Information Warfare has revealed that the battles of today and tomorrow are not merely fought with bullets and bombs, but with narratives, perceptions and the subtle manipulation of minds. Psychological Operations have emerged as a decisive tool in the evolving theatre of Information Warfare.

The transformation of war has ushered in a paradigm shift: from the primacy of kinetic force to the ascendancy of psychological leverage. Where platforms like tanks, aircrafts and ships forged victory, now memes, rumours and targeted messaging penetrate deeper and endure longer. Information, especially when precision-targeted through Psychological Operations (PSYOPS), has become not just a force multiplier but a force in itself.

The advent of the Internet, social media and Artificial Intelligence has revolutionised how information is disseminated and consumed, enabling PSYOPS to operate at an unprecedented scale and precision. In this hyper-connected world, the traditional boundaries between peace and conflict, combatant and civilian, truth and falsehood have blurred into an indistinct grey. Every tweet, every news article, every viral video has the potential to be a strategic asset or a weaponised payload. The rise of deepfakes, algorithmic amplification and real-time Sentiment Analysis has further enhanced the ability to craft compelling narratives that resonate with audiences, often bypassing conscious scrutiny.

While technology provides the tools, it is the human mind that remains the ultimate target. Unlike cyber attacks that target infrastructure or Electronic Warfare that disrupts signals, PSYOPS directly engage with the cognitive and emotional landscapes of individuals and groups. They aim to shape perceptions, erode trust, foster dissent or cultivate allegiance. Whether it is a State actor seeking to destabilise an adversary, a non-State group recruiting new members, or a political campaign vying for public opinion, the objective is ultimately to influence human decision-making.

Psychological Operations, as a subset of Information Warfare, leverage narratives, disinformation, cognitive biases and emotional triggers to manipulate perceptions, induce fear, sow discord or build allegiance to target audiences. The objective is to win without fighting, to cause confusion, dissent and paralysis within the adversary's ranks while consolidating one's own cohesion and strategic narrative. The battlefield has expanded to include not only soldiers and commanders, but also civilians, media personnel, influencers and digital platforms.

THE ROLE OF TECHNOLOGY IN SHAPING THE FUTURE

Technology will redefine the possibilities and perils of Psychological Operations. Emerging technologies, such as AI and Neurotechnology that interact with the nervous system, encompassing both the brain and the peripheral nervous system, as well as invasive brain-computer interfaces, affective computing, which develops systems and devices that can recognise, interpret, process and simulate human emotions and deepfake automation poses new challenges and opportunities. Future wars may see direct manipulation of neural pathways through brain-computer interfaces (BCIs), where adversaries could implant false memories or alter perceptions.

The prospect of "neural PSYOPS," where sentiment is algorithmically engineered or even neurochemically targeted, is no longer purely speculative.

Artificial Intelligence

Artificial Intelligence (AI) holds transformative potential. AI-driven tools can analyse vast datasets to predict behavioural patterns, generate hyper-realistic content and automate influence campaigns at scale. Large language Models (LLM) capable of generating human-like text at scale could automate the creation of persuasive content across multiple languages and cultural contexts. AI also offers tools for detection and counteraction. Deepfakes and synthetic media will challenge the ability to discern truth from falsehood.

As AI technologies become more sophisticated and accessible, the potential for their misuse by terrorist organisations and violent non-state actors continues to grow. The rapid pace of AI development necessitates an adaptive and forward-looking response, one that anticipates future developments rather than merely reacting to current threats.

The stakes of this challenge are high, as failure to effectively counter AI-enabled radicalisation could lead to significant increases in extremist violence and social instability. Success will require extraordinary cooperation between technology companies, government agencies, academic institutions and civil society organisations. This cooperation must be sustained over time and must adapt to the rapidly evolving technological landscape.

Virtual and Augmented Reality Technologies

Virtual and Augmented Reality Technologies may create new frontiers for Psychological Operations, enabling immersive experiences that blur the lines between reality and simulation. A Virtual Reality campaign could place users in a simulated crisis, evoking empathy or fear to drive behavioural change. The integration of these technologies with biometric monitoring could enable real-time assessment of psychological impact, allowing for dynamic adjustment of Information Warfare campaigns based on physiological responses.

The Internet of Things

The Internet of Things and smart city technologies will generate unprecedented amounts of behavioural data, enabling targeted Psychological Operations to track individuals based on their physical movements, consumption patterns and social interactions. This convergence of digital and physical surveillance creates opportunities for Information Warfare that are only beginning to be understood.

Decentralised Platforms and Blockchain-based Communication Systems

The rise of decentralised platforms and blockchain-based communication systems presents both opportunities and challenges. The rise of encrypted platforms (e.g., Telegram, Signal) enables covert coordination of influence campaigns that remain beyond the reach of traditional monitoring. These technologies can enhance the resilience of communication networks against censorship and disruption. Conversely, they can enable anonymous actors to spread disinformation with impunity. Navigating this complex landscape will require a combination of technological innovation, regulatory frameworks and public education, to foster media literacy and critical thinking.

THE ETHICAL AND LEGAL ISSUES

The rise of Information Warfare raises profound ethical, legal and democratic questions. PSYOPS, by design, exploit psychological vulnerabilities and bypass rational discourse. Its ethical boundaries remain blurry, especially in grey-zone operations that fall beneath the threshold of declared war. The fine line between persuasion and manipulation, strategic communication and cognitive coercion, must be navigated with intellectual honesty and institutional restraint.

PSYOPS can promote peace, counter extremist ideologies and foster resilience against adversarial propaganda. However, when misused, they can manipulate vulnerable populations, undermine democratic processes and aggravate societal divisions. States have increasingly blurred this boundary under the pretext of national interest and "information sovereignty."

Information Warfare practitioners must tackle the questions of intent, impact and proportionality. Is it justifiable to manipulate emotions to achieve a strategic goal? How can the line between persuasion and deception be navigated? What safeguards can prevent the abuse of Psychological Operations in ways that erode trust or violate human rights? These questions are important in an era where the boundaries between truth and falsehood are increasingly blurred.

Democratic societies face the particular challenge of maintaining openness and transparency while protecting against adversaries who exploit these very qualities. How does a democratic society defend itself against foreign Influence Operations without infringing upon the very freedoms it seeks to protect?

The use of Information Warfare in democratic societies must be governed by strict oversight, transparency and legal norms to avoid the erosion of trust in institutions or the manipulation of domestic populations for political gain. The challenge lies in striking a balance between operational secrecy, which is often necessary for effectiveness and the need for transparency to maintain public trust.

International norms and agreements regarding Information Warfare are still in their infancy. There is an urgent need for multilateral dialogue to define red lines, establish accountability and prevent the escalation of information conflicts into kinetic ones. The international community must develop new frameworks for governing Information Warfare, establishing norms and agreements that limit the most destructive applications while preserving legitimate uses of information technology. The difficulty of attribution, the global nature of information networks and the varying political systems and values of different nations, complicates this diplomatic challenge.

The Human Element: Resilience and Resistance

Despite the technological sophistication of modern Psychological Operations, the human element remains paramount. It is people, planners, operators, analysts and targets who ultimately determine the success or failure of information campaigns. Understanding human psychology, culture and motivation is as important as mastering the tools of the trade.

Resilience against Psychological Operations is fundamentally a human quality. Critical thinking, media literacy to question narratives, verify sources and recognise manipulative tactics, as well as emotional intelligence, are the best defences against manipulation. Societies that invest in these qualities are better equipped to withstand the onslaught of Information Warfare.

From the days of the Mahabharata to the sophisticated digital campaigns of the 21st Century, PSYOPS have consistently demonstrated their ability to sway minds, alter narratives and achieve strategic objectives without the need for physical force. This book has explored the multifaceted nature of PSYOPS, including the basic foundations of Information Warfare, the tactics, techniques, procedures and technologies employed by practitioners, a detailed overview of Psychological Warfare, the Indian Context, a hypothetical Information Warfare campaign, Recommendations and Conclusion, as a round up.

This book has examined various doctrinal models from the American, Chinese, Pakistani and Indian examples. Despite differences in terminology and emphasis, what unites these models is their recognition of the human mind as the decisive battlefield of the 21st Century.

The case studies, including that of the ISIS in Iraq, the Armenia-Azerbaijan War, Israeli conflicts in Gaza and the ongoing Ukraine War, have revealed discernible patterns. First, asymmetry favours the actor who better manipulates perception. Second, non-State actors, freed from the constraints of statecraft, often innovate more quickly and with fewer ethical considerations. Third, the convergence of Artificial Intelligence and behavioural science is accelerating the efficacy of PSYOPS at an alarming rate. Understanding how these tactics succeed or fail, equips analysts, policy makers and practitioners with the cognitive toolkit to recognise, anticipate and counter psychological campaigns.

This book offers profound insights into the nature, evolution and implications of Information Warfare. The key lessons I want readers to take away, are:

THE CENTRAL ROLE OF INFORMATION WARFARE TODAY

- Information Warfare, especially Psychological Operations (PSYOPS), is no longer peripheral but central to modern conflict and influence.
- The digital age has amplified the reach, speed and impact of Psychological Operations, making them more pervasive and potent.

THE EVOLUTION AND SOPHISTICATION OF PSYCHOLOGICAL OPERATIONS

- PSYOPS have evolved from simple propaganda to complex, technology-driven campaigns.
- Integration with social media, AI and big data enables precise targeting.
- Psychological Operations are now integral to hybrid warfare, combining military, cyber, economic and disinformation tactics.
- Terrorists and non-State actors also use Psychological Operations with remarkable efficiency and democratising influence.

CORE PRINCIPLES OF INFLUENCE

- Credibility is paramount; the effectiveness of any message depends on its perceived trustworthiness.
- Emotional resonance drives impact. Messages that evoke strong emotions, such as, fear, hope, or pride, are more memorable and actionable.
- Repetition and consistency reinforce acceptance and internalisation of messages.
- Exploiting cognitive biases (confirmation bias, anchoring, bandwagon effect) is a common tactic in PSYOPS.

This book has sought to explain the complexities of Information Warfare and the pivotal role of Psychological Operations within it. I hope that readers, whether scholars, policy makers, practitioners, or engaged citizens, will carry forward these insights, contributing to a future where the power of influence is wielded with wisdom and integrity. In an era defined by information, the mind remains the ultimate battleground and the stakes have never been higher.

This book concludes with a set of pragmatic implications:

- **For Practitioners.** Psychological operators must blend psychological insight with technological fluency. Future campaigns should integrate behavioural data analytics, cross-platform narrative engineering and cultural empathy. Training must be reconfigured to prioritise multidisciplinary cognition over legacy tactics.
- **For Policy makers.** The challenge is two-fold: enabling effective Psychological Operations while constraining domestic abuse of the same. Legislative clarity on PSYOPS boundaries, investment in cognitive infrastructure and inter agency coordination will be critical.
- **For Scholars and Educators.** Information Warfare demands a new pedagogy, one that fuses military theory with communication studies, ethics, behavioural science and AI systems. Interdisciplinary research must rise to meet interdisciplinary threats.

Let this book serve not only as a guide to the mechanics of Information Warfare, but also as a call to vigilance, responsibility and ethical action, in the face of ever-evolving threats to truth, trust and freedom.

The final frontier of warfare is not outer space, but inner space—the cognitive and emotional terrains that define human judgement. It is here, that the great contests of our age will be fought and won.

Notes

1 Defense Primer: Operations in the Information Environment, Congressional Research Service (CRS), November 29, 2024 available at: https://sgp.fas.org/crs/natsec/IF10771.pdf

2 Allied Joint Doctrine for Information Operations, Ministery of Defence, Allied Joint Publication-10.1, January 2023 available at: https://assets.publishing.service.gov.uk/media/650c03bf52e73c000d9425bb/AJP_10_1_Info_Ops_UK_web.pdf

3 Allied Joint Doctrine for Information Operations, Ministery of Defence, Allied Joint Publication-10.1, January 2023 available at: https://assets.publishing.service.gov.uk/media/650c03bf52e73c000d9425bb/AJP_10_1_Info_Ops_UK_web.pdf

4 Gary Brown, Addressing Cyber-Enabled Information Operations, RUSI Newsbrief, May 2020, Vol. 40, No. 4 available at: https://rusi.org/sites/default/files/20200501_brown_web.pdf

5 The Conduct 0f Information Operations, Army Techniques Publication (ATP) 3-13.1, October 2018, available at: https://irp.fas.org/DODdir/army/atp3-13-1.pdf

6 Addressing the New Era of Deterrence and Warfare: Visualizing the Information Domain - Part I, ISW Press, Jul 20, 2022 available at: https://www.understandingwar.org/backgrounder/addressing-new-era-deterrence-and-warfare-visualizing-information-domain

7 GAO, Internet of Things: Enhanced Assessments and Guidance Are Needed to Address Security Risks in DOD, GAO-17-668 (Washington, D.C.: July 27, 2017 available at: https://www.gao.gov/products/gao-17-668

8 Ibid

9 Department of Defense, "Summary of the 2018 National Defense Strategy of The United States of America; Sharpening the American Military's Competitive Edge available at: https://media.defense.gov/2020/May/18/2002302061/-1/-1/1/2018-NATIONAL-DEFENSE-STRATEGY-SUMMARY.PDF

10 Ben Quinn, Revealed: the MoD's secret cyberwarfare programme, The Guardian, 16 March 2014 available at: https://www.theguardian.com/uk-news/2014/mar/16/mod-secret-cyberwarfare-programme

11 Dr. Christopher Whyte, Protectors without Prerogative The Challenge of Military Defense against Information Warfare, Christopher Whyte, PhD, available at: https://doi.org/10.21140/mcuj.20201 10108

12 Rid, Active Measures; Clint Watts, Messing with the Enemy, New York: Harper Collins,

2018 available at: https://www.american.edu/sis/centers/security-technology/messing-with-the-enemy-book-review.cfm

13 Adapted from Alex Krasodomski-Jones et al., "Warring Songs: Information Operations in the Digital Age," Demos/ Open Society, European Policy Institute, May2019, p.8 available at: https://demos.co.uk/wp-content/uloads/2019/05/Warring-Songs-final-1.pdf

14 Jarol B. Manheim, Strategy in Information and Influence Campaigns, New York: Routledge, 2011, pp. 68–69 available at: https://library.institutpendidikan.ac.id/wp-content/uploads/2024/08/Strategy-in-Information-and-Influence-Campaigns-How-Policy-Advocates-Social-Movements-Insurgent-Groups-Corporations-Governments-and-Others-Get-What-They-Want-PDFDrive-.pdf

15 James J. F. Forest, Digital Influence Warfare in the Age of Social Media, Praeger Publishers Inc, 2021 available at: https://www.bloomsbury.com/us/digital-influence-warfare-in-the-age-of-social-media-9798765132890/

16 Adapted from Alex Krasodomski-Jones et al., "Warring Songs: Information Operations in the Digital Age," Demos/ Open Society, European Policy Institute, May2019, p.8 available at: https://demos.co.uk/wp-content/uloads/2019/05/Warring-Songs-final-1.pdf

17 The Weaponization of Information - The Need for Cognitive Security, The RAND Corporation, April 27, 2017 available at: https://www.bibliotecapleyades.net/sociopolitica/sociopol_internet261.htm

18 Christopher Paul and Miriam Matthews, The Russian "Firehose of Falsehood" Propaganda Model, Santa Monica, Calif: RAND Corporation, PE–198–OSD, 2016 available at: https://www.rand.org/pubs/perspectives/PE198.html

19 Maj Gen PK Mallick, VSM (Retd), Information, Cyber and Space Domain and its Application in Future Land Warfare, CLAWS, March 2023 available at: https://www.amazon.in/Information-Domain-Application-Future-Warfare/dp/9391490565

20 Army Techniques Publication (ATP) 3-13.1, The Conduct of Information Operations, Headquarters, Department of the Army, October 2018 available at: https://irp.fas.org/DODdir/army/atp3-13-1.pdf

21 Schwille, Michael, Anthony Atler, Jonathan Welch, Christopher Paul and Richard C. Baffa, Improving Intelligence Support for Operations in the Information Environment, RAND Corporation, 2020 available at: www.rand.org/t/RB10134

22 Brian Babcock-Lumish and Leendert van Bochoven, Stephen Gordon, Tim Hofmockel, Frederick Kagan, Nils Peterson and Noah Ringler, Managing the New Era of Deterrence and Warfare: Visualizing the Information Domain, Institute for the Study of War, May 2023 available at: https://www.businessofgovernment.org/sites/default/files/Managing%20the%20New%20Era%20of%20Deterrence%20and%20Warfare.pdf

23 Col David H. Gurney, USMC (Ret.), Military Force and Ethics Joint Force Quarterly. Issue 54, 3rd Quarter 2009 available at: https://apps.dtic.mil/sti/tr/pdf/ADA632102.pdf

24 Josh Luberisse, Controlling the Narrative: The Definitive Guide to Psychological Operations, Perception Management and Information Warfare, Published by Fortis Novum Mundum, 2024.

25 Maj Gen PK Mallick,VSM (Retd), Strategic Communications Opportunities and Challenges, March 18, 2018 available at: https://www.vifindia.org/sites/default/files/SC%20PPT%2018%20mar.pdf

26 The Weaponization of Information - The Need for Cognitive Security, The RAND Corporation, April 27, 2017 available at: https://www.bibliotecapleyades.net/sociopolitica/sociopol_internet261.htm

27 https://www.1stio.army.mil/

28 Mark Pomerleau, Army officially deactivates only information operations command, Defensescoop May 9, 2025 available at: https://defensescoop.com/2025/05/09/army-officially-deactivates-only-information-operation-command/

29 Christopher Paul and Miriam Matthews, The Russian "Firehose of Falsehood" Propaganda Model, Santa Monica, Calif: RAND Corporation, PE–198–OSD, 2016.

30 Cole Livieratos, Bombs, Not Broadcasts, Joint Forces Quarterly, Number 90, 3rd Quarter 2018, pp. 60-67 available at: https://ndupress.ndu.edu/Portals/68/Documents/jfq/jfq-90/jfq-90.pdf

31 U.S. Marine Corps, Changing The Term Psychological Operations to Military Information Support Operations, December 12, 2011 available at: https://www.marines.mil/News/Messages/MARADMINS/Article/887791/changing-the-term-psychological-operations-to-military-information-support-oper/

32 Yanqing Duan, John Edwards and Yogesh Dwivedi, "Artificial intelligence for decision making in the era of Big Data – evolution, challenges and research agenda available at:

33 Dalvin Brown, The United Nations is turning to artificial intelligence in search for peace in war zones, The Washington Post, April 23, 2021, available at: https://www.washingtonpost.com/technology/2021/04/23/ai-un-peacekeeping/.

34 Clarisa Nelu, Exploitation of Generative AI by Terrorist Groups, International Centre for Counterterrorism (ICCT), June 10, 2024 available at: https://icct.nl/publication/exploitation-generative-ai-terrorist-groups

35 Countering Terrorism online with Artificial Intelligence, A Joint Report by UNICRI and UNCCT, United Nations Office of Counterterrorism (UNOCT), 2021.

36 Nic Newman with Amy Ross Arguedas, Craig T. Robertson, Rasmus Kleis Nielsen and Richard Fletcher, Reuters Institute Digital News Report 2025 available at: https://reutersinstitute.politics.ox.ac.uk/sites/default/files/2025-06/Digital_News-Report_2025.pdf

37 Statement of Glenn S. Gerstell* Before the Subcommittee on Cyber, Innovative Technologies and Information Systems of the U.S. House of Representatives Committee on Armed Services Hearing on Technology and Information Warfare: The Competition for Influence and the Department of Defense April 30, 2021

38 Caroline Jack, Lexicon of Lies: Terms for Problematic Information (New York: Data & Society Research Institute, 2017), P6 available at: https://datasociety.net/pubs/oh/DataAndSociety_LexiconofLies.pdf

39 Isaac R. Porche III et al., Redefining Information Warfare Boundaries for an Army in a Wireless World, RAND Corporation, 2013 available at: https://studylib.net/doc/12165232/the-rand-corporation-is-a-nonprofit-institution-that-rese...

40 Maj Gen PK Mallick,VSM (Retd), Strategic Communications Opportunities and Challenges, March 18, 2018 available at: https://www.vifindia.org/sites/default/files/SC%20PPT%2018%20mar.pdf

41 Ibid

42 Jan Kalvik, How the Master Narratives Are Impacting the Meta Narratives on Syria, Defence and Intelligence Norway, Sep 13, 2016 available at: http://www.etterretningen.no/2016/09/13/how-the-master-narratives-are-impacting-the-meta-narratives-on-syria

43 Emily Weinzheimer Conflict Narratives: How Narratives Impacted the Russia-Ukraine and Israel-Hamas Conflicts, Small War Journal, May 21, 2025 available at: https://smallwarsjournal.com/2025/05/21/conflict-narratives-russia-ukraine-israel-hamas/

44 Emily Weinzheimer, Conflict Narratives: How Narratives Impacted the Russia-Ukraine and Israel-Hamas Conflicts, 05.21.2025, Small Wars Journal at https://smallwarsjournal.com/2025/05/21/conflict-narratives-russia-ukraine-israel-hamas/

45 http://www.cnn.com/2024/10/20/middleeast/sinwar-death-narrative-israel-hamas-intl-latam/index.html

46 Koichiro Takagi,What Is Cognitive Warfare? The Future of China's Cognitive Warfare: Lessons from the War in Ukraine, The Hudson available at: https://www.hudson.org/research/17991-the-future-of-china-s-cognitive-warfare-lessons-from-the-war-in-ukraine

47 Maj Gen PK Mallick, VSM (Retd), Defining China's Intelligentized Warfare and Role of Artificial Intelligence, Vivekananda India Foundation available at: https://www.google.com/search?q=Maj+Gen+PK+Mallick%2C+VSM+(Retd)%2C+ Defining+China%E2%80%99s+Intelligentized+Warfare+and+Role+of+Artificial+Intelligence %2C+Vivekananda+India+Foundation&oq=Maj+Gen+PK+Mallick%2C+VSM+(Retd)% 2C+Defining+China%E 2%80%99s+Intelligentized+Warfare+and+Role+of+Artificial+ Intelligence%2C+Vivekananda+India+Foundation&gs_lcrp =EgZjaHJvbWUyBggAEEUYOdIBCzE3MzA5NzBqMGo0qAIAsAIA&sourceid=chrome&ie=UTF-8

48 2024 Annual Report to Congress, U.S.-China Economic and Security Review Commission, available at: https://www.uscc.gov/sites/default/files/2024-11/Chapter_3--U.S.-China_Competition_in_Emerging_Technologies.pdf

49 Josh Baughman and Peter W. Singer, China's social-media attacks are part of a larger 'cognitive warfare' campaign, Defence one, October 17, 2023 available at: https://www.defenseone.com/ideas/2023/10/chinas-social-media-attacks-are-part-larger-cognitive-warfare-campaign/391255/

50 Rid, T. Active Measures: The Secret History of Disinformation and Political Warfare. Farrar, Straus and Giroux, 2020 available at: https://www.cia.gov/resources/csi/studies-in-intelligence/volume-64-no-1/active-measures-the-secret-history-of-disinformation-and-political-warfare/

51 Department of Defense. (2017). Joint Publication 3-13.4: Military Deception. https://www.jcs.mil

52 U.S. Army. (2013). Psychological Operations Tactics, Techniques and Procedures (FM 3-05.301) available at: https://irp.fas.org/DODdir/army/fm3-05-301.pdf

53 Mick Ryan and Peter Warren Singer, The Future of Deception in War: Lessons from Ukraine, Small Wars Journal, June 5, 2025 available at: https://smallwarsjournal.com/2025/06/05/the-future-of-deception-in-war-lessons-from-ukraine/

54 Maj Gen PK Mallick, VSM (Retd), Information, Cyber and Space Domain and its Application in Future Land Warfare, CLAWS, March 2023 available at: https://www.amazon.in/Information-Domain-Application-Future-Warfare/dp/9391490565

55 Itai Shapira. Surprise, Surprise: Misperception, Hubris and Deception in Today's Strategic

Environment, Modern War Institute, June 26, 2025 available at: https://mwi.westpoint.edu/surprise-surprise-misperception-hubris-and-deception-in-todays-strategic-environment/

56 Mick Ryan, Peter Warren Singer, The Future of Deception in War: Lessons from Ukraine, New America, June 5, 2025 available at: https://www.newamerica.org/future-security/reports/the-future-of-deception-in-war/

57 Zineb Riboua, How Israel's Operation Rising Lion Dismantled Iran from Within: A Case Study in the Art of Deception, Hudson Institute, Jun 13, 2025 available at: https://www.hudson.org/defense-strategy/how-israels-operation-rising-lion-dismantled-iran-within-case-study-art-deception

58 Yuvraj Tyagi, How ISPR Expanded Hybrid Warfare Strategy, Suppressing Democracy in Pakistan While Fueling Jihad in Kashmir, 24 February 2025 available at: https://www.republicworld.com/defence/global-defence-news/how-ispr-expanded-hybrid-warfare-strategy-suppressing-democracy-in-pakistan-while-fueling-jihad-in-kashmir

59 Zoya Imam, Grey Zone Ascendancy: Pakistan's Cyber Warfare in the 2025 India–Pakistan Digital Conflict Daily Parliament Times, May 15, 2025, available at: https://www.dailyparliamenttimes.com/2025/05/15/grey-zone-ascendancy-pakistans-cyber-warfare-in-the-2025-india-pakistan-digital-conflict/

60 Maj Gen PK Mallick, VSM (Retd), Defining China's Intelligentized Warfare and Role of Artificial Intelligence, VIF, March 24, 2021 available at: https://www.vifindia.org/paper/2021/may/15/China-s-Cyber-Influence-Operations https://www.vifindia.org/paper/2021/march/24/defining-china-s-intelligentized-warfare-and-role-of-artificial-intelligence

61 Chinese Influence Operations available at: https://www.irsem.fr/report.html

62 Mark Stokes and Russel Hsiao, The People's Liberation Army General Political Department (Washington, DC: 2049 Institute, 2013), 29, https://project2049.net/wp-content/uploads/2018/04/P2049_Stokes_Hsiao_PLA_General_ Political_ Department _Liaison_101413.pdf, also, John Costello and Joe McReynolds, China's Strategic Support Force: A Force for a New Era, (Washington, DC: National Defense University, 2018), p. 17, available at: https://ndupress.ndu.edu/Portals/68/Documents/stratperspective/china/china-perspectives_13.pdf.

63 See, Mark Stokes and Russel Hsiao, The People's Liberation Army General Political Department (Washington, DC: 2049 Institute, 2013), 29, https://project2049.net/wpcontent/ uploads/2018/04/P2049_Stokes_Hsiao_PLA_General_Political_ Departm ent_Liaison_101413.pdf, also, John Costello and Joe McReynolds, China's Strategic Support Force: A Force for a New Era, (Washington, DC: National Defense University, 2018), p. 17, available at: https://ndupress.ndu.edu/Portals/68/Documents/stratperspec tive/china/china-perspectives_13.pdf.

64 Mark Stokes and Russell Hsiao, The People's Liberation Army General Political Department, October 14, 2013 available at: https://www.project2049.net/documents/PLA_General_Political_Department_Liaison_Stokes_Hsiao.pdf

65 Beauchamp-Mustafaga, Nathan, Chinese Next-Generation Psychological Warfare: The Military Applications of Emerging Technologies and Implications for the United States. Santa Monica, CA: RAND Corporation, Jun 1, 2023. https://www.rand.org/pubs/research_reports/RRA853-1.html

66 Maj Gen PK Mallick, VSM (Retd), China's Cyber-Influence Operations, VIF, May 2021 available at: https://www.vifindia.org/paper/2021/may/15/China-s-Cyber-Influence-Operations

67 JeangeÌne Vilmer, A. Escorcia, M. Guillaume, J. Herrera, Information Manipulation: A Challenge for Our Democracies, report by the Policy Planning Staff (CAPS) of the Ministry for Europe and Foreign Affairs and the Institute for Strategic Research (IRSEM) of the Ministry for the Armed Forces, Paris, August 2018 available at: https://bg.ambafrance.org/IMG/pdf/report_information_manipulation.pdf?10364/0ced9e06f6ba84738088accbf0928cbc809ef42f

68 Vishwam Sankaran, Chinese scientists say they have developed new technology to weaponise 6G, Independent, June, 18 2025 available at: https://www.independent.co.uk/tech/china-weapon-6g-electronic-warfare-b2772281.html

69 Karen Allen and Christopher Nehring, *AI-Generated Disinformation in Europe and Africa: Use Cases, Solutions and Transnational Learning* (Johannesburg: Konrad-Adenauer-Stiftung Media Programme Sub-Saharan Africa, 2025), p.89.

70 Starbird, K. (2019). "Disinformation as Collaborative Work." *Proceedings of the ACM on Human-Computer Interaction*, 3(CSCW), 1–26 available at: https://dl.acm.org/doi/10.1145/3359229

71 Dr. Rand waltzman, Prepared Statement, Rand Corporation available at: https://www.rand.org/content/dam/rand/pubs/testimonies/CT400/CT473/RAND_CT473.pdf

72 European Center of Excellence for Countering Hybrid Threats, Tackling the Bureaucratic Vulnerability: An A to Z for Practitioners, European Center for Countering Hybrid Threats, 2020 available at: https://www.hybridcoe.fi/publications/hybrid-coe-paper-3-tackling-the-bureaucratic-vulnerability-an-a-to-z-for-practitioners/

73 Eric V. Larson et al, Foundations of Effective Influence Operations, RAND Corporation available at: https://www.rand.org/content/dam/rand/pubs/monographs/2009/RAND_MG654.sum.pdf

74 Herb Lin, On the Integration of Psychological Operations with Cyber Operations January 9, 2020 available at: https://www.lawfareblog.com/integration-psychological-operations-cyber-operations

75 Maj Gen PK Mallick, VSM (Retd), Information, Cyber and Space Domain and its Application in Future Land Warfare, CLAWS, March 2023 available at: https://www.amazon.in/Information-Domain-Application-Future-Warfare/dp/9391490565

76 Christopher Paul et al., Lessons from Others for Future U.S. Army Operations in and Through the Information Environment, RAND Corporation, 2018 available at: https://www.rand.org/pubs/research_reports/RR1925z1.html

77 Christopher Paul, William Marcellino, Dominating Duffer's Domain, RAND Corporation available at:https://www.rand.org/content/dam/rand/pubs/research_reports/RR1100/RR1166z1/RAND_RR1166z1.pdf

INDEX

Q

R